In *Virginia Woolf and the Visible World* Emily Dalgarno argues that Woolf's subject emerges from a conflict in codes of the visible. Dalgarno examines how Woolf's writing engages with visible and non-visible realms of experience, and draws on ideas from the diverse fields of psychoanalytic theory, classical Greek tragedy, astronomy, photography and photojournalism. The solar eclipse of 1927 marks a dividing line in Woolf's career, after which she portrayed the visible world in terms of light, and shifted her interest from painting to photography. Dalgarno offers analyses of Woolf's individual works, including *To the Lighthouse*, *The Waves* and *Three Guineas*, arguing for the importance of her ongoing interest in translation from the Greek, and exploring the theory of the subject that is apparent in her autobiography.

EMILY DALGARNO is a Professor of English at Boston University, and has also taught at l'Université Paul Valéry in Montpellier. She has published articles on Conrad, Faulkner, Lawrence, and Woolf, among others.

VIRGINIA WOOLF AND THE VISIBLE WORLD

EMILY DALGARNO

CAMBRIDGE
UNIVERSITY PRESS

PUBLISHED BY THE PRESS SYNDICATE OF THE UNIVERSITY OF CAMBRIDGE
The Pitt Building, Trumpington Street, Cambridge, United Kingdom

CAMBRIDGE UNIVERSITY PRESS
The Edinburgh Building, Cambridge CB2 2RU, UK
40 West 20th Street, New York, NY 10011–4211, USA
477 Williamstown Road, Port Melbourne, VIC 3207, Australia
Ruiz de Alarcón 13, 28014 Madrid, Spain
Dock House, The Waterfront, Cape Town 8001, South Africa

www.cambridge.org

First published 2001
Reprinted 2002

Printed in the United Kingdom at the University Press, Cambridge

Typeset in Baskerville 11/12.5pt   System 3b2   [CE]

A catalogue record for this book is available from the British Library

ISBN 0 521 79299 1 hardback

To Andrew Izsák

Contents

Preface

This book represents one moment in my study of the work of Virginia Woolf. At the end of my labors I have an even stronger sense that the intellectual rigor and fertility of Woolf's mind make her a central figure in Modernism. The scope of her reading was wider than is suggested by her essays, and its depth enhanced by her work as a translator. She traces her intellectual lineage to Plato and Greek tragedy. In all of her major works I sense that her translation of *Agamemnon* is the ground of her preoccupation with the division between the visible and invisible worlds of the living and the dead. A topic like beauty, which is central to her representation of gender, takes its place as part of the historical struggle with language that she traces to the *Symposium* and the *Phaedrus*. Other topics – kinship, and the Imperial subject find their echo in writers and philosophers of her era. Yet her inflections are distinctive, in the sense that social problems manifest themselves in her work primarily as problems of language and subjectivity, in a way that has disappointed readers who would have preferred an activist Woolf. Yet the power of her mind to make connections across languages and historical periods accounts in my view for her continuous presence sixty years after the end of her life and career.

I join company with others who have come to understand how the solar eclipse of 1927, the first that had appeared to English viewers in two hundred years, forced Woolf to rethink the nature of the visible, in a way that reshaped her career. It led directly in my view to the strange reconception of character as subject that makes *The Waves* such a formidable yet rewarding reading experience. The intellectual energy that she brought to understanding war photography and the relationship of the retinal to the camera image accounts in part for the new direction and force of *Three Guineas*. My argument about the centrality of vision to all of

Woolf's writing I hope will lead to a fresh recognition of her distinctive contribution to Modernism.

The Albert A. and Henry W. Berg Collection of the New York Public Library, Astor, Lenox, and Tilden Foundations has graciously granted me permission to publish portions of Woolf's holograph notes. Permission has also been granted by the London Society of Authors. The editor of *Novel: A Forum on Fiction* has given permission to reprint in Chapter 5 portions of a version that appeared in the journal in 1994. The editor of *L'Humanité* has given permission to print the figure in Chapter 6.

I acknowledge with deep gratitude the criticism and encouragement of the colleagues and friends who helped to make this a better book. Colleagues in the Department of English at Boston University read and criticized several chapters. My thanks to Susan Mizruchi, Leland Monk, James Winn, and especially to David Wagenknecht. Patricia Hills in the Art History Department drew my attention to an important letter by Leslie Stephen. Mark Hussey of Pace University read and criticized the entire manuscript. Owen Gingerich of the Harvard College Observatory advised me on astronomy. My friends Gillian Cooper-Driver, Anne Gaposchkin, Annette Herskovitz, Arthur Kaledin, Louis Kampf, and Peter Solomon, and my son Andrew Izsák have given me the encouragement that made the difference.

A special thanks to Ray Ryan, Commissioning Editor, Cambridge University Press, for his support and advice, and to the two anonymous referees.

Abbreviations

I have used the Hogarth Press "Definitive Collected Edition" of Woolf's fiction except when otherwise noted. The date of first publication of each work appears in parentheses, and the publisher is Hogarth Press unless otherwise noted.

AP	*A Passionate Apprentice: The Early Journals 1897–1909*, ed., Mitchell Leaksa, Harcourt Brace Jovanovich (1990)
BA	*Between the Acts* (1941), 1990
CDB	*The Captain's Death Bed*, ed. Leonard Woolf (1950)
CE	*Collected Essays*, 4 vols., ed. Leonard Woolf (1966–67)
CR	*The Common Reader* (1925), Harcourt Brace Jovanovich, 1953
CSF	*The Complete Shorter Fiction*, ed. Susan Dick, Harcourt Brace Jovanovich (1985)
D	*The Diary*, vols. I–V, ed. Anne Olivier Bell, Harcourt Brace Jovanovich (1977–84)
E I, II, III	*Essays*, 3 vols., ed. Andrew McNeillie, London and New York: Harcourt Brace Jovanovich (1986–88)
GR	*Granite and Rainbow*, ed. Leonard Woolf (1958)
Hol *W*	*The Waves: The Two Holograph Drafts*, ed. J. W. Graham (1976)
JR	*Jacob's Room* (1922), 1990
L	*Letters*, ed. Nigel Nicolson and Joanne Trautmann, vols. I–VI, London and New York: Harcourt Brace Jovanovich (1975–80)
M	*The Moment and Other Essays*, ed. Leonard Woolf (1947)

xi

MB	*Moments of Being: Unpublished Autobiographical Writings* ed. Jeanne Schulkind, New York: Harcourt Brace Jovanovich (1976), 1985
MD	*Mrs. Dalloway* (1925), 1990
ND	*Night and Day* (1919), 1990
RF	*Roger Fry: A Biography* (1940), Harcourt Brace Jovanovich, 1976
RO	*A Room of One's Own* (1929), ed. Michèle Barrett, London, Penguin, 1993
TG	*Three Guineas* (1938), ed. Michèle Barrett, London, Penguin, 1993
TL	*To the Lighthouse* (1927), ed. Hermione Lee, London, Penguin, 1992
TP	*The Pargiters*, ed. Mitchell A. Leaska, New York, Harcourt Brace Jovanovich (1977)
VO	*The Voyage Out* (1915), ed. Elizabeth Heine, 1990
W	*The Waves* (1931), 1990
Y	*The Years* (1937), 1990

Woolf's holograph notes in the Henry W. and Albert A. Berg Collection of English and American Literature, The New York Public Library, Astor, Lenox, and Tilden Foundations are referenced by reel number.

WORKS BY JACQUES LACAN (IN ENGLISH)

E	*Ecrits: A Selection*, transl. Alan Sheridan, New York, W. W. Norton, 1977
FFC	*The Four Fundamental Concepts of Psychoanalysis*, transl. Alan Sheridan, W. W. Norton (1978), 1981
Sem I	*The Seminar of Jacques Lacan: Book I: Freud's Papers on Technique 1953–1954*, transl. John Forrester, Cambridge University Press 1988, W. W. Norton, 1988
Sem II	*The Seminar of Jacques Lacan: Book II: The Ego in Freud's Theory and in the Technique of Psychoanalysis 1954–1955*, transl. Sylvana Tomaselli, Cambridge University Press, 1988, W. W. Norton, 1991
Sem III	*The Seminar of Jacques Lacan: Book III: The Psychoses 1955–1956*, transl. Russell Grigg, W. W. Norton, 1993

CHAPTER I

The hiding places of my power: Woolf's optics

> . . . the hiding-places of Man's power
> Open; I would approach them, but they close;
> I see by glimpses now. . .
>
> (Wordsworth, *The Prelude*, book XI)[1]

In 1928 Virginia Woolf wrote Vita Sackville-West a lighthearted letter about their travel arrangements, which included as well some thoughts on Tolstoy and on her own writing practice. The vocabulary of the letter casually reveals the sense of the visible that is at play throughout her work. She wrote:

> The main thing in beginning a novel is to feel, not that you can write it, but that it exists on the far side of a gulf, which words can't cross . . . a novel, as I saw, to be good should seem, before one writes it, something unwriteable: but only visible; so that for nine months one lives in despair and only when one has forgotten what one meant, does the book seem tolerable.

In the rapid associations of the letter the passage immediately follows a suggestion that Sackville-West in her essay on Tolstoy should have questioned "what made his realism which might have been photographic, not at all; but on the contrary, moving and exciting and all the rest of it . . . some very queer arrangement . . . of perspective" (*L* III:529). It would seem that the visible world might be represented by language that acknowledges the "gulf" between it and the writer, or by a kind of realism that is based on the visual codes of photography and perspective. In Woolf's mind the visible is prior to and contrasted with the writable. It suggests a kind of power that she attributes elsewhere to Septimus Smith, to see beyond the horizon of ordinary perception into a larger world that is only partly available to verbal representation. The visible is a kind of point in space towards which she moves during a period of extraordinary anticipation, that like gestation figures the future that is being

I

brought into existence minute by minute. Her sense of the visible takes no account of the author in the sense of a writer who masters his material; rather it opens the question of the narrator as subject.

The letter illustrates what I see at work everywhere in Woolf's writing, how narrative begins as a response to her sense of being oriented towards an unrepresentable visible. Her career occurred at a moment when historically specific optical codes were undergoing significant change. In her work narrative comes into existence at the point of conflict between two dominant representations of ocular experience, one that is modeled on mathematical perspective, and another on the mechanical regulation of light, for instance in the camera. My study focuses on what Woolf learned from her translation of Greek literature about representing the visible, the struggle to create in her fiction an alternative to nineteenth-century adaptations of Renaissance perspective and notions of beauty, and her interest in astronomy and photojournalism.

The history of the transformation of visual codes has been widely studied.[2] I focus on two moments, the resurgence of interest in perspective just as it was being abandoned by Cézanne and other painters, and the coincidence of changes in the design of the camera with the Spanish Civil War, so that in different cultures photographs might represent differently the conduct of the same hostilities.

A sense of conflict is often represented by Woolf as the inability of two persons to see the same object, and her characters are often differentiated from each other by their ways of seeing. *Jacob's Room* develops the dilemma stated by the narrator: "Nobody sees anyone as he is" (*JR* 25). In *The Waves* Bernard remarks on the disjunction of the gaze, "What I see . . . you do not see" (*W* 159). So in *To the Lighthouse* the two Ramsay children, Cam and James, see the boar's head in their bedroom in entirely different terms. Lucy Swithin and her brother Bart in *Between the Acts* do not share one visual field: "What she saw he didn't; what he saw she didn't" (*BA* 15). The problematic of the visible so construed comprises who sees and who cannot, the seen and the unseen, the relationship of the visible to representation, and the constitution of the viewing subject.

The value of Jacques Lacan to my argument is that he defines the "bipolar structure" (*E* 103) of the subject that is created at the juncture of visibility and language, the subject for whom full expression in language may be blocked by a difficulty in the realm of seeing. The problem occurs in Woolf's work at the level of character, when a speech act permits Lily Briscoe to finish the painting that she had left unfinished ten years earlier. It occurs also at the level of language: for instance after Peter Walsh's dream his repetition of the phrase, "the death of the soul," registers the event both as perception and as consciousness, as the seen and the said.

Lacan argues that psychoanalysis is neither a world view nor a philosophy: "It is governed by a particular aim, which is historically defined by the elaboration of the notion of the subject" (*FFC* 77). That position is strengthened by his claiming a place for his work and Freud's in a genealogy which goes back to Descartes. He stands for the subject defined as "I" and identified with the ego.[3] Descartes is nevertheless the predecessor of Freud in the sense that "Freud, when he doubts . . . is assured that a thought is there, which is unconscious, which means that it reveals itself as absent. As soon as he comes to deal with others, it is to this place that he summons the *I think* through which the subject will reveal himself" (*FFC* 36). Since, according to Lacan, Descartes' thought was directed to the real rather than the true, he remained unaware of the subject, "but we know, thanks to Freud, that the subject of the unconscious manifests itself, that it thinks before it attains certainty" (*FFC* 37).

In this genealogy Descartes also becomes the starting point for a history of optics. His image of the window in *Meditations on First Philosophy* (1641) suggests a frame of reference for Lacan's representation:

But then if I look out of the window and see men crossing the square, as I just happen to have done, I normally say that I see the men themselves . . . Yet do I see any more than hats and coats which could conceal automatons? I *judge* that they are men. And so something which I thought I was seeing with my eyes is in fact grasped solely by the faculty of judgement which is in my mind.[4]

David Michael Levin derives a world view from this image. It is, he argues, the mechanistic vision of a rational and controlling mind that cannot grant speech or humanity to the men seen in the street.

Jacob Flanders has a similar experience when he turns from reading *Phaedrus*, and looking out of the window observes in the street the alien figures of "Jews and the foreign woman." It is perhaps what leads the narrator to comment, "What does one fear? – the human eye" (*JR* 104 and 75). In Levin's argument this detached way of viewing the world creates the environment necessary for scientific endeavor, but it also incorporates in the same

vision an element of madness. "Descartes . . . places a window
between him and the men on the street, a window which disengages
him from the visible world, makes him a spectator, and interrupts, or
rather destroys, all the causal connections that would normally be in
effect."[5] Woolf's moment in history is marked, like Levin's, by her
clear recognition of the potential for destruction in a philosophy of
spectatorship.

Lacan, more concerned with the visual dimension of the window
experience, sees Cartesian meditation coinciding with the moment
when "geometral or flat" perspective was superseded. It is demonstrated by imagining that a set of "ideal threads or lines" can transfer
an image from one plane to another. Since the method is tactile and
could be taught to a blind person, Lacan concludes that it is "the
mapping of space, not sight" (*FFC* 86). In contrast Dürer's *Artist
Drawing a Reclining Woman* (1538) introduces "a correct perspective
image," in the sense that the image of the female brings into
existence what had previously been "immanent in the geometral
division . . . a dimension that has nothing to do with vision as such
. . . the phallic ghost" (*FFC* 87–8). In a way that becomes important
for Woolf, "the phallic ghost" suggests that desire weds the painter
to his subject.

Woolf, who may not have been aware of "geometral" perspective,
represents mathematical perspective in painting in the context of its
late resurgence in the twentieth century. Erwin Panofsky begins his
essay "Die Perspektive als Symbolische Form" (1924–25) with
Dürer's definition of the Latin "perspectiva" as meaning to see
through.[6] Alberti in the first book of *De Pictura* (1435) writes: "I
describe a rectangle of whatever size I please, which I imagine to be
an open window through which I view whatever is to be depicted
there."[7] The fundamental weakness in this organization of space is
the assumption that we look with a single, immobile eye, and that it
takes "no account of the enormous difference between the psycholo-
gically conditioned 'visual image' . . . and the mechanically conditioned 'retinal image.'"[8] After some discussion of the differences
between Plato's and Aristotle's conceptions of space and the various
practices among painters of the Italian and northern Renaissance,
Panofsky accounts for these apparent contradictions: "Thus the
history of perspective may be understood with equal justice as a
triumph of the distancing and objectifying sense of the real, and as a
triumph of the distance-denying human struggle for control; it is as

much a consolidation and systematization of the external world, as an extension of the domain of the self."[9]

Debate over Panofsky's essay has focused on the parallel that he suggests between perspective and other cultural formations. Hubert Damisch argues from the heuristic power of perspective in the work of Lacan and Foucault that its history is plural. Given that few Italian paintings in fact conform to the laws of perspective, he questions whether it became a paradigm, in the sense of a scientific practice that traverses history and provides a model for thought. He replies to Panofsky's claim that perspective dominated the conception of space until Picasso's *Les Demoiselles d'Avignon* (1907), by noting that discussion reached a new intensity just as Cézanne and painters of his era had abandoned it.[10]

One catches an echo of this debate in Roger Fry's analysis of the history of art as "a perpetual attempt at reconciling the claims of the understanding with the appearances of nature as revealed to the eye at each successive period."[11] Fry specifically rejected the significance of perspective: "neither perspective nor anatomy has any very immediate bearing upon art – both of them are means of ascertaining facts, and the question of art begins where the question of fact ends."[12] But his insistence that the processes of art are analogous to those of science, and the vocabulary of "formal relations" that he developed suggest that to some extent he continued to think within the older problematics. In several passages of his *Cézanne: A Study of His Development* (1927) he analyzes the painter's practice in terms of color laid over geometrical shapes: "instead of searching for diagonal perspective vistas, movements which cross and entwine, he accepts planes parallel to the picture-surface, and attains to the depth of his pictorial space by other and quite original methods."[13] In other words Cézanne's originality was characterized, in Fry's interpretation, by the unquestioned necessity to represent spatial depth.

The undercurrent of elegy that runs throughout Woolf's work is often figured as the compelling power of perspective. We see it in *To the Lighthouse* when Lily Briscoe, although she theorizes her painting as "colour burning on a framework of steel," language that owes something to Fry, is yet caught up in an archaic visualization of Mrs. Ramsay as a madonna seen through a window (*TL* 54). Clarissa Dalloway in two important scenes views through a window an old woman preparing for the night, and Septimus dies by plunging

through a window. And again in *The Waves* Percival as the embodiment of desire remains forever out of reach, a kind of vanishing
point that serves to focus the gaze of each character.

The camera was developed in a manner consistent with Renaissance projections of perspective. Joel Snyder writes that although the
pinhole camera had been used since antiquity for the purpose of
observing eclipses, its images, which "do suggest a pictorial appli-
cation to a modern eye . . . did not to the medievals. And they did
not suggest a pictorial use until well into the sixteenth century, when
the principles of linear perspective . . . had taken root in Italy."[14]
Critics and historians of photography agree that the dimensions of
the image and the coincidence of the fixed point with the eye are
analogous to Renaissance monocular perspective.

It is the premise of my argument that Woolf moved from a world
where the philosophical mind might expand the limits of the visible,
to one where seeing was transformed by an apprehension that light
creates the subject as object. The shift cannot be represented in
terms of a decisive historical passage to a new world view. Lacan
comments on "the optical structuring of space," which since Plato
has been tied to "the straight line" as "a space that is not in its
essence the visual" (*FFC* 94–5). The result is that "the relation of the
subject with that which is strictly concerned with light seems, then,
to be already somewhat ambiguous" (*FFC* 94). Astronomical phenomena contribute to the ambiguity. If you wish to see a star of
lesser magnitude, he writes, "You will be able to see it only if you fix
your eye to one side" (*FFC* 102). In a space defined by light, "the
point of gaze always participates in the ambiguity of the jewel" (*FFC*
96). As a result the eye becomes caught up in a dialectic of loss, that
is quite different from Lacan's earlier sense that one lives under the
gaze of others: "*You never look at me from the place from which I see you*"
(*FFC* 103). *The Waves* and *Three Guineas* are in similar terms transitional works, in the sense that in them Woolf too is poised between a
visible that is modeled on the perspective of the desiring subject or
the subject of philosophical reflection, and a quite different visible in
which the subject is witness to an event created by light, that exceeds
the parameters of retinal vision.

Woolf's work opens itself to a new set of questions when read in
the context of the shift in the representation of the visible in the
West. My argument goes like this. Woolf's engagement with the
visible as problematic appears to have begun with her translation of

the Greeks. She learned from them that the visible is one segment of the larger invisible world that is seen by the gods and intermittently by the mad. It is a model that with variations appears in her major novels from *The Voyage Out* to *The Years*. In this scheme death is the event that precipitates the fundamental question: how does language name the figure who is no longer visible? Her translation of *Agamemnon* includes the image of the grieving Menelaos, who awakens from a dream of the absent Helen to find his embrace once again empty, so that his waking vision and his dream confirm one another.

When we recall that Woolf's experience of the deaths of her mother, her half-sister Stella, and her brother Thoby was followed by World War I, it is not surprising to find repeated in her work the trope of the empty arms that embrace both the invisible world of the dream and the waking world. The image of a character who, seeking to exchange a glance with the dead, is revealed for the moment in the position of viewing subject is central to her work. As the visual field splits among dream, vision, and hallucination the individual character is drained of power and the subject may be momentarily glimpsed.

So in *Mrs. Dalloway* Peter Walsh dreams of "spectral presences" that are "visions" of "the figure of the mother whose sons have been killed in the battles of the world" (*MD* 57–8). When he awakens suddenly he mutters "'The death of the soul'" and subsequently feels the words attach themselves to the scenes of which he has been dreaming, so that they become "clearer" (*MD* 58). After a break in the text Peter then spontaneously recalls the failure of his courtship of Clarissa and his "sudden revelation" that she would marry Richard Dalloway (*MD* 61). The dream/vision of the grieving mother and the revelation of Clarissa lost are stories about the authority of instants of extraordinary visibility, joined by a phrase, "the death of the soul," that opens a narrative perspective far beyond anything that Peter can articulate. He is for the moment before he owns the phrase "'the death of the soul'" by repeating it, in the position of subject, and when he has repeated it, he is no longer.[15] The narrative juxtaposes the subliminal effect of the war to Peter's memory of his personal history so as to suggest that a major theme of the novel and the power of its narration are prefigured in the subject's response to the empty embrace.

WHEN THE SELF SPEAKS TO THE SELF . . .

Before turning to the remarkable congruence between Woolf's understanding of the visible world and that of Jacques Lacan I first pose the questions that are addressed in my study in terms that I derive from Woolf's early work. Three of her short stories suggest that in the aftermath of World War I she recognized that the sign was historically constituted, and that as a consequence the visible world could no longer be represented simply as the object of description. The mirror experience – she preferred "looking-glass" – occurs on the troubled boundary between seeing and naming, and achieves its significance less as a phase in the development of the subject than as a moment of self-reflection that necessarily involves misrecognition. My claim in other words is that Woolf's understanding of visibility and subjectivity is grounded in the events and ideology of twentieth-century history.

The stories that I have in mind are fables of representation, in the sense that they explore but leave unresolved problems that are implicit in her novels. Each one situates the relationship of seeing to naming in a particular historical and ideological context. "The Mark on the Wall" (1917) is the narrator's meditation on the relationship of sign to object in time of war, with a digression on the historical significance of the mirror experience. The story suggests that the visible may be historically determined: "in order to fix a date it is necessary to remember what one saw" (*CSF* 77). The visible comes into existence when it is assigned a name in order to commemorate a historical moment. The narrator distinguishes this practice from that of the former owners of the house who favored "an old picture for an old room," as though they merely required a correspondence between objects and their settings for purposes of decoration. The narrator shares their propensity when musing on castles and knights, but also recognizes that objects refer to a particular history. The list of things that the narrator has misplaced figures a life characterized by loss. The Western civilization that writes its history in terms of "the dust which, so they say, buried Troy three times over, only fragments of pots utterly refusing annihilation," necessarily confers on those objects its sense of the problematic and fragmentary (*CSF* 78). Nor can such loss be assuaged or evaded by writing history as the biography of individuals like Shakespeare, for "this historical fiction . . . doesn't interest me at all" (*CSF* 79). The story, which has often been appreciated for its charm, seems to me to lay out the narrator's difficult choices while leaving the relationship of language to the visible both urgent and unresolved.

At this point the narrative admits an apparent digression in order "lovingly" to protect the image of the self from "any other handling that could make it ridiculous." "Suppose the looking-glass smashes, the image disappears, and the romantic figure with the green of forest depths all about it is there no longer, but only that shell of a person which is seen by other people – what an airless, shallow, bald, prominent world it becomes!" (*CSF* 79). The mirror experience suggests Woolf's satiric view of the romantic ego, and increasingly of certain Romantic poets as well. Here as elsewhere in Woolf's work the mirror experience by isolating the individual's appearance reduces the reflected figure to the empty shell that is seen by others.[16] Although mirror scenes are common in European novels, Woolf is distinguished by her engagement with its implications for narrative epistemology. In this story it leads to criticism of novelists who see no further than reflection. They endanger "the real thing" by their willingness to pursue these "phantoms . . . leaving the description of reality more and more out of their stories" (*CSF* 80). The significant limitations of self-reflection become the ground of Woolf's dissatisfaction with realistic narrative.

"The Mark on the Wall" is brought to a close not when the war ends or when the object is saved from destruction, but when the narrator is recalled from her revery by hearing her companion remark: "It was a snail." Assigning a name brings closure in a world in which the importance of the mark is to be seen and named "in order to fix a date." The possibility of smashing the looking-glass marks a moment of resistance to the romantic notion that objects have the power to memorialize the past as a pretty picture. The destruction of the "romantic figure" is a first step towards seeing beyond the mirror, which creates no more than a self-reflecting fiction, "a world not to be lived in." Interrogating the boundary of self-reflection makes possible a new set of questions about naming and the making of history.

Lacan's discussion of structure in *Seminar III* develops a definition of subjectivity in the context of physics that involves a redefinition of the sign. He begins by distinguishing a "closed" structure, which "is always established by referring something coherent to something else, which is complementary to it" from "an open relation." Whereas in the work of Jakob Boehme, for example, God is present and uses the signifier, in modern physics "there is nobody who uses the signifier." In that context "every real signifier is, as such, a signifier that signifies nothing" (*Sem III*: 183–5). Lacan takes the discussion into the area of neurotic delusion, where the signifier may be used "not so as to inform you, but precisely so as to lure you" (*Sem III*, 193). In her story Woolf contemplates at some length the possibility of a signifier "that signifies nothing." The narrative functions to hold open the relation long enough to stimulate a sense of "ignorance" and "knowledge" in a mood of "vast upheaval." The mark starts out as an object that remains sequestered in the realm of vision, and becomes a signified only by the arbitrary act of the other in time of war. The signifier names what had looked like a "nail" a "snail," the rhyme undermining the authority of the "closed relation" by signaling the capacity of the sign for musical nonsense.

It is significant that in *To the Lighthouse* the narrator comments as Lily attempts to restart her painting after an interval of ten years, "Still the risk must be run; the mark made" (*TL* 172). Both story and novel are consistent with Walter Benjamin's discriminations in "Painting, or Signs and Marks" (1917). He begins by distinguishing the mark from the sign, before analyzing the mark as an element of painting. Like Woolf he is concerned with the sign in the state of becoming. The picture is comprised of marks, he goes on, but "if the picture were only a set of marks, it would be quite impossible to name it." Composition enables the picture to transcend its marks by linking it to "*something that it is not*," which happens when a picture is named. The mark in Woolf's story shares none of Benjamin's emphasis on composition as "the entry of a higher power into the medium of the mark."[17] But if the story dismisses conventional narration, neither is transcendental nomination quite adequate to the force and insistence of Woolf's inquiry into the mark on the wall. The difference from Benjamin highlights her sense that the visible is a problem of the phenomenal world, but the story comes to an end just where a narrative that is transformed by this perspective might have begun.

"Solid Objects" (1920) is one of several short experimental pieces written in 1918–19.[18] It represents the speaking and the viewing subject as two positions which emerge from a split in the gaze. The narrator begins by noting "one small black spot" on a semicircle of beach that is seen by an unidentified eye. As the spot approaches it is apprehended as two "bodies" engaged in violent dispute. Charles is preoccupied with a political argument, John with a round shape which he has found in the sand. The story focuses on the shards of china, glass, and rock that John accumulates as he gradually fails to represent in Parliament the needs of his constituents. Finally Charles, convinced that although he and John share a language, they are "talking about different things," abandons him (*CSF* 101). Although commenting in full on the solid objects that John collects, the narrative offers nothing to explain his motivation: John, who had entered a world of discourse in which he represented his constituents, takes steps to leave the world that Charles continues to inhabit. Although both speak the same language, only the unitary subject is fit to represent his constituency. The two men mirror each other, suggesting a world divided between the visible and the intelligible, the artistic and the professional.

I read "Solid Objects" as Woolf's discrimination of the two senses of *representation*, split along lines familiar in German: *vorstellen*, to represent or signify, and *vertreten*, as in proportional representation.[19] How else can we understand John's standing on the brink of a career in Parliament, until he becomes so absorbed by his collection of broken china and iron objects that he fails to win election? The story closes with a moment of incomprehension as Charles asks, "What made you give it up like that," which John denies (*CSF* 100). But although John no longer represents his constituents, his found objects are no more than a collection, and his subjectivity is not apparent.

Objects in the story suggest the distinction between metonymy and metaphor. The "lump[s]" and "shards" which John culls from the "waste land where the household refuse is thrown away," might if enclosed in "a rim of gold" become a jewel (*CSF* 97–8). As mere objects they image metonymy as a series of elements that have become meaningless when they are no longer useful. The metaphoric dimension of language, far less in evidence in the details of the story, remains potential: "any object mixes itself so profoundly with the stuff of thought that it loses its actual form and recomposes itself a little differently in an ideal shape which haunts the brain when we least expect it" (*CSF* 98). Woolf suggests that when a utilitarian culture reproduces itself in a system of objects, metaphor becomes ghostly idealization.[20]

But if metaphor is in trouble, so is the unitary subject that is identified unproblematically with the self. The narrator is an eye that is not an "I," and in fact refuses the use of "I" that is customary in the code of representation. The first person occurs in two passages. John fantasizes a "sense of power and benignity" when he chooses from the road one stone which exults: "'It might so easily have been any other of the millions of stones, but it was I, I, I!'" (*CSF* 98). The passage satirizes the ego as a blindly self-congratulatory stone, and self representation as an amusing fiction. At the end of the story John rejects Charles's sympathetic condolences on losing the election in two sentences, "I've not given it up," and "I don't agree" (*CSF* 100). Here "I" asserts agency in order to say no. It would appear that representation as first-person narration is an absurd limitation of the stony ego which relegates the non-unitary subject to a position of denial.

Perhaps for that reason John in failing to represent the significance of his collection fails also to attain subjectivity. The narrator mimes his failure. As the spot noted in the first sentence draws closer, it splits in two when the eye first discerns the attributes of bodies: "mouths, noses, chins, little moustaches, tweed caps, rough boots, shooting coats, and check stockings" (*CSF* 96). The gaze of the narrator recognizes entities but not identities, as though in Lacan's terms "any center in which information is added up can be taken for a someone, but not for a subject."[21] What in Lacan's terms distinguishes the subject from the someone is that the signifier brings the subject into existence. In Woolf's story the subject in this sense fails to come into existence. Instead she emphasizes the inhibiting effect of a society whose practices assume the unitary subject. It is as though she is saying that within a culture in which representation as *vertreten* is a dominant social value, the subject can emerge only from a split position. Yet in terms of the dominant discourse the refusal to represent signifies social failure. The passionate viewer collects objects and denies that he has failed, but those actions do no more than anticipate subjectivity and representation as *vorstellen*.[22]

"An Unwritten Novel" (1920) explores the limits of a narration that is derived from the unimpeded play of the gaze. A fellow passenger on the train refuses to "play the game" and returns the narrator's gaze (*CSF* 106). On the basis of a few words exchanged the narrator constructs a family story for the woman, "Minnie Marsh – some such name as that?" (*CSF* 111). "Leaning back in my corner, shielding my eyes from her eyes, seeing only the slopes and hollows, greys and purples, of the winter's landscape, I read her message, deciphered her secret, reading it beneath her gaze" (*CSF* 108). The invasive quality of narration under these circumstances is reflected in the invention of a story about Minnie's hostility towards her sister-in-law.

As in "Solid Objects" the position of the narrator seems constructed around the contradictory functions of language, in this story the incommensurate claims of Minnie as *she* and as *you*. Minnie contained by the gaze in the world of social practices is imagined by the narrator as *she*, but when Minnie manages to evade the gaze either by means of a gesture towards the looking-glass ("you avoid the looking-glass" *CSF* 108), or by expressing hatred, she is directly addressed as *you*. The mere possibility of the transgressions that might lead to dialog compromises the narrator's authority: "Have I read you right?" (*CSF* 111). And when at the end of the story Minnie simply walks away with a young man, suggesting another and different story, the narrator concludes with questions about function and identity: "Well, my world's done for! What do I stand on? What do I know? . . . Who am I?" (*CSF* 115).

"An Unwritten Novel" concludes with a meditation on desire. "Wherever I go, mysterious figures, I see you, turning the corner, mothers and sons: you, you, you . . . If I fall on my knees, if I go through the ritual, the ancient antics, it's you, unknown figures, you I adore; if I open my arms, it's you I embrace, you I draw to me – adorable world!" (*CSF* 115). The ending shifts attention to the narrator, and suggests that the relationship of narrator to tale is motivated by desire for what eludes the objectifying gaze. Desire seems to produce the figure of the other that is manifested in the split position: "when the self speaks to the self, who is speaking?" (*CSF* 114). The task of the narrator would seem to be to satisfy both the demand of the gaze that it create a familiar social context for the strangers met on a train, and that it also take note when desire disturbs the horizons of the gaze. Woolf's narrator does not enjoy a wider frame of reference or easier access to intellectual or unconscious realms than the character. Rather, the author of an unwritten novel is defined as the locus of the contradictions that imply but have yet to produce the subject.

Woolf suggests how contemporary culture naturalizes the gaze. On a railway journey it shares the appeal of the newspaper: "But the human face – the human face at the top of the fullest sheet of print holds more, withholds more" (*CSF* 111). And at the other end of the spatial range, when the narrator engages Minnie's gaze, "there's a break – a division," which is imaged as a hawk hovering over the down, "alone, unseen; seeing all so still down there" (*CSF* 111). The image idealizes the distant gaze, and from that perspective the narrator comments in language that Lacan would recognize: "The eyes of others our prisons; their thoughts our cages" (*CSF* 111). The human gaze is caged within the smaller range of the human other, its confinement expressed as Minnie's anger over small rooms and locked doors in her sister-in-law's house. Whereas Minnie may look through the window of her bedroom "as though to see God better," the narrator sees the secular world comprised of roofs and sky (*CSF* 109). But when the gaze is the view from space, the viewer is "alone, unseen."

Woolf saw two of these stories as pointing the way towards "some idea of a new form for a new novel . . . Whether I'm sufficiently mistress of things – thats the doubt; but conceive mark on the wall, K[ew] G[ardens]. & unwritten novel taking hands & dancing in unity" (*D* II: 14). They are consistent with her uneasiness about the conventions of narrative which is apparent in phrases from the notebooks about "the burden of writing narrative" (*D* III: 189), or "my lack of narrative power" (*D* III: 241). And they reinforce her criticism of the realistic novel in her early essay "Modern Fiction" (1919), especially in the work of Wells, Bennett, and Galsworthy. "Our gratitude," she writes, "takes the form of thanking them for having shown us what they might have done but have not done" (*CR* 151). They are "materialists," in the sense that "they write of unimportant things; that they spend immense skill and immense industry making the trivial and the transitory appear the true and the enduring" (*CR* 153). Yet these novelists were useful to Woolf as the other against which she asserted a problematic and independent view of the representation of the visible.

What these three stories add to Woolf's criticism is the sense that for her narration begins in the need to negotiate the boundaries of the visible world. The stories link third-person narrative which situates behavior in the social world to the gaze which objectifies that world as a mirror image of the self, and in so doing her narrative displays ideological process. The would-be artist is drawn by desire to test the boundary of the visible that is determined by social practice and is reflected in grammar. Nor is the narrator free to imagine an alternative to the conventions of visibility, but merely to register the questions suggested by longing for the figure who always turning a corner effectively absents herself from the gaze and thus draws the narrator on to "embrace" a larger world. Yet so keen was Woolf's sense of the obstacles that historically have inhibited the female coming to subjectivity that although marks may be named and objects found, the narrator's split position is often the end of the story.

. . . AND THE LADY SITS WRITING

Toril Moi in a well-known essay defends Woolf against feminist critics whose "traditional humanism" leads them to demand "work that offers a powerful expression of personal experience in a social framework." Pairing Elaine Showalter's criticism of the subtleties of narrative strategy in *A Room of One's Own* with the theory of Georg Lukàcs, Moi demonstrates that Woolf's feminism is misunderstood and obscured by critics who associate her work with the autonomous self and a realist aesthetic. In fact "the humanism they represent is in effect part of patriarchal ideology."[23] Although she goes on to suggest readings of Woolf oriented by the work of Derrida and Kristeva, I prefer to begin with Lacan. In his theory the subject arises in language, after a precisely detailed prehistory in the visible.

Woolf's feminism is apparent in her representation of past narrative practice. It is apparent in certain visual images, for instance of the female who looks on at a scene of male reading and writing. Cam Ramsay's position as an observer standing on the threshold of her father's study in *To the Lighthouse* echoes similar moments in the fiction of Jane Austen. Reading such images within the realist aesthetic suggests an argument and a plea for female education. But Woolf's study of Greek, which I explore in Chapter 2, was both a lesson in the power of patriarchal institutions to exclude women, and a revelation about the possibilities of a position outside the university. The subject arises when an outsider, usually female, attempts to enter the realm of the symbolic. But Woolf shows that a position rather than a character is gendered when she reveals that Bernard is defined, and to some extent all art feminized, by a particular position within the boundary of the imaginary.

Accordingly my argument that the subject arises from a split between conflicting formulations of the visible world does not accord with those studies of Woolf that assume the unproblematic nature of character and seeing. While I share Alex Zwerdling's focus in "The Enormous Eye" on Woolf as "an original and important social observer," with a strong interest in history and public issues, I take issue with the assumption that Woolf was a writer who tried "to expand the theory and practice of realism," for whom the act of seeing involved "vision" in the metaphorical sense of "insight."[24] My focus differentiates this study as well from work on Woolf's relationship to painters and painting.[25] Nor is my representation of the theory of the visible in the work of Jacques Lacan unproblematic, for although I make use of his optical models of the visual field, Woolf's work suggests a different structure of the Imaginary that makes the female's transition to the Symbolic problematic. Woolf's emphasis on the would-be artist in the characterizations of Lily Briscoe and Bernard suggests that her goal was not to achieve the Symbolic. Rather the narrator accommodates the paradox of Woolf's position as novelist while exploiting the productive contradictions of the visible world.[26]

My project is not unlike Harvena Richter's in *Virginia Woolf: The Inward Voyage*, but although we are drawn to many of the same aspects of Woolf's work, she employs a formalist vocabulary. I would agree with her emphasis on "Virginia Woolf's insistence on perspective – the spatial relationship of the object to its surroundings," and to its importance in *To the Lighthouse*. But whereas she sees perspective as "what separates her most clearly from the Post-Impressionists," I see it as already archaic and so inhibiting the work of Lily Briscoe.[27] Whereas in Richter's chapters on "The Mirror Modes," and "The Voice of Subjectivity," she acknowledges Woolf's interest in Freud and sees the self as "multipersonal," the concept of the subject has been reconceived in visual terms in the work of Lacan.

My entire understanding of Woolf owes a good deal to Makiko Minow-Pinkney's *Virginia Woolf and the Problem of the Subject*. She traces in Woolf's essays the emergence of her feminism and her Modernist aesthetic, which both began with a challenge to phallocentrism. She argues that *A Room of One's Own* (1929) and its earlier version "Women and Fiction" are Woolf's first attempt to present "what was once a generational issue in terms of gender difference." Tracing a path through Woolf's stories I arrive at a position consistent with her conclusion that "Modernism may be seen as an attempt to reintroduce the repressed Imaginary into a symbolic order identified with an oppressive Victorianism by modern writers."[28]

But in the essays Woolf often cast herself in the role of the common reader[29] and when in some essays she presents herself as a writer, she suggests that the obstacles that impede her are ethical in nature. In "Modern Fiction" she introduces the well-known image of the "luminous halo" with a plea for freedom:

> if a writer were a free man and not a slave, if he could write what he chose, not what he must, if he could base his work upon his own feeling and not upon convention, there would be no plot, no comedy, no tragedy, no love interest or catastrophe in the accepted style . . . Life is not a series of gig lamps symmetrically arranged; but a luminous halo, a semi-transparent envelope surrounding us from the beginning of consciousness to the end. (*CR* 154)

Whereas Woolf's essays reveal her public position as reader and writer, it may be that only in fiction does she reveal her particular attraction to the border between the seen and the said as the territory of the potential subject.

I prefer to interpret Woolf's configuration of the relationship of the visible to the invisible as an historically contextualized version of similar ideas in the work of Jacques Lacan. I locate her feminism principally in the way that she genders the experience of the Imaginary. Daniel Ferrer studies madness and suicide as they are manifest in the language of Woolf's major novels in Lacanian terms. I would agree with his interpretation, for example, of the painting of Lily Briscoe in *To the Lighthouse*, that while it is "ostensibly situated outside the field of language . . . ordered by the father," it is "articulated with the space organized by the symbolic system, in which it will eventually find its place,"[30] but I put more emphasis on the imaginary, from which I distinguish Woolf's visible as the region of struggle between modes of representation in the course of which the subject becomes briefly apparent in the language of the narrator. In particular Lacan's interest in optics and his structuralist account of the relation of the subject to the gaze, to painting, and to light make it possible to identify in Woolf's work an interpretation of the same psychic phenomena from the perspective of fiction.

Much of the general resemblance between ideas of the visible in the work of Lacan and Woolf may be attributed to their position as twentieth-century readers of Plato, in particular of the discussion of the visible in Book VII of *The Republic*.[31] Though living in the era of the camera and an intensely ocular culture, both reached back to Plato for the central image of the mind as configuring the relationship of the visible to the invisible. Lacan writes that the gaze is limited by "the phantasy to be found in the Platonic perspective of an absolute being to whom is transferred the quality of being all-seeing" (*FFC* 75). In comparison human vision suffers certain limits: "I see only from one point, but in my existence I am looked at from all sides" (*FFC* 72). It follows from the assumption that the invisible is in a sense primary that both Woolf and Lacan represent the visible world apparent in the gaze as a problem of boundaries. In Woolf's notes on her reading of Plato and other Greek texts as she was writing *Mrs. Dalloway* she identifies the visible with the sane view, whereas madness and dreams test the limits of the visible world. Lacan demonstrates the limits of the visible by distinguishing the gaze from the seeing that goes on in dreams. In the waking state there is "an elision of the fact that not only does it [the gaze] look, *it* also *shows*. In the field of the dream, on the other hand, what characterizes the images is that *it shows*" (*FFC* 75). It is significant that in the work of both writers the subject is lodged precisely at the intersection of two specular realms where, following Plato, the invisible is situated in the perspective of a larger, potential, visible that becomes apparent only at the expense of the unitary self.

Lacan developed the concept of the Imaginary from his work on the mirror experience as an exemplary function. In his paper "The Mirror Stage" (1936, 1949 and reprinted in *Ecrits*) he attributes to the child of eighteen months an experience of his reflection that may be characterized as the experience of unity by a being in discord. Long before the infant can control its motor reflexes it sees before it a coordinated body, which is in fact a misrecognition, a fiction that may represent its future aspirations. The subordination of the child to its image, to fiction, and to the gaze of others alienates subject from self, in a gap which can never be bridged. The mirror experience thus represents not a phase of infant development, but a paradigm of the illusory nature of autonomy and the self that is identical with itself from which no subsequent development entirely frees the individual.

In "A Sketch of the Past" Woolf figures the female subject who comes into existence at the age when she becomes aware of the limits imposed by reflection in the looking-glass. Her half-brother

Gerald is the figure who represents the limitations of the vulnerable female body, and the limitations of kinship in a family which authorized the desire of the male for the young female. As a result of actions which Woolf called "violent," she was able to escape the entrapment of the family and recognize her kinship with an historical line of "ancestresses" whom she resembled not in body but in mind and spirit.

In "The Topic of the Imaginary," a seminar of 1954, Lacan follows a suggestion made by Freud that images come into being in the mind in a manner similar to the way that the camera produces images. Lacan illustrates this mechanical production of the image by introducing a well-known optical diagram, "the experiment of the inverted bouquet" (*Sem* 1: 75–8). When the viewer occupies a specific position inside the diagram of a cone formed by drawing a line from an upside down concealed vase to the surface of a curved mirror he sees a second, upright vase that is created by reflection. The illusion that the imaginary includes the real is apparent from only one position. Lacan draws the conclusion "that in the relation of the imaginary and the real, and in the constitution of the world such as results from it, everything depends on the position of the subject. And the position of the subject . . . is essentially characterised by its place in the symbolic world, in other words in the world of speech" (*Sem* 1: 80). Depending on its relation to speech, the subject may be in the cone and see the illusion, or outside the cone where it is not visible. Woolf's comment on the female who attempts to glimpse the real from the angle of incidence provided by the mirror is apparent in Mrs. McNab, who in *To the Lighthouse* becomes significant as the female character who attempts to gain control of language and of her place in history by standing at an angle to the mirror.

Lacan uses the drawing, with its angles and curves and flowers, to explore the refraction of light and hence of the image, from what seems the fixed and single position of the viewer. "Everything depends on the angle of incidence at the mirror. It's only from within the cone that one can have a clear image" (*Sem* 1: 140). Oddly, the potential to shift the angle of incidence does not suggest that in fact each eye sees from a slightly different angle, or that a female figure like Mrs. McNab might for obscure reasons approach the mirror "sideways" (*TL* 142, 143). Lacan seems for the moment caught between two positions, that of the diagram, and a realization that the visual field is defined by light, with the result that "The picture

... is in my eye. But I am not in the picture" (*FFC* 96). The effort to situate the viewer somewhere other than in "the place of the geometral point" (*FFC* 95) produces the notion of the viewer as the "screen" or the "stain" (*FFC* 97).

Woolf constructs the domain of the visible from a less mechanical vantage point, that of the desiring subject. Throughout her work she constantly suggests the possibility that beyond the gaze lies a space that is defined not by what the eye can or cannot see but by what it desires to see. Her subjects find themselves at the intersection between the monocular vision that is implied by mathematical perspective and something else, which may be a visual memory or a dream, or in her later writing an experience of light. In her work the subject occurs on the site of a split that is located not in the symbolic but in conflicting codes of the visible. In fact many of the most emotionally charged moments in her work occur when a character crosses out of the territory of the visible, as at the end of "An Unwritten Novel," or when Septimus sees Evans.

In Woolf's fiction the historicity of the subject attributes temporal consequences to perspective. The window image in her fiction figures Lacan's future anterior tense: "What is realized in my history is not the past definite of what was, since it is no more, or even the present perfect of what has been in what I am, but the future anterior of what I shall have been for what I am in the process of becoming" (*E* 300). Woolf's window figures death, her particular representation of the limits of the subject. At the end of *The Years*, when the party is breaking up at dawn and the family is dispersing, Maggie and Sara glimpse "the old brothers and sisters" framed in the window, seen for an instant as their own funerary statues: "The group in the window, the men in their black-and-white evening dress, the women in their crimsons, golds and silvers, wore a statuesque look for a moment, as if they were carved in stone. Their dresses fell in stiff sculptured folds. Then they moved" (*Y* 432–3). Clarissa Dalloway's meditation on the old woman seen through the window during her party figures the perceptions of death in the novel. Together with the image of the window in the opening paragraphs it links Clarissa both to Septimus and the old woman, the two figures of death. In the context of a discussion of the historical function of the subject, Lacan writes of death "not as an eventual coming-to-term of the life of the individual . . . but, as Heidegger's formula puts it, as that 'possibility which is one's

ownmost, unconditional, unsupersedable, certain and as such inde-
terminable for the subject'" (*E* 103). Woolf represents death less as
the achievement of the perfect tense that earlier had evoked
Clarissa's fear of her narrow bed, than as a shall-have-been that
becomes less fearful when the subject represents it as history.

Lacan argues that painting has the power to change the terms on
which the viewer enters the world of the gaze. He reverses the
common sense perception that the viewer makes the painting the
object of his gaze by asserting that in the painting "the artist intends
to impose himself on us," in the sense that the painting "invites the
person to whom this picture is presented to lay down his gaze there
as one lays down one's weapons" (*FFC* 100–1). Rather than dis-
arming the aggressive gaze the painting is understood as suggesting
a "dialectic of eye and gaze," in the following manner: "You never
look at me from the place from which I see you" (*FFC* 102–3).

The dialectic suggested by painting shapes important scenes in
Between the Acts. In one the Swithin family and their guests view two
paintings, of a male ancestor, and a lady. The painting of the
ancestor is a "talk producer" that leads to discourse about mimesis,
about the historical identity of the horse and the dog (*BA* 24). The
painting of the unknown lady, a kind of spectacle, prompts a
different response: "They all looked at the lady. But she looked over
their heads, looking at nothing" (*BA* 32). She does not meet their
gaze. In Lacan's terms, "in front of the picture, I am elided as
subject of the geometral plane" (*FFC* 108). That is, the viewer
recognizes when he shifts his position that something has disrupted
the economy of the gaze. The scene prepares the reader for the
village pageant at the end of the novel, when the players reverse the
theatrical conventions of viewing by turning their distorting mirrors
on the audience. "The young, who can't make, but only break;
shiver into splinters the old vision; smash to atoms what was whole"
when their mirrors blur the distinctions between the whole body and
its parts, players and spectators, men and animals (*BA* 183). The
mirrors like the paintings have the potential, unrealized in this novel,
to bring the viewer into the active position suggested by Lacan's
"dialectic."

That potential is realized in *The Waves*, when Bernard after
hearing the news that Percival is dead seeks to console himself by
visiting the Italian room at the National Gallery. Bernard, who
comes to experience the gaze of others as oppressive, asks that the

"cold madonnas . . . lay to rest the incessant activity of the mind's eye, the bandaged head, the men with ropes, so that I may find something unvisual beneath" (*W* 156). The scene suggests that Bernard finds the activity of the gaze a burden of which in his experience the paintings of the madonna have the power to relieve him. His sense of "something unvisual" that lies "beneath" the paintings recalls Lacan's idea that the picture "competes with what Plato designates for us beyond appearance as being the Idea" (*FFC* 112).

Lacan's elaboration of the subject arose in the context of his battle with the psychoanalytical establishment. To their notion of "self" he opposed "subject."[32] Subjectivity is a position that resists the claims of the ego to self-identity. In the 1950s and early 1960s Lacan made an attempt to identify a signifier of the subject in the linguistic shifter, the "I" as the grammatical subject of the sentence. He later abandoned that attempt when he came to see the subject as split between the ego's false sense of self and the functioning of language in the unconscious.

Woolf expresses in several works her reservations about the capacity of the linguistic shifter to represent the subject of discourse.[33] In "Solid Objects" "I" is the language of the stone; in *A Room of One's Own* "I" is a linguistic designation, "a convenient term for somebody that has no real being" (*RO* 4); in *To the Lighthouse* "I–I–I" satirizes academic criticism (*TL* 115); and in *The Waves* "I–I–I" identifies Louis and for a time Bernard as the subjects of an Imperialism that misrepresents difference as identity.[34] In 1933 she praised Turgenev for recognizing that "there are many different 'I's' in the same person . . . [so that] the man who speaks is not a prophet clothed with thunder but a seer who tries to understand" (*CDB* 61).

Lacan came to see the subject as a process of production, which "anchored in language itself . . . does not depend upon the conscious intention of the subject," which gives no access to unconscious meanings and often signifies something apart from the subject's intentions.[35] The narrator of *To the Lighthouse* suggests a comparable process of production in an image of the mental process of Lily Briscoe: "to follow her thought was like following a voice which speaks too quickly to be taken down by one's pencil, and the voice was her own voice saying without prompting undeniable, everlasting, contradictory things" (*TL* 29). These contradictions dance like gnats in Lily's mind until her thought "exploded of its own intensity," and the process is interrupted by her hearing a shot (*TL* 30). Her thought process, apparently unmotivated, is both authoritative and contradictory. In the mode of repetition characteristic of the dreamer who while still asleep hears in his dream the knock on the door that awakens him, Lily's thought coopts from outside itself the occasion for closure. It exhibits what Lacan calls the *pulsative* function of the unconscious, that is "the need to disappear that seems to be in some sense inherent in it" (*FFC* 43). Lily does not represent her thought process to herself, as though the condition of subjectivity were a function of the text that calls for a narrator, rather than a mode of self-reflection within the expressive capacity of the character.

Woolf's narrator becomes the site of conflict between the subject and the demands of the symbolic. But before going further I wish to explore the differences between Woolf and Lacan in their definition of the symbolic. Lacan formulated in "The function and field of speech and language in psychoanalysis," (also known as the "Report to the Rome Congress," 1953) the definition which he later elaborated. The acquisition of language that marks the entry into the symbolic is part of the Oedipal process which acknowledges the power of the father. The relation of Imaginary and Symbolic is reciprocal: the Imaginary is inscribed in the Symbolic, and without the Imaginary the Symbolic, writes Weber, "would self destruct."[36] The portion of the report that pertains to my argument associates the order of language with kinship systems and "the name of the father . . . which, from the dawn of history, has identified his person with the figure of the law" (*E* 67). In Western history in which kinship is based on a philosophical notion of the father, the female who occupies the role of wife or mother is hardly in a reciprocal position. Although Woolf on occasion acknowledges the female as voracious and destructive, Mrs. Ramsay for instance, the image of the female who stands outside a room where men read or write vividly figures in almost every one of her novels her identification of "the name of the father" with male education and male privilege. On the matter of gender Woolf and Lacan are essentially divided.

And she resisted the implication that the symbolic might assign a definite meaning and so produce closure. After Roger Fry had read *To the Lighthouse*, he wrote to Woolf to praise the novel for its movement "backwards and forwards in time," and for his sense that "arriving at the Lighthouse has a symbolic meaning which escapes me."[37] She replied,

I meant *nothing* by The Lighthouse. One has to have a central line down the middle of the book to hold the design together. I saw that all sorts of feelings would accrue to this, but I refused to think them out, and trusted that people would make it the deposit for their own emotions – which they have done, one thinking it means one thing another another. I can't manage Symbolism except in this vague, generalised way. Whether it's right or wrong I don't know, but directly I'm told what a thing means, it becomes hateful to me. (*L* III:385)

Her letter suggests a general resistance to accepted meanings, and is consistent with her emphasis in the essays on the collaborative status of the reader. The function of Lily Briscoe, the figure who draws "a central line," is to make the structure of the sign visible, while leaving its referent somewhat open to the reader. In Pamela L. Caughie's reading of the novel's "fictiousness," "we are no longer concerned with *the* connection or *the* correspondence between two realms but with the connections we posit among a variety of elements selected from a range of possibilities."[38]

One scene from "The Window" suggests that Woolf saw the symbolic as part of an outmoded notion of transcendence. Lily sees Mr. and Mrs. Ramsay at a moment when meaning "descends on people, making them symbolical, making them representative . . . and made them in the dusk standing, looking, the symbols of marriage, husband and wife" (*TL* 80). In the manuscript they are revealingly "Crucified & transcendent" (*TL* 240 n.66). The power of the symbol would seem to derive from a momentarily idealized father. The two senses of "representation" that elsewhere Woolf discriminates are in the half light of dusk combined. The Ramsay couple both visibly images, and invisibly stands for, a constituency of married pairs. The composite symbol owes its power to religion. The Ramsays are pictured as a Christian icon, its authority derived from that of God the father in a secular culture where its significance is perceived by the artist.[39]

That scene is balanced by another from "The Lighthouse" which makes clear how the Oedipal experience divides Cam from James. During the scene in the boat James's fantasy of killing the father divides brother and sister. James fears that "I shall be left to fight the tyrant alone," while Cam is left to wonder "how to resist his entreaty – forgive me; care for me; while James the lawgiver, with the tablets of eternal wisdom laid open on his knee (his hand on the tiller had become symbolical to her), said, Resist him. Fight him. He said so rightly; justly . . . Her brother was most god-like, her father most suppliant. And to which did she yield, she thought, sitting between them " (*TL* 183). The symbolic is a position enforced by filial bonds. Lily's painting on the other hand requires neither the language of justice nor that of forgiveness, a mediation of the symbolic that is not visible to the young girl still at sea.

The word *symbolic* occurs again in Woolf's novels, in *The Waves*, in a passage which suggests its inevitable link to male vision and to ideology. " 'The gardeners sweep with great brooms and the lady sits writing.' Thus he directed me [Bernard] to that which is beyond and outside our own predicament; to that which is symbolic, and thus perhaps permanent, if there is any permanence in our sleeping, eating, breathing, so animal, so spiritual and tumultuous lives" (*W* 248–9). Like Bernard's wish to find "something unvisual" beneath the painting, this passage suggests his desire for the symbolic as a sign of "permanence" in the animal world.

Patrick McGee writes of the passage,

> This is the symbolic not as it has been inscribed with meanings by a given culture but as the material trace, the historical condition of the possibility of meaning. The woman writing embodies the relation to the symbolic as radically other, material, subject to historical reshaping, and she writes where the gardeners, that is, the subaltern classes, sweep up the remains of patriarchal culture . . . The woman writing occupies the border of the symbolic.[40]

Although McGee is elsewhere concerned with gender, in this portion of his argument he underestimates its force. The woman writer who creates a utopia out of waste materials is the joint creation of Bernard and an "observant fellow" who whispers the image to him. In other words the image is created out of the desire of men, in a passage that balances the writing woman against a "witless servant" laughing in the attic (*W* 248). It is Jane Eyre and Bertha Mason once again, both created by Mr. Rochester; Bernard's image in effect makes the symbolic a more remote possibility for the female artist.

Woolf's symbolic realm can become the object of resistance. To pair the woman writing with the woman of witless laughter suggests an Imaginary that is too dangerous to be paired with the Symbolic. In *To the Lighthouse* the moment when the Ramsays become "the symbols of marriage" is imaged by the narrator as an explosion, "a sense of things having been blown apart, of space" (*TL* 80). In "the failing light" boundaries are stretched; distances seem to increase so that space looks larger; a star appears. The passage imagines the destruction of perspective as a way to open a view of the sky. In both novels the symbolic is so entangled with the ideology of kinship and gender that the female subject remains confined to the visible world, and the symbolic is scarcely a form of articulation equally available to both genders. The severe disjunction between Woolf and Lacan at this point demonstrates her recognition that ideology hinders the mutual reciprocity of Imaginary and Symbolic.

Lacan's Imaginary and Symbolic are interdependent: "the imaginary and the symbolic constitute neither an ethical opposition nor an ontological hierarchy, but a differential relationship that disorders each of these 'orders,' as Lacan often calls them; each order sets itself apart *from* the other, but in so doing reveals its dependency upon the other and thereby sets *itself apart*."[41] Woolf customarily represents the interdependence of the visible and the intelligible as an unresolved paradox that functions so as to differentiate. Sometimes it occurs in language, as the difference between Minnie as *she* and *you*, or the double sense of *representation* in "Solid Objects." In a more complex way Woolf suppresses one set of photographs from *Three Guineas* and prints another, as a kind of test of the referentiality of any text to documentary wartime photographs.

Elizabeth Abel's reading of Lily Briscoe's painting also engages the problem of the symbolic. By noting that Woolf shifts the focus of the novel from linguistic to visual representation Abel reads the painting as a challenge to the Oedipal narrative of Freud and Lacan. "Lily's sustained and recuperative matricentric story offers a powerful alternative to James's and Cam's Oedipal fictions."[42] Whereas Cam is "unable to find a language for her own split desire," Lily is able in painting to represent "the simultaneity of maternal absence and presence."[43] If a female's access to the symbolic is blocked by the Name of the Father, painting offers a possible alternative. But Abel is caught up by the necessity to read the painting within a narrative of personal development and feminist choice. Lily's earlier image of Mrs. Ramsay is "a moment of origin," which when she works it through ten years later results in a painting that is a "palimpsest."[44] "Having redefined her medium in metaphors drawn from a moment unrepresented in 'The Window', Lily reconstructs the crucial scene that had been framed as a tableau beneath her canvas."[45] The notion of an origin "beneath her canvas" suggests that mimesis is linked to a history of developmental stages, precisely the formulation that occludes the subject.

In the context of a painting that represents its own history the gaze achieves its significance as an inspiration: "Lily constructs a reciprocal gaze," so that she and Mrs. Ramsay gaze at one another across time and space and "the mother–daughter gaze across a mutually constituted intermediate space fosters painting; the father–son dialogue across a silent female body transmits the knowledge of language and law."[46] The gaze so imagined imparts to painting an authority equivalent to that "of language and law." But Abel does not contrast the gaze with other modes of vision, for instance Lily's vision of the dead Mrs. Ramsay. Nor does she acknowledge the possibility of misrecognition and self-deception inherent in the gaze, of which, as we have seen, Woolf was keenly aware. And most importantly, to overlook the distinction between the character and the narrator elides the subject that may be inferred from the language of the text.

In my reading, Lily's completing the painting is contingent on her becoming a subject. She recognizes that self-division is the first step: "She felt curiously divided, as if one part of her were drawn out there [with Mr. Ramsay]" (*TL* 171). But completing her painting has as much to do with the mimetic problem of representing the figure of the dead as with Mrs. Ramsay's maternal presence. While Lily "felt an obscure distress," wondered what was "wrong with the design," and hunted for the "something that evaded her," the narrator comments "But what she wished to get hold of was that very jar on the nerves, the thing itself before it has been made anything" (*TL* 209). Desire forces Lily to operate in the self-deceptive modes of the gaze and hallucination; we are told in the third person of her impossible wish to get hold of the Real. Lily recognizes the division between her social roles as painter or female, but it falls to the narrator to "locate the subject in a place where it can never arrive."[47] The narrator functions to represent without resolving the paradox of the novelist who "implicitly affiliates her writing with a mode of representation that her representation of language contradicts."[48]

The emergence of the subject from the imaginary is demonstrated when the structure of the visible world is reoriented away from geometral space. Two of Lacan's essays from 1964, "The Line and Light" and "What is a Picture?," suggest that the visual field when defined by light repositions the subject in relation to the gaze. "What determines me, at the most profound level, in the visible, is the gaze that is outside. It is through the gaze that I enter light and it is from the gaze that I receive its effects. Hence it comes about that the gaze is the instrument through which light is embodied and through which . . . I am *photo-graphed*" (*FFC* 106). Whereas the visible created by geometral space is a "trap," light resets the boundaries of the visible. Space that is defined by light provides an alternative:

That which is light looks at me, and by means of that light in the depths of my eye, something is painted – something that is not simply a constructed relation, the object on which the philosopher lingers – but something that is an impression, the shimmering of a surface that is not, in advance, situated for me in its distance. This is something that introduces what was elided in the geometral relation – the depth of field, with all its ambiguity and variability, which is in no way mastered by me. (*FFC* 96)

In the character of Bernard, Woolf represents a mutation in subjectivity figured as the return of light after a solar eclipse. At the moment when Percival departs for India, Bernard acquires a sense of his identity that is consistent with "a world that our own force can subjugate" (*W* 246). But in his summing up after the death of Percival grief and desire release for an instant this recognition of himself as subject: "What is startling, what is unexpected, what we cannot account for, what turns symmetry to nonsense – that comes suddenly to my mind, thinking of him" (*W* 243). The death of the self that was founded on an Imperialist notion of "identity" is imaged as an eclipse. When light returns Bernard experiences the difference: "I saw but was not seen" (*W* 286). Yet the coming to subjectivity is not permanent: "How describe or say anything in articulate words again? – save that it fades, save that it undergoes a gradual transformation " (*W* 287). In Lacan's terms "the subject only appears, insofar as it *fades*."[49] When the moment has passed Bernard reverts to his old habits. Woolf's preference for the would-be artist suggests that she found in the visible the phenomenon of subjectivity which with all its contradictions and impermanence was of more compelling and immediate interest to her than work achieved in the symbolic.

Woolf's resemblance to Lacan is most easily grasped in her manner of representing resistance to the ego that inhabits the grammatical first person. But whereas Lacan's subject negotiates entry into the symbolic by means of the signifier, the acquisition of language in Woolf's fiction seems securely linked to the formal education of men. Like Cam Ramsay, the female lingers on the threshold of the symbolic, experiencing the contradictions of the scopic regime but barred from the symbolic by the kinship structures that are replicated in language. Lily is able to complete her painting as the result of a speech act in which she repeats the words uttered by Mr. Banks, as though the female experiences the symbolic as ventriloquism.

Among the public for whom representation signifies primarily electing a member to Parliament, the sense of *vorstellen*, to image or stage, may be occluded so that it no longer refers to the artist's achievement. After listing Woolf's artist figures, Caughie asks "Why all these failed artists?" in order to pose a new question: "Instead of asking what the text is about, we can ask how it comes about and what it brings about."[50] Woolf apprehended her power in terms like those of Wordsworth in *The Prelude*: "the hiding places of Man's power/Open; I would approach them, but they close;"[51] From this perspective the imaginary partakes of the full powers of the mind in comparison with which the symbolic is a compromised public utterance. In her work the artist who experiences the unresolved dilemma of becoming a subject is a privileged figure.

A more striking resemblance to Lacan is that Woolf never conflates the subject with the self. As a result her representation of the visible situates her work among twentieth-century debates about the coming into existence of the subject. Like Marx and Freud she was drawn to the camera obscura as an image of the way that the eye turns the visible world upside down. She shares with them a sense that ideological distortion characterizes all representation. The subject materializes fiction from the essential contradictions of ocular experience. Subjectivity is a fleeting moment of motivating power, unaccompanied by awareness of the process, which is revealed by the narrator after the fact.

The chapters that follow do not trace a consistent pattern in the representation of the visible throughout Woolf's career, nor do I consider the novels one by one. Each chapter establishes a different angle of vision and brings into play a somewhat different constellation of texts. In Chapter 2 I show that Woolf's study of Greek language and literature emphasized her social circumstances; that is as a female she was not eligible, nor would her father have considered her fit for, university education. Woolf comments directly on the quality of that education in the character of Jacob Flanders, whose reading of Plato in effect insulates him from problems of class and gender. In fact the rudiments of the feminism that Woolf later developed may be discerned in some of her earliest notes about classical Greece. But thanks to the rigor imposed by her tutor Janet Case, Woolf became more than an amateur reader like Sara Pargiter in *The Years*. She translated *Agamemnon*, the most refractory of Greek texts, and appropriated from it an image of loss as deprivation of the visible that recurs in her fiction at moments of great intensity.

She also created for herself an intellectual position outside the university. Study of Greek gave her the sense, since theorized by Walter Benjamin, that the translation that reorders the signifying practices of the translator's language is to be preferred to the translation that merely communicates the sense of the original text. In Woolf's case translation gave her the authority to represent madness as an irruption from the world of dream and vision that confers the ability to see beyond the bounds of the visible world.

As Woolf was drafting *Mrs. Dalloway* she was also translating *Agamemnon*. In both works we see in detail how the sign is destabilized in postwar society. The semiotic confusion of the opening strophe of the play is revised in the opening scene of the novel, in which commercial advertisements written in smoke and the signal of a new religion demonstrate the historical contingency of the sign, and each of the major characters is identified with a particular mode of seeing. The scene precedes the introduction of Septimus, who represents the Greek idea that the mad see what the sane cannot. Sacrifice as a manipulation of the codes of naming is apparent in the ease with which Sir William Bradshaw renames Septimus's illness, so that the warrior becomes victim. In the mind of Clarissa Dalloway he precipitates a redefinition of postwar kinship as the recognition of the self in the other. Among the several misrecognitions that go on during her party it is significant that Clarissa reacts to the death of a young man she has never met, and to the image seen through a window of a nameless old woman preparing for the night.

To the Lighthouse may be read in part as a study of the changes in the conception of beauty, from its valuation in the *Symposium* as the form that leads to the philosophical ascent of the mind, to its status in Victorian culture, where it is associated with Mrs. Ramsay. In the third section of the novel Lily Briscoe is able to complete her painting by a speech act that recuperates beauty for ordinary language. After Woolf's representation of the shifts in its meaning occasioned by war, in "Time Passes," Lily removes beauty from among the "master signifiers," and redefines it for her artistic purposes.

In *The Waves*, discussed in Chapter 4, Woolf represents the historical conditions of personal "identity" under Imperialism and its relation to the subject, especially as that was defined by Heidegger in his 1938 essay, "The Age of the World Picture." Although Rhoda is the character who expresses most openly the savagery of Imperialism, my argument focuses on Neville and Bernard, whom Woolf paired in her early drafts of the novel. Neville expresses his grief for the death of Percival in the language of William Holman Hunt's *The Light of the World*, a well-known image of the light of Christ shining into darkness. Although Bernard turns as well to paintings to mourn his friend, his subjectivity arises out of his response to the unknown African traveler, whom I interpret as the Conrad of "Heart of Darkness." He supplies Bernard with the language of the subject who at the moment of the death of the other is enabled, in Marlow's phrase, to "step over the threshold of the invisible." In that position Bernard images his newfound subjectivity as a solar eclipse, in which light comes and goes and the subject becomes a transparent witness. But the position is not sustained, and the novel ends with a satiric challenge to the image of death.

Chapter 5 reads the mirror scene in "A Sketch of the Past" as a study of the female writer's coming to subjectivity under patriarchy. The mirror experience in Woolf's fiction suggests that the subject comes into existence as a response to the limitations of the Romantic self. Woolf wrote "A Sketch" during the events of 1939–40, in part as a relief from writing the biography of Roger Fry. Not surprisingly his image of the mirror as making it possible to view one's life as a spectator, and her sense that the biographer cannot reveal intimate details had their effect on the narrative of her own life. Looking into the glass Woolf sees not herself but the lineal members of her family. The "ancestral dread" that checks her response to the beauty of her mother and Stella is balanced against her recourse to "ancestresses" to relieve her of the violence implicit in family life, in particular her molestation by her half-brother Gerald.

The female subject is gendered by her particular response to that violence. Gerald's role becomes necessary to the subject's sense that in the context of the Victorian family the female is driven to recreate her kinship and genealogy. I read Woolf's autobiographical exploration of the double image of the female subject, and the circumstances that precipitate entry into the symbolic in the context of *Agamemnon*. Like Cassandra, she is spoken as animal, and when she speaks addresses an audience that fails to comprehend. Woolf concludes her account of the painful and violent experience of her childhood with a study of her attempt to "put the severed parts together," which I interpret as a trope of sign-making.

At the end of her career Woolf revised her image of the visible world. It is refigured in *Three Guineas*, the subject of Chapter 6, in terms of two lifelong interests, in the camera, whose design and function were undergoing change at this time, and in Greek tragedy. As Woolf composed the text, she shifted her emphasis from a Wordsworthian visual perspective to a sense that the camera makes visible what the retina cannot see, and in so doing she renamed the subject as correspondent. Her essay is illustrated with five photographs of men wearing the costumes of their professions, but it also makes repeated allusion to photographs of the "dead bodies and ruined houses" of the Spanish Civil War. The text mediates between two sets of photographs: one printed, and the other more disturbing because not visible. Woolf was well aware that the French and the British represented the war in different terms, and in a holograph note we see that she toyed with but rejected the temptation to follow the lead of journalists in *L'Humanité* and write propaganda. The "Third Guinea" weaves together a reading of *Antigone* with two sets of photographs, of which the more disturbing are those photographs of the atrocity of war that, owing to the conventions of British journalism, were invisible to the English reader save in her text.

CHAPTER 2

On the far side of language: Greek studies, and "Jacob's Room"

Conceive, then . . . that there are these two entities, and that one of them is sovereign over the intelligible order and region and the other over the world of the eye-ball . . . You surely apprehend the two types, the visible and the intelligible.

Plato, *The Republic*, Book VI[1]

ON HEARING THE BIRDS SING IN GREEK

In the memoir of her life, "Old Bloomsbury," published post-humously and probably presented to the Memoir Club sometime in 1921–2, Woolf recounts that during her second serious breakdown, in 1904, she lay in bed "thinking that the birds were singing Greek choruses and that King Edward was using the foulest possible language among Ozzie Dickinson's azaleas" (*MB* 162). Her biographers read the trope of birds singing Greek choruses as a sign of her madness. But it is also a powerful and poignant representation of a moment of her life as an image from classical literature. Leonard Woolf in *Beginning Again* alludes to her hearing "the birds outside her window talking Greek."[2] The same phrasing appears in Quentin Bell's biography: "she lay in bed, listening to the birds singing in Greek and imagining that King Edward VII lurked in the azaleas using the foulest possible language."[3] Although this chapter largely concerns Woolf's translation of Greek literature and its impact on the development of her narrative technique, in her biography Greek stands for the most distant horizon of intelligibility, the point beyond which the sane mind does not reach. Birdsong is communication in a language that the listener does not know, and to acknowledge it as language albeit unknown compromises the listener's social identity in a way that invites being labelled insane. Considered this way, insanity does not signify so much self destructive behavior as a mode of cognition unrecognized by society. So to be considered mad is in part a question of semantics and semiotics, what the words mean and how they mean.

Roger Poole's *The Unknown Virginia Woolf* was written before the publication of Woolf's memoirs, in order to redress what he considered the destructive attitude of her biographers towards her so-called "madness." He interprets the image of the birds as Woolf's reaction to the privilege enjoyed by Leonard and his friends of learning Greek at Cambridge: "Greek was a symbol for everything that she personally would never be able to attain to. Greek was an ideal, a touchstone, an abstraction of pure intellection."[4] He suggests as well that the birds' song in its allusion to Philomela imaged a failure of husband and wife to speak of the troubled nature of their sexual relations, which after her breakdown of 1913–14 Leonard had decided to terminate. Poole's biography is a persuasive and compassionate interpretation of her life.

I argue that the trope of the birds singing in Greek is grounded in Woolf's work of 1922–24, when in addition to "Old Bloomsbury," she was writing *Mrs. Dalloway* (1925), and the essay "On Not Knowing Greek," included in *The Common Reader* (1925). The essay and the novel together represent her studied and passionate engagement with Greek literature. When Woolf writes in the essay about birds singing in Greek she means the nightingale, the ancient figure of female lamentation.[5] Philomela was raped by King Tereus, and later together with her sister Procne, took revenge by serving him at dinner the flesh of his son Itys. Sophocles' Electra, Woolf wrote, "speaks of that very nightingale: 'that bird distraught with grief, the messenger of Zeus'" (*CR* 29), that is the representation of the divine. Birdsong is associated as well with the Chorus of the Greek play, who "sing like birds in the pauses of the wind" and "allow the poet to speak himself" (*CR* 30). The nightingale and the wren figure in a rough note on the ending of *The Waves:* "What a song they sing to love – /We who observe things without being part of them" (Hol *W* 760). The song of the bird, she wrote, supplies for the playwright "another side to his conception" (*CR* 30).[6] As a female and as someone who had had the experience of hearing voices, Woolf was intent on exploring a way of representing the language of the other that stressed the pain associated with the Greek myth of Philomela.[7]

Mastery of the Greek language was a compelling if unattainable ideal which left Woolf permanently in the position of the amateur. She writes of Greek as a trope of the forever untranslatable. In Sophocles' Electra we hear "the nightingale whose song echoes through English literature singing in her own Greek tongue" (*CR* 29). In her diary Woolf noted of Sir Richard Claverhouse Jebb's translation of *Electra* (1894), that "the particular charm of Greek remains as strong & as difficult to account for as ever. One feels the immeasurable difference between the text & the translation with the first words" (*D* 1:184). In one sense hearing the song of the nightingale echo throughout two cultures signifies the experience of reading a translated text with enough knowledge of Greek to recognize the deficit.

Woolf's trope of the birds singing in Greek, so oddly paired with an image of the king of England speaking in obscenities, suggests the interaction of lyric and satire in Aristophanes, although her notes on one reading of the Greek text may possibly have been written somewhat later.[8] Sometime after 23 February 1924 (*D* II:292), in preparation for writing the essay, Woolf read *The Birds*, which pairs the lyrical with the violent and obscene. She and Leonard had just purchased 52 Tavistock Square; they were preparing to move house; and her reading was rather rushed. In a half page on the play she notes "translated by [B. B.] Rogers," and "Read at a gallop." Although her reading was hasty, she noted the pairing of the lyrical with the satiric, and welcomed the addition of laughter to Greek literature: "Very lyrical, & intellectual. He laughs at the gods" (Berg Reel 13). Although the notes were written in haste, in the essay she adds that Aristophanes' laughter and humour are "closely bound up with a sense of the body" (*CR* 38).

Woolf's reading of Aristophanes contributes to the sense that the trope of birdsong in Greek points away from her medical history and towards her knowledge of Greek literature. In *The Birds* (414 B.C.) two characters, Peisetairos (Persuader-friend) and Euelpides (Hopeful), weary of their life in Athens, set out to find a quieter place to live. After some amusing episodes including being fitted with wings, they end up persuading the birds they meet to found a bird metropolis, Cloudcuckoobury in Rogers's translation. It is planned to wrest power from the gods, thus potentially replicating the violence of the life they had hoped to leave behind. Like others of Aristophanes' comedies the *Birds* allows for the ventilation of strong feelings, especially concerning sex and aggression, and draws the viewer into a larger perspective on life, all by virtue of what Kenneth Reckford calls "a healing touch of madness."[9]

For our purposes it is significant that Peisetairos and Euelpides meet two of the principals in the story of the nightingale, Procne, and King Tereus, who has apparently shed his nefarious history and turned into the Hoopoe. In order to convene the birds he summons the nightingale, "my mate." Since she is unable to speak, she communicates with the sound of the flute, which the audience hears played from behind a thicket. The two visitors are enchanted and ask to see her; Euelpides would like to steal a kiss, but remembers that her beak is sharp. Then in one of several reminders that birds after all are good to eat, he replies that he "would treat her like an egg, and strip/The egg-shell from her poll, and kiss her so" (lines 670–2). His response to the nightingale is matched by a scene near the end of the play in which Euelpides and Peisetairos roast some captured birds and dress them with oil and cheese. The comic/sadistic view of violent ingestion contrasts with the idealizing vision of the Chorus, who treat the nightingale as the inspiration for their story of the creation of the birds from Love.

Christine Perkell notes that the birds' lyrics are endowed "with a traditional poetic and religious character . . . probably to elicit a certain nostalgia for and awe of an earlier time, seductive in its apparent simplicity."[10] She refers to the often noted pastoral dimension of the play which offsets the theme of power and military conquest. But in other utterances "the birds collaborate with Euelpides' fantasies, portraying their lives as unimpeded opportunities for self-indulgence." Promising freedom for adultery

the birds base their appeal specifically on the pleasure of illegitimate action . . . As an example, they allow the audience to believe that a great advantage to be derived from wings is the satisfaction of sexual desire which is specifically adulterous. The freedom for adultery, escaping debts and father-beating suggests that, from the perspective of the city, birds represent their lives as virtually criminal.[11]

As the Chorus explains:

> All that here is reckoned shameful, all that here the laws condemn;
> With the birds is right and proper, you may do it all with them.
>
> (Rogers, lines 755–6)

Although the lyrics portray the gods with reverence, in the play they are beset with problems which suggest a "disparity between the birds' beautiful image of the gods and the facts of reality as they appear in the play's action [which] throw into question the truth of the birds' lyrics."[12]

F. E. Romer pays particular attention to the compelling moment near the end of the play when Peisetairos is seen preparing cooked birds to serve to the other birds. The scene plays on the themes of sacrifice and trickery in the myths of origin in Aesop and especially Hesiod. In Hesiod's *Theogony* the three generations of the gods, Ouranos, Kronos, and Zeus "bespeak a pattern of male violence typified not only by violence against fathers but by violence from fathers against females and children as well."[13] Peisetairos' plan to overthrow the gods and restore the rule of the birds simply installs new actors in familiar roles, thus maintaining the status quo. In the barbecue scene as he prepares to serve a meal of cooked flesh to the gods, his double role as trickster and usurper "emerges both from the reinvention of sacrifice in this play and from Hesiod's account of the first sacrifice ever."[14] In *Theogony* Prometheus tempts Zeus with two portions, one meat and one fat and both disguised, but Zeus, who is not fooled plays his own trick on mankind. I hear an echo in another scene of beginning again, when Bernard near the end of *The Waves* sees himself at dinner, "Lord, how unutterably disgusting life is! What dirty tricks it plays us, one moment free; the next, this . . . Disorder, sordidity and corruption surround us. We have been taking into our mouths the bodies of dead birds. It is with these greasy crumbs, slobbered over napkins, and little corpses that we have to build" (*W* 196). Whether Bernard is also a cannibal and a trickster is a question for another context.

Finally in "On Not Knowing Greek" Woolf quoted *Agamemnon*, which she was translating during this same period. In the essay she quotes in Greek Cassandra's "naked cry" as she foresees her fate at the hands of Clytemnestra. The scene links the death of Cassandra to communication. Clytemnestra has earlier suggested that Cassandra is a "barbarian," speaking an "incomprehensible" language that requires interpretation (lines 1050–1). But even the Chorus, which views Cassandra with sympathy, cannot see the death scene that is before her eyes. It believes her to be possessed, singing "the wild lyric" of the nightingale, but Cassandra is not to be saved by metamorphosis. As she moves closer to her death, the Chorus confesses itself unable to comprehend oracles and prophecy: "From divination what good ever has come to men?/Art, and multiplication of words drifting through tangled evil bring/Terror to them that hear" (lines 1132–5). Cassandra, whose prophetic vision leaves her in no doubt of her fate, replies in Woolf's translation, "Yet I know Greek; I think I know it far too well" (line 1254).[15]

In this context the title of Woolf's essay and the trope of her madness suggest the multiple meanings of translation, as movement to another location, which might include metamorphosis. As an intellectual activity translation freed Woolf from some of the constraints of gender in her culture, but without any concomitant increase of social freedoms. In the plays that she read she could observe what happened to women who used language to transgress gender boundaries: they were sacrificed or hid behind a bush in Cloudcuckooland. The title of Woolf's essay suggests the paradox of an authority associated with the risk to the female who knows Greek. Debate over knowing Greek suggests that the safety of those in the Chorus may be sustained by their inability to read Cassandra's meaning.[16] Knowing or not knowing Greek brings together the questions of language that are central in Woolf's work: the relation between sanity and insanity as modes of discourse, the construction and stability of the sign, and the special position of the female subject.

These questions are of a different order from those considered in Woolf's biography, where the debate is organized around the question of whether those who are sane can do any more than label her utterance as proof that she was mad. The image of Greek birdsong was revised by her husband to suppress its literary quality when he omitted mention of the Chorus and substituted "talking" for "singing." It suggests that she saw herself, like her character Septimus Smith, as having a wildly romantic sensibility. In the manuscript of *Mrs. Dalloway* Septimus hears his dead friend Evans say "this is Greek poetry. Then all the birds laughed."[17] Quentin Bell, by identifying the king as Edward VII, appealed to what the reader might know of his amorous career in order to stress the absurdity of Woolf's experience. The image introduces Bell's much quoted sentence, "All that summer she was mad."[18] Both accounts were written under the assumption of philosophical objectivity, without any attempt to discover what experience of her state of mind Woolf was representing when she wrote her memoir.

Walter Benjamin's essay on translation "Die Aufgabe des Ubersetzers" (1923) ("The Task of the Translator") suggests some of the uses to which Woolf put her knowledge of Greek. He writes of translation as a phenomenon of the work which "has reached the age of its fame" when it manifests the kinship between languages. Translation is always "unsuited to its content, over-powering and alien," so that an "adequate translator" is unlikely. The fundamental task of the translator does not consist in getting the sense right, but in revealing not only differences of meaning, but divergent ways of meaning from language to language. The more elusive aspects of Benjamin's argument concern "pure" language and the necessity to reproduce not content, but "lovingly and in detail [to] incorporate the original's mode of signification." Translation in his argument "must refrain from wanting to communicate." Rather it becomes itself a mode of representation. "It cannot possibly reveal or establish this hidden relationship [between languages] itself; but it can represent it by realizing it in embryonic or intensive form. This representation of hidden significance through an embryonic attempt at making it visible is of so singular a nature that it is rarely met with in the sphere of nonlinguistic life."[19]

In Benjamin's essay communication is no longer the primary function of language. The first paragraph of his essay explicitly denies the reader's response: "No poem is intended for the reader, no picture for the beholder, no symphony for the listener."[20] Texts which convey information, where the translator might be tempted to communicate to the reader by getting the (presumably simple) sense right, are less translatable: "The lower the quality and distinction of its language, the larger the extent to which it is information, the less fertile a field is it for translation, until the utter preponderance of content . . . renders it impossible."[21] Like Benjamin, Woolf used translation as a model of the functions of language in which communication and what it implies about information presented for the convenience of the reader is devalued, in favor of the notion that translation represents "divergent ways of meaning." Woolf's singing of the birds and Benjamin's idea of "pure" language both represent the ideal of translation as a boundary beyond which practice cannot reach.

Perhaps Woolf's biographers have focused exclusively on the human cost of the rare phenomenon which Benjamin outlines in abstract terms. Did the Woolf who heard birds singing in Greek hear a "pure" language? Did she make "visible" in her work the untranslatable, "hidden significance" of Greek? More specifically, how can the reader understand the traditional poetic image of the nightingale in the context of foul language uttered by King Edward? Is the pairing of Philomel with the king of England a form of ludic protest against the social mores which granted males almost un-limited sexual access to dependent young females? What is the significance of sacrifice in twentieth-century Britain? And more broadly, how can the authority associated with madness in Greek literature be translated into the literature of another time and place?

FROM TRANSLATION TO NARRATION

The biography of Woolf's early life has usually been written from the perspective of her family relationships, and the psychological damage caused by a series of deaths, of her mother, her half-sister Stella, and her brother Thoby. But a biography that focused on her intellectual development would give priority to her study of the Greek language and literature, although it went on largely outside educational institutions. Her brother Thoby introduced her as a small child to the Greeks, telling her the story of Hector and Troy as they walked up and down the stairs "outside the water closet" (*MB* 125, 138). In her early letters she already reveals a keen and continuous interest in the study of Greek, and in her notes on Greek texts her awareness of the degree to which knowledge of Greek was linked to British debates about gender.

Woolf's studies may be set against the background of the changes taking place in British university education. Christopher Stray analyzes "the timing of class formation in relation to industrialization."[22] Since the Industrial Revolution came to England relatively early in comparison to its appearance in Germany and France, it did not necessitate the same kinds of change in university education as were needed later when scientific training was more clearly necessary. He describes the changes that took place in Britain in terms of the politics of culture. As boundaries between classes shifted, the university offered a means "to self-recognition": education and in particular classical learning "became a crucial status marker, providing the means to distinction and social exclusion. As we shall see this use of education was characteristic of the emergence of successive bourgeois groups through the century, each seeking distinction in relation to its perceived superiors and inferiors."[23] If we add women to the list of excluded groups, we gain a sense of the politics of Woolf's lifelong sense of her position as an "outsider."

Roy Lowe develops the

hypothesis that in England a diverse and highly-stratified system of higher education developed partly as a consequence of the unreadiness of existing universities to respond fully to social change. In the process, the role of the emergent university colleges was crucial. In the event, their aspiration to break from the "technocratic" model and to conform with that of the Oxbridge college drove a wedge between "humane" and applied studies which was to prove immensely significant for English society in the twentieth century.[24]

Woolf seems to me to exhibit the contradictions implicit in a plan to admit large numbers of students to an education designed for an elite class. Although she did not and could not attend Cambridge, the university attended by her father, her brother, her husband, and several of her family and friends, she supported the notion that Greek was the center of humane study. It is ironic that although denied a university education, she was tutored in the language that was mandatory for all students at Oxford and Cambridge. But had she been admitted, one wonders how she would have used an education designed to train men for the leadership of church, state, and empire.[25] Women had entered Cambridge University as teachers and students since the early 1870s, when Newnham and Girton Colleges were established, but although they were admitted to the tripos in 1881 and given a certificate, they could not until 1948 receive degrees.[26]

In this climate, tuition in Greek and other languages, and some courses in history comprised the whole of Woolf's formal education.[27] She began her study of Greek and history at King's College (London) in 1897 (*L* 1:10). In January 1898 she "went to Greek for the first time" with Dr. George Warr (*L* 1:12). Although her letters express her pleasure in learning Greek, a recently uncovered letter from Leslie Stephen to Dr. Warr suggests the limitations that he imposed on his daughter's instruction. In November 1897, when she had just begun her study, he wrote:

My daughter is attending your Greek class. I hope that you will allow me to give you one hint. She has been in a very nervous state, wh., though explicable, has given me some anxiety. I have allowed her to go to the class, for wh. she was very anxious; because I think that it does her some good to have the occupation. At the same time, I have found that anything like a strain from having to do tasks tells upon her in a degree, wh. is greater than would be at all possible if her health were quite right. I should be grateful if you would just remember this & let her off with light work. Of course, it does not come to much by itself in any case, but I have to be exceedingly careful for the present.[28]

Stephen's fatherly note asks that Greek be taught as a kind of therapy for a convalescent young girl, and in the phrase "it does not come to much by itself" seems to suggest that he did not believe a daughter would become proficient. In the event Woolf moved on rapidly to new and more demanding instructors: first Clara Pater, with whom she studied Latin and Greek, and then in 1902, Janet Case, who became Woolf's lifelong friend (*L* 1:26, 64).[29]

Case's intellectual training and tastes help to account for the fact that Woolf approached the Greeks with the translator's rigorous attention to language. She spent the hours from ten to one daily preparing for her bi-weekly lesson (*MB* 127–8). According to a sketch that she wrote, Case was a scholar, who insisted that her reluctant pupil begin by mastering the details of Greek grammar (*AP* 183). As a result Woolf came to Greek texts not as a reader like Sally in *The Years*, who carelessly misreads the text of *Antigone*, but as a reader trained in translation. Her journals for this early period show her at work on a series of projects translating Plato, Aristotle, Thucydides, and Sophocles. Woolf's passion for Aeschylus, in whose work her own is most deeply grounded, was instilled in her as well by Janet Case.[30] When Woolf's ambitious engagement with Greek texts, the essay "On Not Knowing Greek," appeared in *The Common Reader*, she wrote to her old teacher: "I was rather nervous lest you should curse my impertinence for writing about Greek, when you are quite aware of my complete ignorance" (*L* III:191). The letter suggests as well that as a translator she was well aware of the terms of the debates being carried on within the universities on the value and the possibility of "knowing" Greek.

The feminist arguments that Woolf developed throughout her career began in her early notes on the Greeks. Her understanding that British attitudes to gender evolved from the interpretation of Greek texts is apparent in her notes on Alfred Zimmern's *The Greek Commonwealth* (1911), a widely read text. Woolf's six pages of notes from 1922–24[31] respond to the revealing analogies that he draws with Edwardian Britain. For instance he writes of the Greek city as "like an English college . . . a men's club," where life-sustaining friendships "sometimes make history."[32] His remarks on gender are especially challenging to the modern reader. In the chapter on population he notes that "while the years of Athens's greatness were for men one of the happiest periods in the whole history of the world, the women who worked beside them were restless, uneasy, and perplexed. Something was wrong."[33] In addition to wives there were "professional women," who worked as "companions," so that

Demosthenes distinguished between "companions for the sake of pleasure [and] wives to bear us lawful offspring."[34]

Readers of Woolf's polemical essays are familiar with her argument that patriarchy encourages female prostitution. In *Three Guineas* (1938) she writes apropos of the influence said to be exerted by wives, that "many of us would prefer to call ourselves prostitutes simply and to take our stand openly under the lamps of Piccadilly Circus" (*TG* 130). That view survived unchanged from her notes many years earlier on Zimmern's analysis of the role of women: "the domestic woman did not earn her living. did not have rights. the pros. did earn her living."[35]

It has been noted that Woolf often softened her feminist criticism when she revised a manuscript for publication. She also waited some fifteen years to publish the criticism of British gender practices that developed from her early recognition in these notes of the way in which her male contemporaries had put their Greek studies to ideological use.

Woolf read the Platonic dialogs in her twenties. Her notes on *The Phaedrus, The Protagoras, Euthyphro,* and *The Symposium* are preserved, and there are ample indications in her work that she had read *The Republic* as well. The dialogs made an important contribution to a representation of the visible world that she could not have derived from the conventions of realistic fiction. She would probably not have interested herself in philosophical questions, for instance whether "physical beauty is not a more 'accurate' or 'immediate' likeness of the corresponding Form than are instances of justice in relation to *their* corresponding Form,"[36] for she wrote of Plato primarily as a poet and image-maker. His concept of beauty as a divine Form manifest to the eye and mind allowed her to imagine a visible world which includes the seen and the unseen, as well as the viewer who under certain circumstances can see both and articulate their common ground.

A good deal about the relationship of the visible to the invisible in Plato's work may be found in Walter Pater's *Plato and Platonism* (1893). A copy of the book appeared in Leslie Stephen's library around 1898, when Woolf began her studies with Pater's sister, and in March 1905 Woolf purchased for herself the Edition de Luxe of Pater's works.[37] In the chapter of *Plato and Platonism*, entitled "The Genius of Plato," Pater describes a philosopher whose genius was to mediate philosophical abstraction and the visible world.

Just there – in the situation of one, shaped, by combining nature and circumstance, into a seer who has a sort of sensuous love of the unseen – is the paradox of Plato's genius, and therefore, always, of Platonism, of the Platonic temper. His aptitude for things visible, with the gift of words, empowers him to express, as if for the eyes, what except to the eye of the mind is strictly invisible, what an acquired asceticism induces him to rank above, and sometimes, in terms of harshest dualism, oppose to, the sensible world.[38]

The Platonic paradox of a philosopher who enjoys "a sort of sensuous love of the unseen" is manifested in the modern world, he argued, in the metaphysical dimension of the poetry of Wordsworth or Tennyson.[39]

Perry Meisel, noting that Woolf rarely mentioned Pater in her formal writings, sees him in terms of the absent father whose name is repressed.[40] Although Meisel makes little of *Plato and Platonism*, the configuration of visible/invisible, terms that appear over and over in Chapter Six, suggests a context in which Woolf read not only Plato but the Greek tragedians and nineteenth-century English poetry as well. When for instance Woolf counters the tendency to abstraction in *Mrs. Dalloway* by insisting in her notes that her characters be made visible, or when she attacks Wordsworth's interpretation of reflection, she orders the notion of what is visible/invisible in the fictional world in terms that are consistent with Pater's.

Woolf's serious engagement with the *Oresteia*, which she first read with Janet Case in 1903 (*L* I:72), came somewhat later, while she was writing *Mrs. Dalloway* and preparing the essays in *The Common Reader*. A line by line translation of *Agamemnon* (lines 1–1550) is among the reading notes which Brenda Silver dates 1922–24.[41] The Greek text has been printed on the right side of the page with a few words translated in the margin in Woolf's hand, and on the left side appears a clear uncorrected translation, "mostly copied from Verrall," she wrote, "but carefully gone into by me" (*D* II:215).

What can be the significance of a translation which was prepared with such effort by a professional writer and left among her personal papers? There was no shortage of available translations of *Agamemnon* into English: since 1824 at least ten had been published in Britain, including Robert Browning's in 1877, and a few more had appeared in the United States. The first British edition of the Loeb Classical Library bilingual edition of Aeschylus, translated by an American, Herbert Weir Smyth, was published in London, volume I in 1922, and II, which contained *Agamemnon*, in 1926. Working in the period 1922–24 Woolf would have had available as a model of the bilingual text the work of A. W. Verrall, his English/Greek *Choephori* in 1893, and his English/Greek *Agamemnon* in 1889 and 1904. Verrall printed the Greek text on the right side of the page, a prose translation on the left, the notes in the lower half of the page. Much of the format of the bilingual edition as we know it appears to have been his.

But Verrall's text and his scholarship were not acceptable to everyone. Walter Headlam, also a professor at Cambridge, published an attack on what he called the "mischievous" results of Verrall's edition. In *On Editing Aeschylus. A Criticism* (1891) he attacked Verrall's scholarship on the grounds of grammar, metre, and punctuation. He criticized Verrall's method as unscientific, in particular his "reckless-ness of assertion without care to verify; arguments invented to serve a present turn; citation of such evidence as may seem to bear out a proposition, and omission of the rest."[42] In his reply *"On Editing Aeschylus" A Reply* (1892) Verrall argued that Headlam's criticism was "gross," "libellous," and "actionable," and defended himself by describing his research step by step.[43] I wonder, given the heated arguments at this time about the study of Greek as maintaining social boundaries, whether the unacknowledged issue was not Verrall's having made Greek texts available to the Greekless reader.

In 1906 Woolf had been courted by Walter Headlam (1866–1908), an old family friend who was sixteen years her senior.[44] Her letters say that he volunteered to read all her "unpublished works," and was planning to dedicate his translation of *Agamemnon* to her "in gratitude for 3 pages of the finest criticism known to him which I wrote and despatched 4 years ago!" (*L* 1:259). Two years later, when her interest had waned, Headlam died rather suddenly, and Woolf wrote to Madge Vaughan that "it is tragic, for he always seemed disappointed and aggrieved with the world. Last time I saw him he complained as usual, but thought that he was becoming known, and he had almost finished some edition of Aeschylus" (*L* 1:335–6).[45] In fact Headlam's verse translation of *Agamemnon* was published in 1910. It was a bilingual edition, Greek text on the right side of the page, Headlam's verse translation on the left, and dedicated to Swinburne.

Agamemnon is reputedly the most difficult of ancient Greek texts. Although Woolf's choice of a play and the decision to translate seem to have arisen out of personal tastes formed in relation to friends and to her teacher, to have undertaken it at all was in itself a kind of intellectual credential. Instead of becoming merely the dedicatee of an edition of *Agamemnon*, a role which would have cast her as the girlish recipient of a romantic tribute, she would be the translator, a role that she associated with Headlam. When after his death she was able to stand back and see his sense of disappointment as injured vanity, she chose to model her translation on that of his rival. In so doing she imitated a prose translation rather than a poetic, perhaps put off by the recurring awkwardness of Headlam's phrasing, for instance in these lines: "To prayers is not an ear in Heaven; one frown/All conversant with such calls guilty and pulls down."[46] Yet in the context of his attack on Verrall's scholarship, Woolf's phrase "carefully gone into by me" acquires added significance.

Woolf read still other Greek plays in translation. When in 1901 she wrote to Thoby that she had read *Antigone*, she remarked that her father had offered to get from the library the translation of R. C. Jebb (*L* 1:42). It is unlikely that she read it in Greek, for an undated note on *Antigone* reads: "This one wd be worth reading in Greek," and another on *Oedipus at Colonus*, "I imagine the Choruses need to be read in Greek."[47] In notebook XIX, containing her notes for *The Common Reader* prepared 1923–24, Woolf lists an edition of the *Baccae* in Greek, but five plays by Sophocles: *Antigone, Oedipus Coloneus, Oedipus King, Trachiniae,* and *Ajax,* all in the French translation of Leconte de Lisle.[48] His *Traduction Nouvelle par Leconte de Lisle* was among the books in her personal library (*D* 1: 178 n.2) She also read Sophocles in the English translation of Sir Richard Jebb. His name appears in notebook XIX in connection with "specimen passages," although later notebooks, XLVII from 1923, XLV from 1934, and LX from 1933–37, x from 1931–39 all refer to his English translation of *Antigone,* in Part III of *Sophocles. The Plays and Fragments* (1891). In his edition the Greek appears on the left side of the page, an English prose translation on the right, and at least half of every page is given over to notes. A note in *Three Guineas* confirms that she read *Antigone* in this translation.[49] Thus Woolf knew the plays of Sophocles in two modern languages, but not without misgivings, for having read *Oedipus Coloneus* in French she wrote, "I suppose that Sophocles loses more in translation than most."[50]

But even when she read in English translation Woolf responded to language as a translator. She criticized Jebb to Saxon Sydney-Turner in 1918: "I'm not at all pleased with Jebb by the way, he never risks anything in his guesses: his sense of language seems to me stiff, safe, prosaic and utterly impossible for any Greek to understand. Now surely they launched out into flowering phrases not strictly related, much as Shakespeare did. Jebb splits them up into separate and uncongenial accuracies" (*L* II:221). In Benjamin's terms Jebb is the translator who gets the sense right but disregards entirely the possibility that Greek and English tragedy might exhibit comparable modes of signification.

The bilingual editions of Greek texts that were beginning to be published by the Loeb Classical Library seem to have been intended for a reader like Woolf who knew some Greek. In her review essay "The Perfect Language" she greeted with enthusiasm the publication of Volume II of the Loeb Classical Library, *The Greek Anthology*, translated by W. R. Paton (1917). "To those who count themselves lovers of Greek in the sense that some ragged beggar might count himself the lover of an Empress in her robes, the Loeb Library, with its Greek or Latin on one side of the page and its English on the other, came as a gift of freedom to a very obscure but not altogether undeserving class" (*E* II:114). Thus the common reader was "given the means of being an open and unabashed amateur, and made to feel that no one pointed the finger of scorn at him on that account . . ." (*E* II:114). In practice the bilingual edition enabled a reader "with some knowledge of the language" to read an entire play quickly while still remaining aware of the limits of translation. It represented a good compromise between the demands of the reader to apprehend the entire text and the love of the translator for the beauty of Greek words. A few years later in 1923, after twenty years of study, Woolf wrote appreciatively of the bilingual edition: "I now know how to read Greek quick (with a crib in one hand) & with pleasure" (*D* II:273).

It is not clear that university education would have altogether benefited Woolf. Reba N. Soffer reveals that women, at Newnham for instance, were educated as though they were men: "Instead of developing education for women as women, Newnham deliberately adopted the dominant university culture of civic, national and imperial responsibility" although few jobs other than teaching were open to its certificate holders.[51] In an era when textual study at the university was narrowly focused, and reading in translation was not quite respectable, Woolf's position as an outsider gave her the freedom to move in a different direction. Although she was aware of and participated in contemporary arguments about translation, she was more interested in representing in her fiction the new modes of signification which she had discovered while translating the Greeks. Her interests have more to do with recent studies of what has been called the changing discourse of viewing in ancient Greek culture than with debates about the professional importance of training in the classical languages.[52]

Jean-Pierre Vernant provides an example. He examines the extent to which the ancient Greeks recognized "an order of reality corresponding to what we call image, imagination, and the world of the imaginary."[53] I summarize his long and complex argument, in which Plato's attack on the image shows him both the heir and destroyer of archaic culture.[54] Plato writes of the *eidolon* as a replica, a duplicate, or an incarnation. When Odysseus attempts to grasp his loved ones he embraces the air, a double that belongs to the other world. "For archaic thought, the dialectic of presence and absence, same and other, is played out in the otherworldly dimension that the *eidolon*, by being a double, contains, in the miracle of something invisible that can be glimpsed for just an instant."[55] Plato treads a fine line between an archaic conception of the image as an "irruption of the supernatural" in the form of dreams and phantoms, and the philosophical consideration of the image as mediating between "the two poles of being and nonbeing, between the true and the false."[56] The result of opposing the image to reality instead of considering it a dimension of the real is "its disqualification from the point of view of knowledge."[57]

Much of Woolf's fiction may be interpreted within a similar problematic of the image as in part an irruption from the world of dreams and madness, and also as mediating between the realms of fiction and history. The image of birdsong in Greek owes much of its power to its capacity to function in these several realms. In her fiction the subject comes into existence in just such a momentary glimpse of the invisible, its function translated by the narrator into the language and structure of the novel. For instance in *Mrs. Dalloway* the narrator represents Peter Walsh's dream and Septimus Smith's delusions, in language that associates both the dream of a mother seeking her lost son, and the hallucinated "giant mourner" with the recently ended war. In fact the novel was structured so as to argue for the authority of the "irruption of the supernatural."

In a sense learning Greek provided for Woolf one of the social functions of university life. It assuaged her solitude by allowing her to overcome a sense of exclusion from European intellectual traditions. At age twenty-one she wrote "I think I see for a moment how our minds are all threaded together – how any live mind today is of the very same stuff as Plato's & Euripides. It is only a continuation & development of the same thing" (*AP* 178). This perception is linked to "A Dialogue upon Mount Pentelicus," an unpublished piece written sometime around 1906, the year in which she traveled to Greece with Thoby.[58]

The dialog begins in the manner of *Phaedrus* with some attention to the rural surroundings. A group of English tourists visit a marble quarry, where slaves "wore out their lives." Finding themselves unable to converse with their guides in modern Greek, the British pronounce them "barbarians" and the British "the rightful inheritors." The narrator satirizes the young man who having taken "a third in your tripos," and voted against mandatory Greek at Cambridge, nevertheless persists in seeing the Greeks as a reflection of "all that is best in yourself." Their pages "embalm all that you have felt to be beautiful in art and true in philosophy." At that moment in the dialog "a great brown form," looking like a bear but in fact a Greek monk gathering fuel appears, and the British attempt "to return the gaze of the brown monk as one man gazes at another." From the silent exchange of the gaze the narrator creates an image of an avenue on which stand "Plato, Sophocles and the rest" and the English. The narrator imagines that "the flame . . . in the monk's eye . . . had been lit once at the original hearth." The story ends with an ironic twist, as the monk's one utterance, "good evening," confirms precisely the relationship that Cambridge had "disavowed."[59]

Patrick McGee in his study of "Woolf's Other" says very plausibly that Woolf did not make the same use of the university as would someone who had not been denied access.[60] Her satire reflects the outsider's position. "A Dialogue" suggests that owing to a misconception of what it means to be civilized, British institutions do not foster a vital understanding of Greek civilization or of the material of beauty. But "the university neither monopolizes the principle of reason nor can claim its reason as the only foundation for thought broadly defined. For . . . it has also produced for every age in which it has existed an/other thought, a thought beyond authority, legitimacy, convention."[61] McGee bases his argument on the sketch "A Woman's College from Outside" (c. 1920). But "A Dialogue" is a much earlier example, and one that grounds her position in the study of Greek. It suggests the authority of the silent gaze that can imaginatively reenvision Plato and Sophocles. Authority is shifted away from the speakers in the dialog and from speakers generally to the narrator, who, endowed with a power to read the visible world, is able by that means to represent both the invisible and the unsaid. The satire comments on denying women university education by creating a narrator who doubles the subject position; that is she displays the unique power to read both the intelligible world of university men and the still visible world of ancient Greece.

"THE VOYAGE OUT"

In Woolf's first novel we can see how difficult it was to represent the invisible world or the female as divided subject while working within the conventions of the realistic narrative. *The Voyage Out* is in part the love story of Rachel Vinrace and Terence Hewet, who meet on holiday in South America. The most arresting aspect of their relationship is that it ends not in marriage, but with Rachel's death. A parallel narrative develops the relationship between Rachel and her mentor and surrogate mother Helen Ambrose, who undertakes the education of Rachel.

The characters live in a culture in which study of the Greeks is a largely male prerogative. Helen's husband is preparing an edition of the odes of Pindar, and Mr. Perrott reads Greek (*VO* 174). The newspaper reports discoveries on Crete, possibly a reference to Arthur Evans's beginning the excavation of Knossos in 1900. Hirst exhibits the contradictions of the dominant culture. Although he believes that "few things at the present time mattered more than the enlightenment of women [and] almost everything was due to education," he patronizes Rachel before offering to lend her a copy of Gibbon (*VO* 168). Mrs. Flushing and Mrs. Dalloway discuss the difficulty of their ever learning Greek, and Mrs. Flushing draws male scorn for wishing to read the *Symposium* in translation. To Rachel's request for a copy of Gibbon her uncle Ridley replies "But what's the use of reading if you don't read Greek? After all, if you read Greek, you need never read anything else, pure waste of time" (*VO* 177). Although study of Greek seems limited to males and women may be excused for wishing to read translations, Hirst occupies himself during the church service with a bilingual edition of Sappho (*VO* 244).

Small wonder that in such society Rachel considers herself uneducated, and that her reading is confined to what she calls "modern books," that is English literature plus Ibsen (*VO* 126). Her death occurs at an educational as well as a sexual impasse. It puts in question both her musical training which as a female "accomplishment" is a kind of consolation prize, and more importantly the education given her by Helen. As a wife who is devoted to the comfort of her husband and a woman capable of a warm attachment to Hirst, a younger version of her husband, Helen is an ambiguous and disturbing figure, who plays a decisive role in foreclosing Rachel's subjectivity.

A number of scenes of viewing visualize the position of the outsider who looks in on others through a window. In the first such scene Helen and Rachel catch their first glimpse of Terence Hewet through a lighted hotel window; in another Terence observes through a window. Claire Kahane writes that these scenes "confuse the distinctions between voyeur–subject and the object of its look, which shift their point of focalization between male and female, seer and seen, subject and object of the gaze."[62] Perspective, associated with the window, takes on an ideological significance that anticipates *To the Lighthouse*, when female outsiders look on at a scene where two men talk and read.

A more problematic scene of viewing concerns the embodiment of the viewer. Rachel and Terence have confessed their love in a scene marked by their silence and doubt. As the lovers struggle to dispel their sense of the unreality of body and world, Rachel touches his cheek: "This body of his was unreal; the whole world was unreal" (*VO* 301). In the midst of their discussion of the new meaning of "happiness," Rachel undergoes an experience of the "unreal":

Voices crying behind them never reached through the waters in which they were now sunk. The repetition of Hewet's name in short, dissevered syllables was to them the crack of a dry branch or the laughter of a bird. The grasses and breezes sounding and murmuring all round them, they never noticed that the swishing of the grasses gew louder and louder, and did not cease with the lapse of the breeze. A hand dropped abrupt as iron on Rachel's shoulder; it might have been a bolt from heaven. She fell beneath it, and the grass whipped across her eyes and filled her mouth and ears. Through the waving stems she saw a figure, large and shapeless against the sky. Helen was upon her. Rolled this way and that, now seeing only forests of green, and now the high blue heaven, she was speechless and almost without sense. At last she lay still, all the grasses shaken round her and before her by her panting. Over her loomed two great heads, the heads of a man and woman, of Terence and Helen. (*VO* 302)

As an interpreter of Beethoven Rachel has earlier shown that she commands the discourse of art and emotion, but in this scene she specifically fails to participate in the discourse of heterosexual desire. Others may kiss and "speak of love and . . . marriage," but she is able to visualize love only in terms of Helen's "soft body" (*VO* 302). Rachel herself remains "speechless and almost without sense," an observer of heterosexual love that is played out by others. In Kahane's words, "the text abruptly reconstitutes the primal couple as Terence and Helen, with Rachel on the outside, looking in."[63] Although Rachel as onlooker is sexually and socially disempowered, forced into the position of witness she commands the optical point of view that is always a position of privilege in Woolf's fiction.

The scene freezes the moment of awakening, and like a Surrealist photograph, for instance Man Ray's images of female heads, it estranges the moment by rotating the image ninety degrees. In the language of *Mrs. Dalloway* "The cold stream of visual impressions failed . . . The brain must wake now" (*MD* 145). Long before Lily Briscoe completes her painting in *To the Lighthouse* the image has been constructed in a way that questions the Renaissance conventions of perspective. Positioned as an infant on her back, Rachel looks not out, but up at Terence and Helen.

If I may adapt some of the argument of Rosalind Krauss about the viewer of certain works of modern art, Woolf may be seen as working towards a notion in which a dislocation of the body redefines the viewing subject. In a discussion of the aesthetics of Roger Fry in relation to Marcel Duchamp's *Etant donnés* Krauss studies the position of the viewer that is created when Duchamp constructs an erotic image that must be viewed through a keyhole drilled in a door. The voyeur, if we may think of Rachel in this position, discovers her body indirectly, in the process of looking at a sexual scene, as though Woolf were suggesting that vision is always incarnated, if not like Duchamp that vision "is carnal through and through."[64] And although it may be that the scene of Rachel's viewing is not exactly an instance of the "optical unconscious,"

Woolf constructs a visual field that is "both carnally constituted and, through the activity of the unconscious, is the permanent domain of a kind of opacity, or of a visibility invisible to itself."[65] The moment is definitive; when it has passed Rachel fails to recognize once familiar figures standing in the distance. As for Helen, Rachel "had passed beyond her guardianship" (*VO* 306), that is beyond the triangular world of heterosexual lovemaking, although she dies before the reader can discover what her new incarnation might signify.

The problems raised in this scene remain at the heart of Woolf's fiction. Exclusion from formal education is figured in her texts as a problem of the conventions of visual representation, which is manifested in the gendering of female characters and of Septimus Smith. The outsider is forced into a position of spectatorship which Woolf's fiction represents as authoritative. Helen and Rachel identify in the window the male figure who will change the course of their lives, but only by dislocating her visual perspective is Rachel able to recognize her desire in terms of the heterosexual institution that excludes her. The split position that this scene demonstrates recuperates for fiction the position of outsider that in society may be untenable.

PLATO AND "JACOB'S ROOM"

Woolf's reading of Plato was focused on the significance of beauty as Socrates represents it in the *Phaedrus* and the *Symposium*. She was well aware that "beauty" had become in her culture a "master signifier," that is in Lacan's terms "a signifier which is isolated from the rest of discourse," recognizable as that term "that always seems to put an end to associations instead of opening things up."[66] The term seems particularly apropos of the preoccupation with beauty that may be observed in the poetry of Byron, Keats, and Shelley. Yet the generation that survived World War I called several "master signifiers" in question. In *Jacob's Room* the scenes where Jacob reads Plato and then muses on the problems of female beauty and his preference for male society inscribe the master signifier in the context of prewar gender politics. Not until *To the Lighthouse* did Woolf hit on the idea that the visual representation of beauty might be used to figure the historical and generational change through which she had lived.

Woolf's notes on Greek from the period 1907–9 are contained in a little book which includes notes on Juvenal, Homer, Virgil, Sophocles, Euripides, and Aristophanes, as well as notes on Plato, and a comment from 1917, the year when she reviewed one of the early volumes of the Loeb Classical Library. Among her notes on several dialogs, *Phaedrus*, *Protagorus*, and *Euthyphro*, those on the *Symposium* are the most copious.[67] According to her letters, in 1917 she reread her early notes on Plato, and in September 1919 she was reading the dialogs again. In November of 1920 she wrote to Janet Case, "I am reading the Symposium – ah, if I could write like that! . . . This I say to show you how your seeds bear fruit after 20 years – anyhow 17" (*L* II:446). As she began drafting *Mrs. Dalloway*, in August and October 1922, she was at the same time preparing to add a long essay on the Greeks to *The Common Reader*, and in preparation was reading Plato and others throughout the period 1922–23. Thereafter the references to Plato in her notebooks and letters diminish and so presumably her immediate interest.

Woolf's seven pages of holograph notes on the *Symposium*, which she dated "15 July '08," provide her clearest statement on the significance of beauty. Although they are difficult to read, since it appears that her pen was running out of ink, the overall impression is, as Brenda Silver suggests, that Woolf paraphrased the dialog and made a few observations of her own.[68] Her notes follow the order of speakers. After noting the "charming opening" of the introductory dialog, she comments on the speeches of Phaedrus, Pausanias, Eryximachus, Aristophanes, and Agathon. But since she devoted five of the seven pages to the speeches of Socrates, Diotima, and Alcibiades, their discussion of beauty seems to have preoccupied her attention.

Woolf's emphasis in the notes on the theme of beauty (she repeats the word some twenty-eight times) suggests her main interest in *The Symposium*.[69] She summarizes the speech in which Socrates tells his friends the advice he has received from Diotima:

He should learn to love the beauty in one form first; then he will perceive that all beauty is related, and he will love the beauty in all forms equally. Then he will love the beauty of the mind above all others. Personal beauty is only a trifle. Then he will see the beauty of the sciences – he will contemplate the whole sea of beauty. . . . So Diotima spoke.[70]

Woolf focused her attention on Diotima, the prophetess who instructs Socrates in the ascent of love, from love of an individual to a philosophical love whose object is always available.

After Agathon's guests have discussed sex in the language of homoerotic desire, Socrates introduces a story about Diotima, who seems to know more about male desire than do men themselves. David Halperin argues that Diotima represents a thinly disguised male fantasy about female desire. Adapting an argument about pregnancy of the soul, she argues that a man in love with a boy "conceives and gives birth to what he has been carrying inside him for ages . . . he nurtures the newborn; such people, therefore, have much more to share than do the parents of human children, and have a firmer bond of friendship, because the children in whom they have a share are more beautiful and more immortal" (209D). "Diotima's systematic conflation of sexual and reproductive functions," Halperin continues, "indicates that Plato has shifted, intellectually and mythopoetically, to a realm of desire conventionally marked as female."[71] A man and his boy lover together give birth to a love of beauty and moral and intellectual self-expression.[72] But since Diotima assumes without question that pregnancy and birth are the climax of female sexual development, she is no more than a masked version of male desire. "Plato's figuration of Diotima's supposed 'femininity' reinscribes male identity in the representation of female 'difference'; it is a projection by men of their own experience onto women, a male fantasy intended for internal consumption."[73]

The final page of Woolf's notes suggests that she recognized as well the issue of gender in Socrates' quotation of Diotima: "The speech of Socrates is one of the most beautiful I have read. It is an [entire?] expression of something often hinted at in the dialogues. He raises you, more swiftly and simply than with his logic chopping – to the utmost heights – good [that it?] should ever have been written!" After some lines on Alcibiades, who speaks "as though on the stage," she writes of the tragic end of the dialog: "Socrates is above it all, – not to be moved, and acts with a kind of delicate chill irony, which must have maddened. There is an exquisite phrase or two at the end, to finish off the picture . . . Should be read again and again. This is only an outline."[74] Woolf's enthusiastic response to the ascent of beauty described by Diotima is tempered by her realization of the philosophical temperament that the love of Forms seems to produce. In *Jacob's Room* Woolf begins the critical examination of an ideology of beauty that the male who has been educated in Greek history and literature associates with female passivity.

Jacob's life is played out on the map of the Roman Empire, from the moment when Mrs. Flanders takes her sons to play in the ruins of a Roman camp in Cornwall, until his visit to the Acropolis near the end of his life. He suffers a split desire: longing to be in Cornwall, he travels to Greece, and there undergoes a significant trans-formation of gender. Whereas his earlier intimacy with Bonamy was consistent with relationships with women as whores or idealized sisters, in Athens he enters on a heterosexual romance with a married woman, and suddenly finds it too difficult to correspond with Bonamy. Like the journey of a Romantic hero Jacob's journey to Rome leads to self-knowledge and the discovery of the limits of ideology. At the end of a section which puts "character mongering" about Jacob's sexual allegiances together with stark images of death in combat, Woolf concludes with what I take to be an image of the effects of ideology: "It is thus that we live, they say, driven by an unseizable force. They say that the novelists never catch it; that it goes hurtling through their nets and leaves them torn to ribbons. This, they say, is what we live by – this unseizable force" (*JR* 151). "Unseizable" characterizes both Jacob's sexual identity and its relation to the image of men who die "uncomplainingly" in battle (*JR* 151). Woolf refuses here and throughout the novel to fabricate in her fiction the connection between sexual identity and heroic death. The driving force although it remains "unseizable" in the sense of unrepresentable assures the destruction of Jacob.

Woolf anticipates here Althusser's discussion of education in his well-known essay "Ideology and Ideological State Apparatuses" (1969).[75] The war in which Jacob dies is an event prepared by an education which teaches young men a destructive myth about their relationship to ancient Greece, that is compounded by their relative ignorance of Greek texts. Jacob "knew no more Greek than served him to stumble through a play. Of ancient history he knew nothing" (*JR* 70–1). His ignorance is coupled with an idealization of "manly beauty" that is perpetuated by governesses, and satirized in the scenes where one or another of Jacob's young women friends visits the British Museum to "reinforce her vision" of Jacob.

The scene in which Jacob reads the *Phaedrus* suggests that his education in effect shields him from the problems of class, nation, and gender which are being enacted in the street below. Plato's dialog motivates him as a solitary reader to drive the darkness away, while dialogs of another kind are going on in the street. He hears "the woman battering at the door and crying 'Let me in!' as if a coal had dropped from the fire." When he finishes his reading he steps to the window and observes where "the Jews and the foreign woman, at the end of the street, stood by the pillar-box, arguing" (*JR* 104). This Cartesian scene suggests that Jacob's education has led to a certain deafness, and the separation of the intelligible from the social world, which appears to him as a distant spectacle.

The myth of Greece that celebrates "manly beauty" in effect segregates men from women, who remain in Woolf's figuration the outsiders. Rachel Bowlby observes that "the undecided identity of the sex to be educated in the beauties of the Greek male prepares the way for . . . the overtly female identification of the narrator."[76] She enjoys a view of the transcendent potential of the beauty observed in men and women that is intuitively closer to that of Diotima than the defensive view of the male student who can barely read the text. In the novel British education leads to the death of young men, and more generally to the emptying of the male position, represented by the image of Jacob's empty room and his empty shoes with which the novel ends.[77]

The split position of the narrator of *Jacob's Room* comes into existence as a reaction to the exclusive cult of males who study Greek. The narrator rather than Jacob is able to unite a theory of beauty and passion. Although ideals such as justice and self-control are difficult for all but a few to perceive, beauty presented through the sense of sight is apparent to all: in the language of *Phaedrus*, "Beauty alone has this privilege, to be the most clearly visible and the most loved." The view of Woolf's narrator is that beauty is a transcendent quality that becomes visible momentarily. In the street although one may see "beauty itself . . . No one can count on it or seize it or have it wrapped in paper. . . Thus if you talk of a beautiful woman you mean only something flying fast which for a second used the eyes, lips, or cheeks of Fanny Elmer, for example, to glow through" (*JR* 110). Jacob's response is by contrast narrowly personal: "The body is harnessed to a brain. Beauty goes hand in hand with stupidity . . . He had a violent reversion towards male society, cloistered rooms, and the works of the classics; and was ready to turn with wrath upon whoever it was who had fashioned life thus." When Florinda lays a hand on his knee, he pleads a headache, and the narrator concludes: "The problem is insoluble" (*JR* 76). Woolf clearly implies that gendered education has contributed to a division between beauty as embodied or transcendent, that has crippled the relationship between men and women.

Although *Phaedrus* seems to function in *Jacob's Room* as a kind of satiric subtext, there is a suggestive if not fully demonstrable link between Woolf's representation of female desire and Socrates' grotesque image of the madness of the lover. In his second speech Socrates distinguishes kinds of madness. The prophetess and priestess are mad; madness brings relief from troubles; and poets are possessed by the Muses. The fourth is "that which someone shows when he sees the beauty we have down here and is reminded of true beauty" (249D). It is "the ultimate vision, and we saw it in pure light because we were pure ourselves, not buried in this thing we are carrying around now, which we call a body, locked in it like an oyster in its shell" (250C). If while in the fourth state of madness a man see his young boy he becomes swollen and feverish, because beauty "opens the sluice-gates of desire and sets free the parts that were blocked up before" (251E). The sensation itself is that heat revivifies the places where once the soul had wings:

as nourishment flows in, the feather shafts swell and rush to grow from their roots beneath every part of the soul (long ago, you see, the entire soul had wings). Now the whole soul seethes and throbs in this condition. Like a child whose teeth are just starting to grow in, and its gums are all aching and itching – that is exactly how the soul feels when it begins to grow wings. It swells up and aches and tingles as it grows them. But when it looks upon the beauty of the boy and takes in the stream of particles flowing into it from his beauty (that is why this is called "desire"), when it is watered and warmed by this, then all its pain subsides and is replaced by Joy. (251B and C)

The notion of feeling desire in the places where one's feathers once grew is a preposterous image of androgyny that is allegorical according to G. R. F. Ferrari, perhaps inspired by Sappho.[78] Although the soul that falls in love begins a lifetime of growth, the feelings of love are analyzed in terms of their effect on the lover, rather than in terms of a relationship. Whereas the ordinary lover may imagine the frustration of his plans, "the philosophic lover has no ready outlet . . . for his encounter elicits, not the prospect of a well-established goal, but an aspiration towards a way of life, the goal of which he must learn to specify as he goes along."[79]

Woolf seems to have interpreted Plato's sense of philosophic love as disembodied androgynous desire in the image of solitary orgasm. Clarissa Dalloway, recognizing that her feeling for young women is "what men felt," experiences

a tinge like a blush which one tried to check and then, as it spread, one yielded to its expansion . . . and felt the world come closer, swollen with some astonishing significance, some pressure of rapture, which split its thin skin and gushed and poured with an extraordinary alleviation over the cracks and sores! Then, for that moment, she had seen an illumination; a match burning in a crocus; an inner meaning almost expressed. (*MD* 27)

The experience that begins in the language of the body, "like a blush," leads to her vision of transcendental coupling in the image of the flower. Mrs. Ramsay has a similar experience in response to the beams of the lighthouse: "some sealed vessel in her brain whose bursting would flood her with delight" (*TL* 72). The experience though intensely erotic owes nothing to genital practice. Sexuality becomes specular, an "illumination" of the natural world created in response to the desire experienced by an individual in solitude.

Rhoda expresses desire in similar terms, in a passage from *The Waves* in which she anticipates leaving school.

There is some check in the flow of my being; a deep stream presses on some obstacle; it jerks; it tugs; some knot in the centre resists. Oh, this is pain, this is anguish! I faint, I fail. Now my body thaws; I am unsealed, I am incandescent. Now the stream pours in a deep tide fertilising, opening the shut, forcing the tight-folded, flooding free. To whom shall I give all that now flows through me, from my warm, my porous body? (*W* 35)

The image of fertilizing moisture also recalls the song of the woman in *Mrs. Dalloway* who stands outside the Regent's Park Tube station, singing "the old bubbling burbling song, soaking through the knotted roots . . . fertilising, leaving a damp stain" (*MD* 71).[80] But whereas Plato says that desire without a transcendental outcome leads to making babies, in Woolf's writing we note that the fertilizing stain drives the woman to a solitary position on the margins of society.

Brenda Lyons argues that Woolf's "writings do not engage with Platonic arguments, but rather draw from the dialogs to inspire, complicate, and support her own aesthetic ends."[81] I agree that Woolf's representations of Plato suggest that she attributed to him poetic rather than philosophical and intellectual authority. If our discussion ended with *Jacob's Room*, I would agree as well that the

Phaedrus and other dialogs function "as its parodic unconscious."[82] But Woolf's essay "On Not Knowing Greek" gave her a mastery of Plato and the Greeks that prepared her to represent war in "Time Passes" in part as an evacuation of the ideal form of beauty.

"ON NOT KNOWING GREEK"

"On Not Knowing Greek," is an ambitious essay of 7000 words, written especially for *The Common Reader* (1925), which otherwise is a collection and revision of Woolf's earlier work. By the time it was finished she had read four Platonic dialogs, two plays each by Aeschylus, Euripides, and Aristophanes, and everything of Sophocles. She read a few texts in Greek, others in French, or in new English translations. In May 1925 she saw performances of Euripides' *Helen* and *Cyclops* (*D* III:16). By 1925 her knowledge of Greek tragedy though not exhaustive was sufficiently extensive to permit her to generalize for example about the qualities of Aeschylus, and to quote some lines in Greek.

In the essay Woolf domesticates the Greeks – Sophocles, Euripides, Aeschylus, and Plato (she also mentions Homer and Thucydides) by considering them in the context of British history, geography, and literature. She provides enough of the text, for instance a summary of the *Symposium* that stresses the party, to satisfy the unread, while at the same time appealing to the scholarly reader by quoting the occasional line in Greek. An argument whose appeal is so diverse courts contradiction. In her assertion that "It is useless, then, to read Greek in translations," Woolf takes sides against her own habits as a reader in order to join her argument to the public debate (*CR* 37).

Among numerous books and reports that debated compulsory study of Greek is one entitled *The Living Languages: A Defence of the Compulsory Study of Greek at Cambridge* (1891), by James Kenneth Stephen. According to Quentin Bell, he was Leslie's favorite nephew, who after an injury to his head went mad.[83] Although I have found no evidence that Woolf owned or read the book it seems unlikely that she would not have had some acquaintance with its content. Stephen defends the study of Greek against the demands of some teachers and parents that it be replaced by the study of science. His argument is unabashedly and insistently inflected by questions of class and gender. A university education is reserved for those who are either the sons of wealthy parents, or clever enough to qualify for scholarships. The two categories of Greek students whom he discusses are boys in public schools and university men, who will gain "entrance into a favoured class."[84] The system operates to exclude boys who are "stupid,"[85] and of women there is no mention. The style is extremely repetitive, the basic vocabulary stressing *boys, men,* and their *knowledge*: "I particularly wish it to be understood that by 'the value of a knowledge of Greek' I mean the value not merely of knowing Greek – which may at any given moment be practically nothing whatever – but of *having known Greek*, which I take to be always considerable."[86] That is, although Stephen himself no longer recalls much of the language that he studied for ten years, he argues that the study of Greek prepares the mind to assimilate rapidly other kinds of knowledge. It would appear that learning Greek, once problematic for females, had become problematic in the culture.

Woolf's opening sentence reads like a response to her cousin: "For it is vain and foolish to talk of Knowing Greek, since in our ignorance we should be at the bottom of any class of schoolboys . . . All the more strange, then, is it that we should wish to know Greek, try to know Greek, feel for ever drawn back to Greek, and be for ever making up some notion of the meaning of Greek, though from what incongruous odds and ends, with what slight resemblance to the real meaning of Greek, who shall say?" (*CR* 24). Excluded by reason of gender she could not defend the study of Greek in school, and remained skeptical about the meaning of *knowledge* as it refers to a culture that is racially and linguistically distant. Rather her tactic is to make knowing problematic, while giving the common reader a kind of capsule appreciation of the Greek writers who were studied in public schools and in universities.[87]

Her final sentence joins her essay to an argument about Hellenism and Hebraism. We turn to the Greeks for relief "when we are sick of the vagueness, of the confusion, of the Christianity and its consolations, of our own age" (*CR* 39). The idea of reading the Greeks as an alternative to Christianity owes something indirectly to Benjamin Jowett, whose translation of *Protagoras* is mentioned in Woolf's notes. As a Victorian clergyman and don he "in large measure transformed Plato's thought into a surrogate for Christianity."[88] His translations and teaching dominated Oxford, where "he taught a generation or more of teachers and students to find lessons for contemporary life in

Plato . . . and through Plato to view themselves as the servants of a higher social ideal."[89]

Although Woolf was concerned to argue the value of Greek literature, she was well aware of the contradiction inherent in the position of the translator. In two much revised paragraphs she discussed the problems. "We can never hope to get the whole fling of a sentence in Greek as we do in English." Shelley requires twenty-one words to say what a Greek can in thirteen. And when Professor Mackail writes "wan," he makes the Greeks sound like the Pre-Raphaelites. "It is useless, then, to read Greek in translation," she concludes (*CR* 36–7). But as I point out, Woolf read Greek tragedy in French and English as well as Greek, and welcomed the advent of the Loeb Classical Library bilingual editions. Translation paradoxically makes available texts which the serious reader will find inadequate. The contradiction is compounded by questions of class and gender, for in 1925 it still was not easy for a woman to learn Greek, and reading a translation might be considered as much a mark of social exclusion as of the reader's personal choice.

Woolf wrote her "Greek chapter" and *Mrs. Dalloway* "side by side," sometimes writing "fiction before lunch & then essays after tea" (*D* II:310). Since she shuttled back and forth between the novel and her Greek studies, it is not surprising that "On Not Knowing Greek" cleared the way for an altogether larger consideration in *Mrs. Dalloway* of the significance of the Greeks in postwar British society. Greek tragedy suggested to Woolf a way of representing the effects of war. English attitudes were expressed, she wrote, in the "sidelong, satiric manner of Wilfrid Owen and Siegfried Sassoon," whereas the Greek vocabulary allowed suffering "to be looked at," so that we read the Greeks searching "for what we lack" (*CR* 36). Woolf's representation of the visible effects of the war in the novel is grounded in her translation of Greek tragedy.

In the essay Woolf refers to an image in *Agamemnon* of the disorder of the visual field that occurs after loss, an experience that lay, she wrote, "on the far side of language" (*CR* 32). She quotes in Greek a line in which the Chorus images Menelaos' dream after Helen has eloped with Paris. In Woolf's holograph translation the passage reads:

He shall pine for her that is far beyond sea, till he seem, but a phantom lord of the house. Grace of beautiful [*sic*] the husband hateth: with the want of the eyes all the passion is gone. Dream-forms stay with him a while, convincing semblances, & offer delight in vain; for lo, when vainly he thinks to grasp the phantom, the vision escapes through the arms and is gone that instant on wings that follow the passing of sleep.[90]

In the essay Woolf interprets the line: "It is the meaning which in moments of astonishing excitement and stress we perceive in our minds without words." So Aeschylus gives us, "not the thing itself, but the reverberation and reflection which, taken into his mind, the thing has made, close enough to the original to illustrate it, remote enough to heighten, enlarge, and make splendid" (*CR* 32). The language of reflection and illustration suggests that the dream troubles the sign, simultaneously stressing the capacity of language to translate the visible and stimulating its rhetorical power.

George Devereux praises the passage from *Agamemnon* as one of the most persuasive representations of a dream in Greek literature. He interprets the dream as arising from the deep depression of an indecisive man. His paraphrase is intended to represent the multi-faceted richness of Aeschylus' language:

The yearning for her, who is beyond the seas, will make it seem that a phantom (mis)governs the palace (and makes Menelaos himself also seem ghost-like). The fair forms of the statues (of lovely girls) seem hateful to the husband. In the inanimate (but, perhaps, also hungrily searching) gaze of his eyes, all of Aphrodite (libido) is gone to wrack and ruin. Mournful dream apparitions seem to bring joys that are vain, for vainly, when in fancy one sees what is good, the vision, slipping sideways out of the (dreamer's) arms' embrace is gone – never again to assume (follow, imitate) the winged gain ("allure") of sleep.[91]

It is a "*typical* mourning and sexual frustration dream," in a culture which valued dreams. Aeschylus, whose brother died at Marathon, would have known at firsthand the effect of loss and grief.[92] "At first, Menelaos negates the reality of his loss simply by means of a stunned disbelief; later on, he does so by means of a dream, whose *first half* manifestly begins to restore the *status quo ante.*"[93] After discussion of the grammatical subtlety of the representation of Helen as dream image and/or phantom, Devereux argues that

the most logical – and most moving – conception is that Helene is hallucinated by Menelaos who, *by* hallucinating her, not only becomes himself like unto a phantom, but also *mediates* his hallucination to his household. In the negative sense, this means that the household is adrift, as though a mere phantom held the reins; little of what should normally be done is accomplished – and even less is done well.[94]

The dream is "the nocturnal counterpart of his waking depressive symptoms."[95] In other words Helen both appears in response to Menelaos' wishes, and she eludes his embrace, as frustrating in the dream as in waking life.[96]

The images of the response to the loss by death of a beloved that appear several times in Woolf's work seem to me prefigured by the image of Menelaos' waking to find his embrace empty.[97] In these images of mourning, absence literally disfigures the visual field and deranges the gaze of the mourner. The passage from *Agamemnon* calls to mind most specifically the scene of her mother's death in "A Sketch of the Past," in which her father "staggered from the bedroom as we came. I stretched out my arms to stop him, but he brushed past me, crying out something I could not catch; distraught" (*MB* 91). Mr. Ramsay has a similar experience: "[Mr. Ramsay stumbling along a passage stretched his arms out one dark morning, but, Mrs. Ramsay having died rather suddenly the night before, he stretched his arms out. They remained empty.]" (*TL* 140). In both "A Sketch" and the novel the family becomes adrift as a result of the father's particular mediation of loss. Since the father fails to translate the image, the daughter is figured as an outsider, who comments on a scene in which she plays no part. So when Abel Pargiter makes a similar gesture in *The Years*, his daughter Delia observes "It was like a scene in a play" (*Y* 39).

In each of these passages mourning is attributed to the father as actor from the position of the daughter as chorus. The result seems a shift towards spectacle as the daughter stands aside, and death in her representation is conflated with desertion by her parents. After the death of the mother the shift in the visibility of the signified leads to misrecognition. In "Reminiscences" Woolf complained of the family rituals of mourning that "did unpardonable mischief by substituting for the shape of a true and most vivid mother, nothing better than an unlovable phantom" (*MB* 45). Bernard expresses a similar anxiety after the death of Percival in *The Waves*: "Let us commit any blasphemy of laughter and criticism rather than exude this lily-sweet glue; and cover him with phrases, I cried" (*W* 177). What Woolf in the latter passage calls the "symbolical" is language that demonstrates the potential to obliterate a once living presence. The image raises the question, how can a living language represent without mischief the presence of the dead?

Clarissa's response to the death of Septimus resets the question suggested by the image of the embrace: "Death was an attempt to communicate . . . There was an embrace in death" (*MD* 163). Here the image resonates far beyond the details of a marriage, as we see in the parody of the embrace, when Peter imagines a farewell to Daisy as she spins away in the dog-cart: "her arms are outstretched, and as she sees the figure [of Peter] dwindle and disappear still she cries out how she would do anything in the world, anything, anything, anything" (*MD* 140). Rather it suggests the dimensions of Woolf's project to write a novel about life and death. *Mrs. Dalloway* represents the desire for "communication" between male and female, soldiers and noncombatants, the insane and the sane, the dead and the living. Since an early scene in the novel demonstrates the limitations of the sign to communicate in the new circumstances of postwar culture, what are we to make of Clarissa's sense of "an embrace in death"? If the arbitrary sign is said to be "unmotivated," perhaps it represents the motivated sign, in the sense of setting the enabling conditions for some future significant utterance.

"On not knowing Greek" maintains Woolf's earlier emphasis on Plato as the poet of beauty. The *Common Reader* essay represents beauty in a manner remarkably consistent with the attitude she had expressed in her study notes from 1907 and in her 1917 essay on the Loeb bilingual editions. There she notes that the Greeks had a different conception of beauty: "Another power seems to be theirs – the power of gazing with absolute candour upon the truth of things, and beauty seems to come of its own accord, not as an ornament to be applied separately but as an essential part of the world as it appears to them. Theirs is a beauty of the whole rather than of parts" (*E* II: 117). In the *Symposium* Plato "describes how, when a party of friends met and had eaten not at all luxuriously and drunk a little wine, some handsome boy ventured a question . . . and Socrates took it up, fingered it, turned it round, looked at it this way and that, swiftly stripped it of its inconsistencies and falsities and brought the whole company by degrees to gaze with him at the truth" (*CR* 33). The Socrates represented in the dialogs "did not care for 'mere beauty,' by which he meant, perhaps, beauty as ornament" (*CR* 35).

The difference between the two essays is marked by Woolf's claim that the war had altered the expression of emotion, so that "in the vast catastrophe of the European war our emotions had to be broken up for us . . . before we could allow ourselves to feel them in poetry or fiction" (*CR* 35). As a result, she asks whether we are "reading into Greek poetry not what they have but what we lack?" (*CR* 36) By 1925, after some seventeen years of reading Plato, Woolf had taken the first step towards the disquieting examination of the postwar redefinition of "beauty" in *To the Lighthouse*. There, until Lily Briscoe can recuperate the term in ordinary language, Beauty as it was understood by Victorian males functions to inhibit the completion of her painting.

The scene of reading *Phaedrus* contributes significantly to the antiwar theme of *Jacob's Room*. But following Woolf's extensive review and rereading of Greek texts, her joining the public debate over the importance of studying Greek, and her translation of *Agamemnon*, she created a broader context for the realization of her Greek studies. In *Mrs. Dalloway*, I argue, Septimus is Jacob returned from Flanders as though to answer the question implicit in the earlier novel, what would he have made of the Greeks if he had been born in the working class and survived the war?[98]

CHAPTER 3

No god of healing in this story: "Mrs. Dalloway" and "To the Lighthouse"

THE "ORESTEIA" AND "MRS. DALLOWAY"

While Woolf was planning *Mrs. Dalloway* she was also engaged in translation: "I should be at Aeschylus, for I am making a complete edition, text, translation, & notes of my own – mostly copied from Verrall; but carefully gone into by me" (*D* II:215). Among her notes is a line-by-line translation of *Agamemnon*,[1] which Brenda Silver dates 1922–24. The Greek text is printed on the right side of the page with a few words translated in Woolf's hand in the margin, and on the left side appears a clear, largely unrevised translation. My contention is that the Greek texts in which her own are most deeply grounded are those few – *Agamemnon* and *Choephori*, as well as the *Phaedrus* and *Symposium*, that she read slowly word by word in Greek, as though in comparison to reading the practice of translation shaped her language more intimately.

Agamemnon may be read as a study of the relationship of signifier/signified in the immediate postwar era. The theme of communication is explored in the context of narratives of history, prophecy, and gender. It opens with a long speech in which the Watchman fearfully attempts to read the signs of the night sky that might predict the victory of Agamemnon. The Chorus, believing that all will come clear in the daylight, struggles to construct an historical narrative of events in the House of Atreus, including the contradictory nature of Agamemnon's motivation to go to war, and the theme of justice. Clytemnestra, although she cannot yet know that Troy has fallen, reads the beacon of fire as an unambiguous announcement of the news. The Chorus remains in doubt until hearing the report of a witness. Agamemnon returns and yields to his wife's seductive entreaty to walk upon the tapestry she has spread on the ground, an honor reserved for the gods. Cassandra, Agamem-

non's slave and concubine, prophesies his murder and goes to her
death comparing herself negatively to the wild bird that the Chorus
has earlier mentioned. Clytemnestra rationalizes her murder by
referring to Agamemnon's sacrifice of their daughter. She and her
lover Aegisthus retire while the Chorus utters threats.

The first speech of the Watchman establishes that the problematic
of the play is the representation of history as it is being made. In the
aftermath of a victorious war the sign no longer communicates but
requires interpretation. The Watchman hopes for the return of the
king, but in the Verrall/Woolf translation: "The rest/Shall be
unspoken {my tongue hath upon/it an ox-foot weight}, though the/
house itself, if it could find a voice,/might declare it plain enough;
for I/mean to be, for my part, clear to who/knows & to him who
knows not blind" (lines 34–40). The authority of speech belongs
conditionally to the House of Atreus, a notion that is echoed in
"Time Passes." Otherwise the Watchman's history will be understood by those who already know, assimilated in this translation to
those who see. The Watchman sets the scene for a play that until the
entry of Cassandra is fully dialogic, as the characters and the Chorus
both seek and refuse a language in which to speak their common
history.

Each of the principal characters and the Chorus are characterized
by a pattern of semiotic behavior; each seeks to associate a signifier
with a remote signified. Before Agamemnon appears Clytemnestra
gives a verbal picture of the victory in Troy which she cannot yet
know (lines 320–50). The fact that she tells what is Agamemnon's
story is part of the reason that she appears unwomanly. The ease
with which she fabricates history characterizes the woman who does
not hesitate to murder her husband. Her final representation of her
action to the Chorus is correspondingly unproblematic and unin-
flected. Verrall/Woolf translate: "By us he fell,/he died, and we will
bury him" (lines 1152–3). The tyrannous female is characterized not
only by her violent action but in the realm of language by a rush to
closure, and to create narrative at the expense of reflection.

The Chorus gives us another perspective on language when it
makes signification so problematic that it prevents action. Although
throughout the play the Chorus's doubts are a constant reminder of
dramatic irony, that what is ongoing on stage the reader knows as
completed action, it is unable to act even when it hears the king cry
out. It vacillates between fear of tyranny and fear of death, which it

rationalizes as its continuing distrust of divination and guesswork. And while it hesitates the doors of the palace open, the bodies are revealed, and Clytemnestra does not hesitate to admit her lies and to express her indifference to the Chrous's reaction.

In this setting Cassandra creates the role of witness at the limits of the visible. When she fails to respond to a command, Clytemnestra assumes that she must speak a "barbarian" language and asks her to make a sign with the hand, which is apparently refused. Cassandra's repeated "see there" merely baffles the Chorus and leads it to see her behavior as that of the nightingale, an identification with Philomela that she rejects. She is not "a false prophet" (line 1195), and "My teaching shall be riddles no longer" (line 1183). She asks that the Chorus "bear witness" that she knows "the ancient sins of the House of Atreus" (lines 1196–7). In the language of the Verrall/ Woolf translation Cassandra rejects the gendered role of prophet that Apollo created for her. In her last moments she establishes her independence of him as she combines her position as foreign observer and sacrificial animal to create for herself something that sounds like the role of female teacher/historian. It is a role to which Woolf reverts in the autobiographical "A Sketch of the Past."

My reading of Woolf's Cassandra is consistent with Froma I. Zeitlin's interpretation of Clytemnestra's role in the *Oresteia* as affirming the need for patriarchal values that "institutionalize the subordination of women. The point of the myth is not the recording of some historical or prehistorical state of affairs, but rather the demonstration that women are not fit to rule, only to be ruled."[2] Although Clytemnestra's violence is motivated by the sacrifice of her daughter, as the trilogy progresses "the crimes of the males of the house . . . first fade into lesser significance and finally are mentioned no more."[3] At the end of the trilogy, when a jury judges Orestes for the murder of his mother, Athena casts the vote that frees him. "Once objectified and projected outward, the myth [of the destructive powers of the androgynous female] reinforces, legitimates, and even influences the formation of those impulses by the authoritative power of that projection, especially when it is embedded in a magisterial work of art."[4]

✳The British society of *Mrs. Dalloway* is also divided in its understanding and representation of the war that England has won.[5] The division is apparent in the shift in gender roles among women, especially apparent in the characterization of Miss Kilman and in the future that Elizabeth Dalloway imagines for herself. Septimus has been feminized not only by his reaction to the trauma of the battlefield, but as I shall argue by his education in a Keatsian view of sacrifice. Like Cassandra he glimpses the horror that is not visible to others of his society, and like her he fails to communicate his knowledge. Yet the narrative does not grant him the authority of historian, in part because the use of language as communication is problematic, and in part because when he attempts to speak beyond the commonsense solutions of Sir William he is imprisoned within a Romantic vocabulary of sacrifice.

In Verrall/Woolf's translation of *Agamemnon* the themes of the play are refracted by its semiotic dimensions. Although Woolf's notes in the margins of the Greek text suggest that she used a dictionary to prepare an independent translation, on the whole hers follows that of A. W. Verrall save for a phrase here and there. A comparison of their translation with the modern version of Richmond Lattimore calls attention to Verrall/Woolf's greater emphasis throughout on semiotics, often at the expense of easy, idiomatic phrasing. For instance when the Chorus ponders the significance of the wild bird who tears apart the pregnant hare, Lattimore translates, "Grant meaning to these appearances" (line 144). The Verrall/Woolf version by contrast reads, "to this sign thou art prayed to let the event accord," which perhaps because slightly less readable highlights the anxiety of the Chorus about the problematic nature of signification in relation to prophecy. Or the Chorus alluding to its fear in the presence of Cassandra says in the Lattimore version, "Why must this persistent fear/beat its wings so ceaselessly/and so close against my mantic heart?" (lines 975–7). Verrall/Woolf translate: "Why is it that so constantly my auguring soul shows at the door this fluttering sign and the prophet-chant offers itself without bidding or fee?" This version clearly suggests the Chorus's recognition, as for the first time it finds itself alone with Cassandra, that language speaks the prophet.[6] Woolf's translation demonstrates throughout a sense that prophecy is a problem of language, contingent on social circumstances. Her text seems written for the reader with some Greek who will make specific demands on the translated work.

It is in the context of language as communication that *Mrs. Dalloway* revises the *Oresteia* by its figuring of the impact of war on the social consensus of what is seen and can be represented. The structure of the novel like that of the play is grounded in a view of the visible world as always already doubled. Like *Agamemnon* it begins with two scenes that put in question the referentiality of the sign as the prelude to what Simon Goldhill terms a move from surety and certainty to misgiving and doubt.[7] In the novel misgivings center on the significance of the war to its apparent survivors. In a dream Peter Walsh sees himself united with the figure of a mother who awaits "a lost son . . . killed in the battles of the world" (*MD* 50), but he has not been a soldier, and the social reality to which he has returned, to reestablish his friendships and find himself a job, contradicts the dream. Septimus Smith has in fact returned from war like Agamemnon, like him only to be killed by a trick. While he imagines that he has access through the dead to the lost world of ancient Greece, his physicians regard the chthonic powers that enthrall him as symptoms of his illness.

The clearest imprint of the entire *Oresteia* on the novel is the representation of tragedy as the willful manipulation of the language of sacrifice, and the destruction by war of kinship patterns that confuses human behavior by subverting the capacity of the sign to refer to the visible.[8] These circumstances disrupt the semantic field so that the reader becomes aware that character and narrator may use the same word but in different codes. Woolf's narrator recuperates the function of "communication" that Septimus and Clarissa merely idealize, in a world where language is unstable and speech often repressed. In this climate Woolf's satire is directed against the doctor who deals with Septimus by renaming his illness.

In Greek tragedy, among the plays that Woolf read, the visible is the horizon of the human. The gods need no eyes, for they are comprised entirely of sight. They become visible to some men on the border of the seen/unseen. For instance in the *Choephori* Orestes sees the Furies which the Chorus does not (line 1061); in *Ajax* Odysseus cannot see Athena, who has the power to "darken vision." In Euripides' *Bacchae* Dionysus, who is half-divine, sees the God that Pentheus does not (lines 500–1). In fact the play ends with the plea: "And the paths undiscerned of our eyes, the Gods unseal them" (line 1391). Much of the complexity of the characterization of Septimus as well as the structure of *Mrs. Dalloway* is derived from the sense of a world that is visible to the narrator from a perspective that includes the invisible.

Woolf's earliest notes for the novel, dated 6 October 1922, and written on the verso of leaves of the third and final volume of the holograph of *Jacob's Room*, outline a work whose structure was designed from the start to grant cognitive authority to insanity.[9] It was to be focused on "characters, like Mrs. D – much in relief: then to have interludes of thought, or reflection, or short digressions (which must be related, logically to the rest) all compact, yet not jerked."[10] Ten days later she wrote: "Sanity & insanity Mrs. D sees the truth. S. S. seeing the insane truth . . . The pace is to be given by the gradual increase of S's insanity on the one side; by the approach of the party on the other . . . The design is extremely complicated."[11] Thus from the earliest plan insanity, far from being considered an illness, is represented as an authoritative mental state, to be demonstrated by a narrative structure that grants it equivalence with sanity.

During the next nine months, 9 November 1922–2 August 1923 Woolf continued to plan the novel, recording her notes in a small notebook which contained her reading notes on the *Choephori* of Aeschylus, dated January 1907.[12] The notes on the novel document her creation of a narrative that would be flexible enough to express the themes of life and death, and sanity and insanity, while accommodating a number of stories already in draft. The novel was to be structured by a contrast between "the two minds. Mrs. D & Septimus." In the absence of plot both characters were to be represented by the contrast between their "view of things."

Woolf's continuing preoccupation with death as she drafted the novel clearly indicates why she could not work within the conventions of realism. She wrote in the notebook on 2 August "There must be a reality which is not in human beings, at all. What about death, for instance? But what is Death?" That thought helps to explain in retrospect the difficulties that she anticipated with both style and structure: "Some general style must be found, or one's attention is too broken." She was concerned about "the continuous style." In a discussion of "breaks in the texture" she asks "Can one admit rhapsodies?" The notion that a chorus might replace the breaks in narrative that in realistic novels are effected by chapters suggests that she was adapting the structure as well as the world view of Greek tragedy.

In such a refashioning of narrative, the representation of the visible posed a special problem. Notes in the *Choephori* notebook suggest that Woolf's characterization established a particular relationship between the intelligible and the visible. To note that Peter Walsh "must *think*: not merely see" suggests a world divided between the intelligible and the visible, and a character limited by the horizon of the visible. Of Septimus she wrote, "He [is] only real insofar as she [Rezia] sees him. Otherwise to exist in his view of things . . ." How Septimus might otherwise be seen is suggested by Bradshaw's questions and answers which objectify the ill. "Mrs. D must be seen by other people" suggests the degree to which Woolf associated the social identity of a character with visibility. Overall the unseen character seems in danger of becoming socially invisible as though the social fabric were a matter of sight lines.

Woolf's major characters are paired in terms of their capacity to see, in the language of her essay, "on the far side of language." She begins the novel by discriminating between Clarissa's and Septimus's sense of the visible. Clarissa has "a sense of being herself invisible, unseen; unknown" (*MD* 8). Her position, "outside, looking on" (*MD* 5) although in part the result of social exclusion, from Lady Bruton's luncheon for instance, gives her the sense of control that comes from establishing a perspective. Septimus lacks the control conferred by the gaze, and without a clear position he responds helplessly to his wife. Whereas she five times bids him to look, he hears another voice: "Look the unseen bade him, the voice which now communicated with him who was the greatest of mankind"(*MD* 21).

Peter Walsh on the other hand suffers the constraints of the merely observant mind. As Clarissa in the act of bringing him unseen to her side recalls, "Peter never saw a thing of all that. He would put on his spectacles, if she told him to; he would look" (*MD* 5). Yet on first meeting Richard Dalloway Peter has a "revelation" that Clarissa will marry him (*MD* 53), and the narrator represents him as rejecting "the crude beauty of the eye" (*MD* 144). The sight of the ambulance which bears the body of Septimus Smith leads him to "a moment, in which things came together; this ambulance; and life and death" (*MD* 134). Although Peter has the ability to transcend visual experience, the limits of his "observing" the London scene are made clear: "The cold stream of visual impressions failed him now as if the eye were a cup that overflowed and let the rest run down its china walls unrecorded. The brain must wake now" (*MD* 145). The passage denies him the blessing of Psalm xxiii: "My cup runneth over. Surely goodness and mercy shall follow me all the days of my life and I shall dwell in the house of the Lord forever." The blessing of the invisible lies beyond the limits of the visual, the seen of the waking world.

By contrast, after Sally Seton's kiss, Clarissa, who is an atheist, sees the boundaries of the visible world dissolve, so that "the radiance burnt through, the revelation, the religious feeling!" (*MD* 30). Peter recalls her "transcendental theory which, with her horror of death, allowed her to believe, . . . that . . . the unseen part of us, which spreads wide, the unseen might survive, be recovered somehow attached to this person or that, or even haunting certain places after death . . . perhaps – perhaps" (*MD* 135). Mark Hussey notes that Clarissa's ability to constitute her identity in relation to what she calls "apparitions," the reflection of the self by others that can survive death, is represented as a human potential that appears over and over in Woolf's novels.[13] In this context her sense that "Death was an attempt to communicate," that "there was an embrace in death," asserts the power of the unseen (*MD* 163).

Woolf shared several fifth-century attitudes towards madness and its special relationship to vision. Ruth Padel documents extensively the details of the fifth-century view. Madness was not considered an inherent part of human psychology but was caused by something external, just as Septimus's madness has been caused by his experience in battle. When Oedipus blinds himself, the Chorus asks, "What madness came upon you?" (line 1299). Madness might alternate with periods of sanity: Ajax after his madness is once again sane. Septimus also has sane moments, when he chats with his wife as she decorates a hat. Owing to a curse, a few tragic characters – Cassandra, Io, Orestes – are chronically susceptible to madness. As for the vision of the mad, when they see wrongly they see what the sane see, but see it differently, as when Septimus reads the skywriting differently. But the mad also see what the sane cannot, as when he sees his dead friend Evans. As a result the mad are isolated by what they see.[14] And at one point Septimus closes his eyes to prevent his going mad. Padel also notes that in some contexts, as for instance in the *Bacchae*, to be sane is to be mad. One might argue that the only true madman in *Mrs. Dalloway* is Sir William Bradshaw with his sense of Proportion and Conversion, and that measured by his standards it would be madness to be sane.

Padel stresses that the idea of madness as the "broken potential" for greatness did not originate in the fifth century, where madness was seen as a curse, but rather in the Renaissance.[15] Septimus's grief for his dead friend Evans is a fantasy of the relevance of Greek civilization to the present. Sparrows sing to Septimus in Greek. Evans sings to him that the dead await the end of the war in Thessaly. In the manuscript Septimus hears Shakespeare speaking Greek, and Evans when he dies returns to Greece and speaks to Septimus in Greek verse.[16] Yet he reads Aeschylus in translation (*MD* 78), suggesting that Greek for him is less a language or a literature than a sign of his aspirations to education and the status of lyric poet.[17]

The characterization of Septimus as poet is part of Woolf's satire of Romantic attitudes. He sees himself as the Lord, or as a great poet, perhaps like Keats: "beauty, that was the truth now" (*MD* 61). But echoing only the final lines of the "Ode on a Grecian Urn" Septimus ignores the question posed in the previous stanza: "Who are these coming to the sacrifice?" The mute witnesses who "for evermore/ Will silent be" are an ominous comment on Septimus's postwar life and death. Woolf's narrator portrays Septimus as grandiloquent, for instance "finishing a masterpiece at three o'clock in the morning and running out to pace the streets" (*MD* 75). The madness of Septimus suggests less the waste of human potential than his helpless display of the destructive delusions of Romanticism.

In Woolf's earliest notes Clarissa and Septimus "are linked together by the aeroplane." That scene and the episode of the motor car put in question the visible aspects of the sign and the referentiality of language, as a prelude to introducing Septimus into the narrative. Clarissa imagines that the occupant of the motor car is the Queen, the flower-seller the Prince of Wales. Septimus sees the motor car "as if some horror had come almost to the surface and was about to burst into flames," and himself "blocking the way" (*MD* 12). The scene reveals the heuristic gap between Septimus and other readers of signs. From the point of view of Clarissa and the flower-seller the inscrutable appearance of wealth and power is sufficient to signify royalty. Septimus seems unable to create the position of viewer which would detach him from the scene. Rather he hovers on the boundary between subject and object, his body "rooted to the pavement," becoming the object of the gaze (*MD* 12). He imagines himself in an extraordinary interactive visual relationship that threatens his physical safety and forecloses his entry into the symbolic.

The scene of skywriting which follows draws the reader's attention to the process of signifying. Gillian Beer reads the image of the aeroplane in *Mrs. Dalloway* as "the free spirit of the modern age returning the eye to the purity of a sky which has [in the language of *Between the Acts*] 'escaped registration.'"[18] In the scene members of the working class fail to agree on the words or letters of an advertisement written in the sky. While individuals in the street read *Glaxo*, or *Kreemo*, or *toffee*, Septimus, unable to read the inscription as language, sees a signal of "exquisite beauty . . . beauty, more beauty," and understands that "all taken together meant the birth of a new religion" (*MD* 18). The visual suggestion of royalty, commercial advertisements written in smoke, and the signal of a new religion compete for authority. Sight and sign are placed in doubt when the subject position is open to shaping by visions and other forms of (mis)recognition.

These two scenes represent sanity and insanity as two modes of cognition. The attempt by the crowd in the street to read the problematic skywriting grounds sanity in consumer culture. Septimus on the other hand reads skywriting in the mode of the Watchman in *Agamemnon*, as though it were an omen. In the opening lines of the play the Watchman has waited ten years "to read the meaning in that beacon light" which would signal the fall of Troy. Woolf translates the lines in which he measures the year by the seasons: "I know all the nightly company of the stars, chiefly those [signs del.] chief signs that marked by their brightness tell the seasons." Septimus reads the language of advertisement as prophecy, a "signal" of a language he cannot read. The play and the novel suggest that communication of an event cannot always be distinguished from foretelling, a theme that is repeated in Cassandra's dialog with the Chorus near the end of the play.[19]

The scene demonstrates the historical contingency of the sign. Goldhill's comment on the language of *Agamemnon* frames the problem: "the gap between signifier and signified, and the gap between the present (its analysis) and the future (its prediction) are interconnected, again linking narrative and language in the desire for clarity and control."[20] In both play and novel readers of different generations and different genders read differently, and both texts challenge literal discourse by drawing attention to the process of sign making. In the novel tension exists among "the sign as k-e-y," the letters the narrator may have seen, the various readings of the names of commercial products, and Septimus's recognition that the letters signal beauty and more beauty. If the function of the sign is to communicate, then the ambiguity of sign/signal and reading/recognition confounds analysis of the present. The narrator and Septimus together express the tension generated by a glimpse of the future. He sees it as a threat when he closes his eyes to prevent seeing "the meadow of life beyond a river where the dead walk," a vision of his personal future (*MD* 20). In the novel as a whole that tragic conception is imbricated by the "desire for control" represented by a party which is nevertheless marked by death.

The theme of sacrifice is represented in the novel as the willful manipulation of the process of naming.[21] Sir William Bradshaw "never spoke of 'madness'; he called it not having a sense of proportion" (*MD* 85). Renaming illness as deficiency serves to conceal the "insane truth" that Septimus represents, the tragic theme of the warrior become prey. In Sir William's consulting room Rezia reports that her husband had "served with the greatest distinction" in the war, whereas Septimus sees himself as "the criminal who faced his judges; the victim exposed on the heights; the fugitive; the drowned sailor" (*MD* 85). Others speak of Septimus as a warrior; he speaks of himself as prey.

Like Agamemnon and Orestes, Septimus suffers a double social identity. Pierre Vidal-Naquet discusses the way that tragedy restores order after a period of tension by means of a sacrifice that transforms warriors into prey. It is prefigured in *Agamemnon* by the image of two eagles devouring a hare, in the *Eumenides* by the image of the Furies devouring Orestes.[22] Although fifth-century Greece was no longer a hunting society, it still practiced the hunt and turned to it for the myths that represented its social structures.[23] His most striking example, drawn from *Agamemnon*, is the imagery that represents the eating of unborn litters of young, for instance in Woolf's translation of the Chorus's reference to the anger of Artemis: "Artemis the undefiled/is angered with pity/at the flying hounds of her father/eating the unborn young in the hare and the shivering mother" (lines 132–5). The hare with her young is Troy, he argues, Iphigenia sacrificed by Agamemnon, and the children of Procne and Tereus to which the Chorus refers in the scene with Cassandra. The lines "With the sword he struck,/ with the sword he paid for his own act" refer to Agamemnon's murder as payment for the Trojan War and the sacrifice of his daughter.[24]

If as Charles Segal observes of Greek tragedy, "the confusion of hunt with sacrifice and of hunted beast with human being operates as a focal point for major inversions in all the civilized codes,"[25] we may see that idea at work in the way that Woolf represents the inversion of law and justice. At the behest of the law and the police Sir William Bradshaw controls "unsocial impulses" (*MD* 89). In his office Septimus reflects on the irony of enforced socialization by animals: "They hunt in packs. Their packs scour the desert and vanish screaming into the wilderness. They desert the fallen. They are plastered over with grimaces" (*MD* 78). "Once you fall, Septimus repeated to himself, human nature is on you. Holmes and Bradshaw are on you. They scour the desert. They fly screaming into the wilderness" (*MD* 86). Woolf's satire of Bradshaw's legal authority creates for Septimus a subject position which the social code has denied him.

The image suggests the language of the Chorus of Furies in the *Eumenides*, who when they learn that Orestes has murdered Clytemnestra become enraged. It is the language of Clarissa's hatred of Miss Kilman, "one of those spectres who stand astride us and suck up half our life-blood, dominators and tyrants" (*MD* 9). In this instance Septimus's capacity to speak in the code of the hunted gives him access to the Furies. He commands the language that articulates Clarissa's unspoken feelings.[26]

But if madness gives access to the realm of chthonic powers it also impinges on the question of agency, the degree to which Septimus or any character may be said to originate his actions or decisions. Vernant writes that the concept of agency and choice means something quite different in Greek tragedy from our contemporary notions of the autonomous will, and suggests a different orientation towards action and decision. He traces the components of supernatural necessity and personal characteristics as the agents that compel the tragic hero to commit a misdeed. At an early period madness might control the individual, so that far from being the agent of his action he is carried away by a power beyond his control. Tragedy marks "a turning point" in the approach to will and agency that we can observe in the character of Agamemnon. He is compelled to sacrifice his daughter Iphigenia by Ananke and by his own reckless will to military victory. In Aeschylus the tragic decision is motivated both by character and divine power. Vernant concludes,

Tragic guilt takes shape in the constant clash between the ancient religious conception of the misdeed as a defilement attached to an entire race and inexorably transmitted from one generation to the next in the form of an *ate* or madness sent by the gods, and the new concept adopted in law according to which the guilty one is defined as a private individual who, acting under no constraint, has deliberately chosen to commit a crime.[27]

As Holmes mounts the stairs Septimus experiences a crisis of agency. Sir William acts in the name of the law and the police, so that in his presence Septimus feels himself "the criminal who faced his judges" (*MD* 85). Holmes speaks of his suicide in the language of cowardice and blame, as though it represented a choice. The act of suicide is situated between the gaze of the old man who pauses on his staircase as Septimus opens the window and the codes which Holmes and Bradshaw represent. Septimus is a victim to the extent that the scene of his hurling himself on the area railings recalls Apollo's warning to the Chorus in the *Eumenides* to leave the sanctuary where men have been tortured and impaled. Septimus's last words, "I'll give it you," suggest that he gives Holmes and Bradshaw "their idea of tragedy," but not his (*MD* 132). I take his words to mean that he rejects the role of sacrificial victim to which Holmes and Bradshaw have driven him by manipulating the language of the law. As in classical tragedy his action focuses attention on the way that agency reveals a conflict in social codes, in this case the unequal confrontation between the visual image of Septimus's male lineage and the text of the law that Bradshaw represents.

One of the effects of the war on Woolf's generation seems to have been a quickened sense of the instability of the Western kinship system. It becomes a matter of uncertainty and fascination in the work of Yeats and Joyce as well. In the aftermath of World War I living male heirs are simply absent from *Mrs. Dalloway* (although Peter Walsh sees young boys carrying guns), and kinship is undergoing redefinition. The lifestyle of the previous generation is captured in visions that are not communicated. Peter Walsh dreams of a maternal figure in the context of an archaic village scene, about to be swept "into complete annihilation" (*MD* 50). At first Clarissa imagines establishing kinship primarily in the conventional terms of marriage, either to Peter or to Richard, but as the novel develops she manifests a new kind of kinship with Septimus and with the old woman whom she sees through the window.[28]

The climax of the novel, argues J. Hillis Miller, is not the party, but the moment when Clarissa leaves the party and through the window sees the old woman preparing for bed.[29] In an earlier glimpse of her Clarissa recognized a kind of kinship: "that's the miracle, that's the mystery," Clarissa thinks, that is incompletely grasped in religion or love (*MD* 112). When Clarissa sees her again during the party she functions like the old man who witnesses Septimus's suicide, in the place of parents as an image of the previous generation. Preparing for the night, she offers Clarissa a more peaceful sense of her retirement to the narrow bed that she has earlier seen as prefiguring her coffin. The presence of the old woman is entirely specular; when Clarissa sees her during the party she communicates only by drawing her blind. It is significant that at the boundary of the visible so marked Clarissa's thoughts are diverted to Septimus.[30]

Bennett Simon considers the historical and social implications of kinship in the *Oresteia* as the erosion of family ties. Clytemnestra and Agamemnon scarcely speak to each other. When Orestes appears on the scene in the *Choephori*, Clytemnestra does not at first recognize her son, and does so only as he is about to kill her. Agamemnon, having murdered his daughter Iphigenia, does not after his death respond to appeals from Orestes and Electra, his surviving children. Cassandra's silence when faced with Clytemnestra signifies that her family history is too painful to be told. Kinship and identity are more often affirmed in the *Oresteia* "in acts of violence and retalia-tion."[31] The resolution of the problem of destroyed kinship "involves a new form of reallocation of power within the family and within the extended kinship system of gods and man. That new form is the city and its laws."[32]

The structure of *Mrs. Dalloway* links the theme of kinship and sacrifice to communication. The image of Clarissa and Peter as two horses pawing the ground "before a battle begins" (*MD* 44) suggests, in the terms of Vidal-Naquet, a society whose social structures are unconsciously sustained by the myth of battle. Septimus has been feminized by the sacrifice of his life in the war, and subsequently by his taste for feminine occupations. When Clarissa gives a thought to the Armenians as "hunted out of existence," her language recalls Septimus's "They hunt in packs," but "she could feel nothing for the Albanians, or was it the Armenians?" (*MD* 106). Although Clarissa may be able to deny the violence in history, her hatred of Miss Kilman is the "brutal monster" which gives her "physical pain"

(*MD* 9). Yet the novel asks us to believe in the significance of her response to the mere mention of an event in the life of a sacrificed male whom she has never seen. If we pose Bennett Simon's question about the reallocation of power after the destruction of existing patterns of kinship, the answer seems to me that Clarissa's party suggests a future in which prewar relationships although strained remain fundamentally unchanged, and kinship as the ability to communicate has become the supreme fiction that masks the unwritten acceptance of violence.[33]

Kinship can also be interpreted as a question of recognizing the self as other than it is known to be. In *Agamemnon* Clytemnestra reveals a male capacity for decisive action, but the revelation of her hidden self is not the occasion for action either by herself or by the Chorus, which initiates no action in the play. Rather the discovery of kinship occurs in the *Choephori*, where in Simon Goldhill's reading recognition is a question of shifting from signifier to signified in a metaphoric linking. After a long exile Orestes returns home and lays a lock of his hair on the grave of his father, Agamemnon. The scene in which his sister Electra goes to the father's tomb and recognizes her brother's hair and his footprint is important for how and what she recognizes. She did not treat the trace "as a sign of Orestes directly . . . but compared the footprint and lock with her own."[34] Recognition is a process whereby Electra metaphorically links her brother to herself. She uses language to assert her kinship with Orestes and to deny filiation with Clytemnestra. "The recognition scene, then, not only develops the problematic of the sign and the reading of the sign . . . but also marks the importance of such a topic in the discussion of a relation between language and discourse, between a subject and society's language."[35]

Such a scene of recognizing the self as other figures briefly in *To the Lighthouse*. James echoes Electra's recognition of the footprints that resemble her own (*Choephori*, lines 105–6) when he uses the figure from the play to express his recognition of the bond that he shares with his father: "there he had come to feel, quite often lately, when his father said something which surprised the others, were two pairs of footprints only; his own and his father's. They alone knew each other" (*TL* 200). So James metaphorically links himself to his father and marks the relationship "between a subject and society's language."

Zeitlin stresses the theatrical aspect of recognition. She defines tragedy as charting "a path from ignorance to knowledge, deception to revelation, misunderstanding to recognition."[36] In the process the tragic hero discovers the world and himself to be other than he had imagined. In tragedy "recognition is the overtly theatrical event that condenses the epistemological bias of the entire phenomenon of drama. Thus, recognition extends along a far wider spectrum, embracing the world, the other, and the self."[37]

The party that concludes *Mrs. Dalloway* is the theatrical event that is the occasion for several moments of visual recognition and misrecognition. Lady Rosseter is at first unrecognizable as Sally Seton. In the eyes of Mrs. Hilbery Clarissa resembles her mother. Richard admires "that lovely girl" at the party, just as he realizes that he has failed to recognize his daughter. Peter's experience is more complex. Feeling "terror" and "ecstasy" he recognizes Clarissa, "For there she was" (*MD* 172). The tense of the verb suggests that true recognition involves more than "the cold stream of visual impressions," which lead to misrecognition. Under the conditions of terror and ecstasy what had been visible becomes intelligible, linking past and present.

The narrator presents the reader with the more complex terms of the metaphoric linking that leads to recognition. Clarissa and Septimus quote the same phrase from *Cymbeline*, "Fear no more the heat o' the sun" in passages of indirect discourse, a phrase which serves to recall Clarissa from the scene in which she observes the old woman to the news of Septimus's death (*MD* 186). The reader may measure against the narrator's assertion of "the enormous resources of the English language" to communicate feeling (*MD* 157) the difficulty of social communication that Clarissa, Richard, Septimus, and all the characters experience. Richard does not, cannot, tell Clarissa that he loves her. It is easier for Septimus to communicate with Evans: "'Communication is health; communication is happiness, communication – ' he muttered" (*MD* 82), than with Sir William Bradshaw a few pages later. The narrator represents Clarissa's reaction to news of Septimus's death as her sense that "death was an attempt to communicate" (*MD* 163). Since social communication has been so compromised, it lies with narration to recognize a new kind of filiation between strangers.

Jean-Pierre Vernant poses a question about the contribution that psychology can make to the traditional philological and historical methods of analysis of Greek tragedy. The Greek text achieves depth, he argues, by the circulation of certain words and phrases through the several vocabularies of religious, legal, and political life. Creon and Antigone for instance use the same words to refer to different things. As a result communication between characters is impeded; the Chorus hesitates "rebounding from one meaning to the other;" and only the spectator gets the whole meaning.

> Between the author and the spectator the language thus recuperates the full function of communication that it has lost on the stage between the protagonists in the drama . . . The language becomes transparent and the tragic message gets across to him only provided he makes the discovery that words, values, men themselves, are ambiguous . . . only if he relinquishes his earlier convictions, accepts a problematical vision of the world and, through the dramatic spectacle, himself acquires a tragic consciousness.[38]

The quotation could serve as a summary of the reasons that Woolf looked to Greek tragedy for a sense of the limits of personal communication.

To read *Mrs. Dalloway* as an attack on communication as suggesting the prior identity of the referent is to see it as a central Modernist text. Minow-Pinkney writes of Septimus, "Communication as the exchange of signs is made possible only within the symbolic order, through the split in the subject which is established by the intervention of the phallus in the unity with the mother. In Septimus's madness, the division between signifier and signified is no longer clear. Words and things are confused, imagination and reality no longer distinguishable."[39] Woolf historicizes the stability of the symbolic order in both the car and aeroplane scene and the final scene of the party. When neither public inscriptions nor family and social identity are visible to all in the same way, the modality of the sign makes apparent that characters like readers occupy diverse positions.

It is well accepted that Septimus Smith and Clarissa Dalloway represent aspects of each other.[40] To pair their two characters in effect undermines the characterization associated with mimesis by implying the question, in whose mind are they so paired? Who among the characters in the novel hears Septimus's message that "communication is health and happiness"?[41] A culture that is committed to realistic representation forecloses certain modes of communication. His death reenacts the Romantic association of beauty with sacrifice; it is a gesture that points with anguish towards a view of communication as being in touch with someone who is absent. I see Septimus like Diotima, as a voice that although wearing the mask of the other does not represent an alternative view of the world.[42]

Woolf's sense of theater is manifest in the image of the window that permits Clarissa to become the spectator first of her past life at Burton, and then of her future as an old woman. Yet Woolf denies her subjectivity, and displaces that function onto the narrator. By bringing into question the significance of "communication" not only in the lives of the characters but also in a theory of representation the narrator functions in a manner consistent with the symbolic that has the authority to stage (*vorstellen*) the represented. As theatrical image the window represents the limits of the visible world, beyond which Clarissa cannot see, and through which it is madness to plunge.

The perspective of the window locates both Clarissa and Septimus between past and future, yet in a moment that is clearly sequestered from the present. Perspective in this context would seem the visual representation of the tense that Lacan has named the future anterior, the tense that is neither past definite nor present perfect, "but the future anterior of what I shall have been for what I am in the process of becoming." As a mode of thought as well as a tense, the future anterior defers closure, and implies a synchronic rather than a developmental view of history.[43] Its combined sense suggests the potential of the image of an old woman framed in the window to replace a developmental narrative with an image of the future towards which the action moves, beyond the recognition of the characters. That Woolf represents the aftermath of war neither as the conclusion of a tragic conflict, nor as entry into a new future has consequences for narrative structure. So Septimus and Clarissa walk the same London streets, but neither becomes visible to the other, as though they were moving on parallel tracks which converge beyond the narrative, and beyond the visible world framed by the picture. In *To the Lighthouse* we see the consequences when Lily Briscoe finally abandons perspective as a technique of painting. Then in the chapter called "Time Passes" the narrative sequesters death in parentheses, and the third section becomes a developmental narrative, bringing a kind of closure that at least makes possible a future.

"TO THE LIGHTHOUSE"

In *To the Lighthouse* Woolf deconstructs the term "beauty," which she had found so compelling in her reading of the *Symposium*. The idea of

Platonic beauty which fascinated her has become in *To the Lighthouse* an ideological phenomenon which seems to involve a Romantic misreading that she attributes to Keats and Wordsworth. Beauty, which is attributed by male characters to nature and to Mrs. Ramsay, is, along with mathematical perspective, the obstacle that prevents Lily Briscoe from integrating her aesthetic theory with the practice of painting. When Lily is able to sequester herself from male discourse she redefines the term, a speech act which permits her to complete her work. Coming to a realization of the historical nature of beauty, Woolf represented the painter as redefining the term for Modernism.

"Time Passes" puts the matter in terms of a philosophical change in the nature of perception, in language that resembles the formulation of Maurice Merleau-Ponty:

> Today we no longer believe nature to be a continuous system . . . *a fortiori* we are far removed from thinking that the islets of "psychism" that float over it are secretly connected to one another through the continuous ground of nature. We have then imposed upon us the task of understanding whether, and in what sense, what is not nature forms a "world," and first what a "world" is, and finally, if world there is, what can be the relations between the visible world and the invisible world.[44]

Had Woolf not made herself familiar with the problematic of the visible in her reading of the Greeks it seems doubtful that she would have undertaken to address in "Time Passes" a philosophical question of this complexity and magnitude.

The ideology of feminine beauty in nineteenth-century British culture was so widespread and so amorphous that to pin it down is not feasible. Yet a few instances are indicative. At Cambridge beauty was an issue of culture as well as a philosophical debate. John Maynard Keynes in "My Early Beliefs" (1949) creates a picture of an era at the university when his friends evaluated conduct in terms of the world of Platonic ideas. We lived, he wrote, "in the world of Plato's *Dialogues;* we had not reached the *Republic,* let alone the *Laws.*" Beauty played a significant part in a kind of neo-Platonic ethics. It was mediated through the work of G. E. Moore, of whom Keynes observes, that "he could not distinguish love and beauty and truth from the furniture," and quotes a passage from *Principia Ethica* (1903) on the difficulty of distinguishing "material beauty" from the "merely beautiful." But as 1914 approached, "the thinness and superficiality, as well as the falsity, of our view of man's heart became, as it now seems to me, more obvious."[45]

The dilemma of definition that Keynes notes had its origin in the various historical adaptations of the Platonic idea of beauty. Seth Benardete, studying the concept of beauty in dialogs other than those that Woolf read, notes that Platonic beauty transcends its class, so that it is "both complete in itself and a pointer beyond itself." Beauty has "this double character . . . in the three definitions of Socrates . . . [that] recognize an opposition within a pair of terms that the beautiful, it seems, should but cannot resolve . . . appearing and being, beautiful and good, and aural and visual pleasure."[46] Renaissance discussions of art and artists recognized the double nature of representation in the insistence that a work of art be faithful both to nature and to beauty. Johann Winckelmann wrote of natural beauty in 1755 in terms of Greek statuary: "The imitation of beauty in nature either directs itself toward a single object or it gathers observations of various individual objects and makes of them a whole . . . The second, however, is the way to general beauty and to ideal images of it; and this was the way chosen by the Greeks." Visual art can thus reveal "the highest limits of that which is both humanly and divinely beautiful."[47]

Woolf's constant attention to beauty in her essays and letters suggests that she too recognized its double nature, comprised of both absolute and relative beauty. In a letter to Gerald Brenan about *Jacob's Room* she saw her position as determined by the historical nature of beauty: "the greater beauty: the beauty which comes from completeness," that she saw in the work of Austen, Stendhal, or Tolstoy is not available to the modern writer: "I think I mean that beauty, which you say I sometimes achieve, is only got by the failure to get it; by grinding all the flints together; by facing what must be humiliation – the things one can't do – To aim at beauty deliberately, without this apparently insensate struggle, would result, I think in little daisies and forget-me-nots – simpering sweetnesses – true love knots" (*L* II: 599). Although she rejects overt attempts to create beauty, which in a modern work might lead to sentimentality, she opts instead for the paradox of the failed attempt.

Her Modernism evolved out of that planned failure.[48] In particular her notion of beauty is in line with Baudelaire's definition in "Le Peintre de la vie moderne" (1863) of the double nature of beauty, derived from the opposition between a theory of beauty as absolute and a theory of its historical nature. "Le beau est fait d'un élément éternel, invariable, dont la quantité est excessivement difficile à déterminer, et d'un élément relatif, circonstanciel, qui sera, si l'on veut, tour à tour ou tout ensemble, l'époque, la mode, la morale, la passion."[49] [Beauty is made of an eternal, invariable element, whose extent is extremely difficult to determine, and another that is relative, circumstantial, which will comprise, one might say, by turns or together, the era, the style, morality, and passion (translation mine).] Such beauty may be understood as beautiful in the manner of antique statuary, or ugly in the manner of caricature. The conception is at the heart of his definition of modernity: "La modernité, c'est le transitoire, le fugitif, le contingent, la moitié de l'art, dont l'autre moitié est l'éternel et l'immuable."[50] [Modernity is the transitory, the fugitive, the contingent, the half of art of which the other half is the eternal and immutable (translation mine).]

In "The Narrow Bridge of Art" (1927) Woolf echoes Baudelaire in her distinction between Romantic and contemporary beauty. In Keats's "Ode to a Nightingale" sorrow is the shadow which accompanies beauty. In the modern mind beauty is accompanied not by its shadow but by its opposite" (*GR* 16). Modern skepticism has redefined the term, so that "Beauty is part ugliness" (*CR* 16). Septimus's too literal reading of Keats's "Beauty is truth, truth beauty" stresses its absolute value and neglects the ephemeral aspect of beauty, with dangerous consequences for himself. In Baudelaire's essay the painter must extract the mysterious beauty of the costume of a bygone era which might easily be declared ugly (Section IV: La Modernité). So when Rezia observes a well-dressed French woman, "'Beautiful!' she would murmur, nudging Septimus, that he might see. But beauty was behind a pane of glass" (*MD* 77). The moment represents the division between the ephemeral beauty of dress and the absolute beauty that draws Septimus, but is framed by the narrator as out of reach. Yet the division seems a matter of temperament and timing; before Septimus's death he and Rezia come together in the scene where they trim a hat in the moment before he plunges through the frame. Clarissa's comment on his death, "He made her feel the beauty, made her feel the fun," suggests, in the context of Keats and Baudelaire, the union of eternal sorrow with her appreciation of ephemeral circumstance.[51]

Jürgen Habermas reads this passage of Baudelaire's essay as part of the debate between ancients and moderns, and the shift "between the absolutely beautiful and the relatively beautiful" as the key to his definition of modernity. As a result, he argues, "the authentic work is radically bound to the moment of its emergence; precisely because it consumes itself in actuality, it can bring the steady flow of trivialities to a standstill, break through normality, and satisfy for a moment the immortal longing for beauty – a moment in which the eternal comes into fleeting contact with the actual."[52] That passage seems to me to describe the transition from the notion of transient beauty in *Jacob's Room* to the focus in *To the Lighthouse* on a new definition of beauty that is "radically bound to the moment of its emergence." Woolf's emphasis on the fleeting moment of Lily Briscoe's realization rather than on her completed painting suggests the representation of beauty and loss as "the point where time and eternity intersect."[53]

The controversy over beauty in *To the Lighthouse* was located as well in Victorian culture. Aestheticism, which has been characterized as "the use of a beautiful woman as an image of the poet's introspection," suggests the fundamental contradiction inherent in bourgeois culture, "that it promises alternatives to that culture, but provides them only in the realm of the ideal."[54] In that context the image of the beautiful woman is "the basis of an entire ideology of art that rests on the possibility of simultaneously knowing and not knowing that art serves no function and yet is bought and sold."[55] The aesthetic of "The Window" appears to be that the female figure and her infant son although they inspire "tribute" are unrepresentable by Lily. And in the chapter called "The Lighthouse" she specifically rejects the possibility that her work will be displayed, the first step to economic valuation. The painting itself represents the contradiction of these two positions, and Lily's temporary inability to complete it locates ideology in her lived experience of the work of painting.

The frequent and unvarying emphasis on the beauty of Mrs. Ramsay suggests that the word had become, in Lacan's terms, a "master signifier." I understand Lacan's term to mean that "beauty" although it continues to circulate in the culture is no longer actively referential. Somewhat later Lacan's "master signifier" had become "a positional notation . . . a signifier which is isolated from the rest of discourse," recognizable in analysis as a term "that always seems to put an end to associations instead of opening things up."[56] Lacan's term fits the use of "beauty" in "The Window," where it seems that removed from the stress of historical circumstance the sign has become "a positional notation," that is, more significant in identifying the speaker's position than capable of registering shifts in meaning.

Orlando (1928) suggests that Woolf saw the "master signifier" as unique to a culture and so untranslatable. After Orlando becomes a woman, she goes to live with the gipsies. But when she attempts to express her sense of beauty, she discovers that in its place they use "good to eat." Out of this misunderstanding over a contested meaning was born her desire to write a long blank verse poem.

As used by the characters in *To the Lighthouse* "beauty" is a fixed term that represents the ideology of gender. To Mr. Tansley Mrs. Ramsay "was the most beautiful person he had ever seen" (*TL* 18). Her children and guests "pay tribute to her beauty" (*TL* 90). " 'But she's no more aware of her beauty than a child,' said Mr. Bankes" (*TL* 34). Her husband notes "the sternness at the heart of her beauty" (*TL* 71), and associates her beauty with ignorance. When he imagines that she reads without understanding Shakespeare's Sonnet 98, "her beauty seemed to him to increase" (*TL* 131–2). As a "positional notation" *beauty* is repeated over and over by the male characters in a gesture that praises while it often belittles Mrs. Ramsay.

The narrator provides another perspective, writing of Lily Briscoe's love of the Ramsays, "it is so beautiful, so exciting, this love" (*TL* 111). The narrator also questions whether Mrs. Ramsay's beauty might provide for her a mask: "What was there behind it – her beauty, her splendour?" (*TL* 34). But the question does not effectively put the term in play, or "open things up" among the characters. Throughout "The Window" Mrs. Ramsay remains socially identified as the beautiful woman, the object of the gaze.

Woolf's characterization of Mr. Bankes is a wonderful send-up of mimesis as a pious tribute to beauty. When in 1914 Woolf read Clive Bell's *Art*, she praised the theoretical chapters. He preferred his term "significant form" to "beauty," on the grounds that the latter is confused by the man in the street with "desirable." Mr. Bankes similarly confuses beauty with his own ideas of the desirable when he praises a painting hung in his home, on the grounds both that it commemorates the landscape where he had spent his honeymoon, and that its market value has increased. From the "notational position" that locates art at the intersection of family and real estate values, he taps "the triangular purple shape" on Lily's canvas and ponders whether a woman "famous for her beauty – might be reduced . . . to a purple shadow without irreverence" (*TL* 59).

Although Lily replies that "she had made no attempt at likeness" (*TL* 59), she is unable to act on her theoretical notion of painting as "colour burning on a framework of steel" (*TL* 54) while her work is under the "gaze" of Mr. Bankes, and she herself can hear in her mind Charles Tansley repeating " 'Women can't paint, women can't write' " (*TL* 54). The male gaze, epitomized in the image that reproduces the norm of female behavior as maternal, seems to have frozen her in the position of female resistance. And there matters remain, with Lily resisting the demand for mimesis, until the death of Mrs. Ramsay frees her to redefine beauty.

Lily's dilemma may be read as a moment in the history of art characterized by the abandonment of the belief that linear perspective necessarily represented the visual field. By the end of the nineteenth century the visual conventions which had prevailed since the fifteenth century were called in question. Art that was no longer produced in a religious context did not invite a specific response. In painting a woman seated with her male child Lily is attempting to represent the madonna in the window within the frame of mathematical perspective. Produced in those outmoded conventions her painting of Mrs. Ramsay fails to move to what Hans-Georg Gadamer in his essay, "The Relevance of the Beautiful" calls a painting that can be read. That is, when Lily thinks of her painting as "rolled up and stuffed under a sofa" (*TL* 173), she acknowledges its failure to become a painting that relies for its reception not on a religious context but on its capacity to become "the focal point of recognition and understanding."[57] That failure, which she experiences as personal, is deeply imbedded in a culture dominated by a male gaze that has made a fetish of female beauty. As "Time Passes" suggests, only after World War I was she free to reimagine her relationship to the beauty of her model, abandon outmoded visual conventions, and thus complete her work.

In "Time Passes" Woolf shifts the focus away from individual characters in order to address a problem that Plato did not contemplate. How does a Form become drained of content, so that beauty, which once promised the philosopher ascent to the highest level of understanding, has in contemporary culture become reduced to signifying gender ideology? The narrator first phrased the problem in "The Window," in connection with Lily's attitude towards Mrs. Ramsay: "Was it wisdom? Was it knowledge? Was it, once more, the deceptiveness of beauty, so that all one's perceptions, half-way to truth, were tangled in a golden mesh?" (*TL* 57). Here visible beauty would appear to block the path to wisdom. In "Time Passes" Woolf locates the problem more generally: the empty house and the looking-glass which no longer reflects a face have become lifeless forms.

> Now, day after day, light turned, like a flower reflected in water, its clear image on the wall opposite. Only the shadows of the trees, flourishing in the wind, made obeisance on the wall, and for a moment darkened the pool in which light reflected itself . . . So loveliness reigned and stillness, and together made the shape of loveliness itself, a form from which life had parted. (*TL* 141)

Woolf has revised the image of Plato's cave, in which reflection governs men's vision, to comment on the social reality of a world depopulated by war and disease, whose attributes in the absence of human viewers are light and shadow.

The narrator represents the effects of war as cultural ruin. Books have decayed; the Waverley novels have been rescued from "oblivion." The building itself might shortly have housed vagrants. And both the witless Mrs. McNab and the visionaries who walk the beach are socially marginal. Following the appearance to those who seek a vision of "divine bounty" of the "ashen-coloured ship" that sinks at sea, the narrator records the destruction of beauty as a master signifier: "This intrusion into a scene calculated to stir the most sublime reflections and lead to the most comfortable conclusions stayed their pacing. It was difficult blandly to overlook them, to abolish their significance in the landscape; to continue, as one walked by the sea, to marvel how beauty outside mirrored beauty within" (*TL* 146).

I read the passage as in part an attack on Wordsworth's assertions about beauty. Woolf's phrase echoes the image of the mirror in Wordsworth's "Preface of 1800," in a passage where he describes the powers of mind of the poet: "He considers man and nature as essentially adapted to each other, and the mind of man as naturally the mirror of the fairest and most interesting qualities of nature."[58] Whereas Plato's cave suggests the limits of human understanding, Wordsworth fosters the "comfortable conclusion" that outward vision serves to confirm inward. His image of the mind as mirror achieves its optimism by reducing the three-dimensional complexity of perception in the cave, where men see only shadows, to a two-dimensional model of reflection. In comparison Wordsworth trivializes the relationship of the soul to beauty, which for Plato is tentative, governed by the human capacity for madness, subject to rhetorical conventions, and best expressed in the *Phaedrus* as the theme of a prayer for inward beauty.[59]

Woolf's attitude towards Wordsworth seems to have been undergoing a change at this time. Ellen Tremper records how Woolf at first identified her love of the poet with her father's reciting from memory his major poems.[60] After the death of Stephen's wife in 1875 he had turned to Wordsworth for his moral qualities, writing in a letter to Charles Eliot Norton that he "seems to me the only consoler. I despise most of your religious people, who cultivate their maudlin humours, & despise even more your sentimentalist of the atheist kind; but old W. W. is a genuine human being, whom I respect."[61] A few years later, along with Ruskin, Arnold, and others of their generation he helped to found the Wordsworth Society (1880).[62] In Woolf's essay "How It Strikes a Contemporary" (1923), she takes a position consistent with her father's: Wordsworth is "the philosophic poet," grouped with Austen and Scott as a writer of "unabashed tranquility" (*CR* 243). In 1929 she inscribed in her diary lines from Book VII of *The Prelude*, "a very good quotation I think" (*D* III:247–8). And as late as 1936 she wrote of the poem to Ethel Smyth, "so good, so succulent, so suggestive" (*L* VI:73).

But the image of Wordsworth in the novel and in *Three Guineas* strongly suggests that she had established a view of the consolations he offers that was independent of Leslie Stephen's, perhaps in response to what she perceived as Wordsworth's unfair treatment of his sister Dorothy.[63] In the passage of "Time Passes" where "the mirror was broken," the narrator queries reflection itself: "[was] the mirror itself . . . but the surface glassiness which forms in quiescence when the nobler powers sleep beneath?" (*TL* 146). While granting the possibility that "nobler powers" exist, Woolf questions the cultural adaptation of the ethics of reflection, which the war had apparently shattered.

Before Lily can complete the painting begun and left unfinished ten years earlier she must achieve the condition of subjectivity. When Mr. Ramsay has departed with Cam and James for the lighthouse, she recognizes her divided position: "She felt curiously divided, as if one part of her were drawn out there" (*TL* 171). The price of solitude is a certain anguish as she turns her back on society. "Always (it was in her nature, or in her sex, she did not know which) before she exchanged the fluidity of life for the concentration of painting she had a few moments of nakedness when she seemed like an unborn soul, a soul reft of body, hesitating on some windy pinnacle and exposed without protection to all the blasts of doubt. Why then did she do it?" (*TL* 173). The image of a naked soul waiting to be born suggests the pure immanence of the subject, which in this passage Woolf images in terms of past human cost rather than future production.

Lily must also come to terms with beauty. In "The Lighthouse" the narrative divides; Mr. Ramsay leaves with his children for the lighthouse, and Lily remains on the lawn to paint. Each portion of the divided narrative is focused on a question about what is "real." The question addressed by Mr. Ramsay to McAlister, "about the great storm last winter" (*TL* 178), is balanced by Lily's question addressed to herself, "What is the meaning of life? That was all – a simple question" (*TL* 175). Mr. Ramsay's arrival at his destination reflects a world of male discourse that is diachronic and achieves closure (in *The Waves* closure is figured as a train arriving at the station). Lily's discourse is synchronic. She puts in play, to recall Lacan's term, a consideration of the historical nature of beauty. Historical perspective at first frees her. She thinks of the dead with a little "contempt," of Mrs. Ramsay that "even her beauty, became for a moment, dusty and out of date" (*TL* 190). But following the apparition of Mrs. Ramsay Lily's historical sense retreats in the face of visibility: "Fifty pairs of eyes were not enough to get round that one woman with, she thought. Among them, must be one that was stone blind to her beauty" (*TL* 214). The consideration of beauty as historically specific is limited to Lily's discourse; the word does not appear on the voyage to the lighthouse. The answer to her question would seem to involve not a great "revelation," but "little daily miracles" (*TL* 175–6), as though the intersection of the eternal with the actual might be expressed in the language of spirituality.

The completion of the painting is accomplished by an act of ventriloquism, in which Lily appears to resemble Cam, repeating to herself the words of the father. Lily begins her analysis of beauty by recalling Mrs. Ramsay in the language of William Bankes.

The figure came readily enough. She was astonishingly beautiful, William said. But beauty was not everything. Beauty had this penalty – it came too readily, came too completely. It stilled life – froze it. One forgot the little agitations; the flush, the pallor, some queer distortion, some light or shadow, which made the face unrecognizable for a moment and yet added a quality one saw for ever after. It was simpler to smooth that all out under the cover of beauty. (*TL* 193)

As a master signifier associated with the male gaze, beauty freezes life, masking the face by denying it variety and motion.[64] In the context of her experience Lily resists the "eternal" quality of beauty, and like Baudelaire prefers to shift the emphasis to the fugitive and passing.

Lily's alternative response to beauty is to experience the loss of Mrs. Ramsay on her body, which I understand to mean that female desire in effect bypasses the problematic of beauty. In a line that I find the most painful in all of Woolf's work, the narrator says of Lily, "To want and not to have, sent all up her body a hardness, a hollowness, a strain. And then to want and not to have – to want and want – how that wrung the heart, and wrung it again and again!" (*TL* 194). She echoes the division experienced by Mrs. Ramsay at the end of "The Window," where the text repeats that she "wanted something more" which she cannot identify, but with an intensity unmatched by Mrs. Ramsay (*TL* 127). Lest the reader suppose that Woolf puts too much emphasis on Lily's bodily anguish as the price of subjectivity, the parallel narrative of Cam's reaching the light-house in the company of her brother James and Mr. Ramsay suggests the tragedy of the Oedipal plot, in which a female fails to achieve subjectivity on any terms.

The language of Lily's vision of Mrs. Ramsay echoes the ambiva-lence of Menelaos' experience with the Helen of his dream. "Ghost, air, nothingness, a thing you could play with easily and safely at any time of day or night, she had been that, and then suddenly she put her hand out and wrung the heart thus" (*TL* 194). Lily's pain, tears, and anger produce not exactly a hallucination of Mrs. Ramsay, but a sense of her presence that owes something to "some trick of the painter's eye" (*TL* 197). "For days after she had heard of her death she had seen her thus putting her wreath to her forehead and going unquestioningly with her companion, a shadow, across the fields. The sight, the phrase, had its power to console" (*TL* 197). But it is interrupted by the view from the railway carriage or a voice that intrudes, so "that the vision must be perpetually remade" (*TL* 197). It would appear that nothing less than irrevocable loss by death frees the painter or her model from a stultifying notion of beauty.

In "The Lighthouse" the female painter and her model represent a world in which "beauty" is no longer a master signifier, but has become a term that Lily reserves to discuss problems of representation. The appearance in history of the female painter would seem to have altered the status of beauty as a master signifier, and raises the question whether its static quality derived from its lodgment in the discourse of both male desire and art. The female painter, undergoing a different process of socialization, and educated in a different vocabulary of the emotions, is able to restrict her use of "beauty" to the discourse of aesthetics, where unlike the master signifier it serves to open debate.

Lily reviews her canvas in an attempt to identify a problem that has been eluding her: "Phrases came. Visions came. Beautiful pictures. Beautiful phrases. But what she wished to get hold of was that very jar on the nerves, the thing itself before it has been made anything" (*TL* 209). She effectively returns "beauty" to ordinary language, just as earlier she had done with "perspective," when she is able "to get her canvas – so – into perspective" (*TL* 187). But beauty prompts Lily's desire to encounter the Real, what has not yet been represented. It is probably impossible to relieve "beauty" of its ideological burden, which has rather been shifted to another aspect of the unrepresentable. "Get that and start afresh; get that and start afresh; she said desperately" (*TL* 209). What she gets is a position as subject: "She was astonishingly beautiful. Let it come, she thought, if it will come" (*TL* 210). In my reading of this elusive passage Lily is able to impersonate male desire for her own gendered purposes which are the very opposite of mastery. We recall that Mr. Bankes on their outings "would tell her things, about perspective, about architecture," so that she naturally "saw through William's eyes, the shape of a woman, peaceful and silent, with downcast eyes" (*TL* 192). Repeating the phrase which Mr. Bankes has used twice (*TL* 192, 193), in an act of ventriloquism she dons the mask of the male who remarks Mrs. Ramsay's beauty, but without the wish to patronize or dominate her. What we mean when we talk about beauty is a question that Lily has until now suppressed. The transformation which finally brings about the long delayed completion of the painting is in fact a speech act.

In the literature of Modernism we learn that following World War I several master signifiers came under attack. After "Time Passes," Lily participates in that cultural moment when by shifting the discourse of beauty towards the historic and the ephemeral she is able to recuperate the term for the female artist. The eternal element of beauty would appear to be linked to the woman as madonna, and to the death of the other that is experienced in dreams and hallucinations. Woolf represents it as a moment of history whose absolute closure cannot be represented in modern art. Instead Lily, sounding for the moment like Bernard at the end of *The Waves*, asserts against death art as continuing process. Whereas the painting that is a matter of paint and canvas "would be rolled up and stuffed under a sofa" (*TL* 173), the painting that matters as "actuality" in Habermas's term "can be constituted only as the point where time and eternity intersect. In this way, modernity is rescued, not from its infirmity surely, but from triviality; in Baudelaire's understanding, it is so disposed that the transitory moment will find confirmation as the authentic past of a future present."[65]

If the act of ventriloquism seems limiting, the verbal equivalent of the imaginary in which the subject is spoken by the language of the other, Gilbert D. Chaitin suggests that in Lacan's work such repetition may be the necessary first step towards the creation of metaphor. If in fact "catechretic metaphor" occurs when "a signifier takes as its signified another signifier which has been emptied of its signified," then Lily's echoing Mr. Bankes effectively masks the fact that on her lips "beauty" refers no longer to a quality of Mrs. Ramsay, but to another signifier now detached from its former meaning. Beauty then is no longer an imaginary identification attributed to a woman that reflects male metaphor. Chaitin recapitulates Lacan's argument: "In order for a metaphoric transfer of meaning to take place, the attributes customarily attached to a person or thing, a 'subject' in the grammatical sense, must first be detached from their usual mooring and then reattached to the new location."[66] Lacan emphasizes the movement of the signifier to a new position rather than the conventional notions of metaphor as registering apparent similarity or difference. The process of completing the painting is the image of Lacanian metaphor.

"ANTIGONE" AND "THE YEARS"

The important scenes of reading and writing in *The Years* represent the joint response of the common reader and the translator to Greek as the language of desire.[67] Both Edward and Sara have acquired their models of love from *Antigone*, a classical text which has been interpreted by a culture that uses the Greeks to enforce the segregation of the sexes. Woolf has captured the passion of the translator in a scene in which Edward Pargiter works on a Greek text: "He caught phrase after phrase exactly, firmly, more exactly, he noted, making a brief note in the margin, than the night before. Little negligible words now revealed shades of meaning, which altered the meaning. He made another note; *that* was the meaning . . . There it was clean and entire. But he must be precise; exact; even his little scribbled notes must be clear as print" (*Y* 42). Edward is an example of Benjamin's translator who is so intent on getting the sense right that he is apparently blind to the possibility of divergent ways of meaning.

We see the limitation of his imagination when he identifies his beloved Kitty with the dead Antigone. Reconsidering his evening's work over a glass of wine, Edward yields to the impulse to appropriate the Greek heroine. He imagines the figure of a girl, half Greek half English, in fact his cousin Kitty. "She was both of them – Antigone and Kitty; here in the book; there in the room" (*Y* 43). Although Edward's lived experience of the text responds to the erotic dimension of the play, his terms are different from those of Haemon, Antigone's lover, who dies. The position of translator while it allows for a response that does not involve identifying with any character nevertheless reveals the paradox at the heart of Edward's desire for the woman whose marriage bed is her tomb. In the novel Kitty goes on to become Lady Lasswade, and although Edward weeps at the news, he remains a bachelor don.

Edward's nephew North, who has spent his life farming in Africa, is an outsider in the university world. During the party scene at the end of the novel he sits at the feet of his uncle. Edward has just quoted to his sister Eleanor, in Greek, Antigone's most famous line, that makes Creon believe she has lost her wits. R. C. Jebb translates the line: " 'Tis not my nature to join in hating, but in loving."[68] North asks for a translation which Edward refuses. When North asks to be told about Aeschylus and Sophocles and the Chorus, his uncle replies, " 'My dear boy . . . don't ask me. I was never a great hand at that. No, if I'd had my way' – " (*Y* 373–4). The sentence goes unfinished, perhaps because the Chorus, according to Jane Marcus, "curses the old men who use big words."[69] Or perhaps the line reflects Edward's misgivings and confusion about loving and hating.

What is the reader to make of a translator who refuses to translate, and in fact disavows a life spent working on Greek texts? Does the Greek unintelligible to Edward's listeners signify to himself the private disappointment that he has sublimated in intellectual work? The play seems to encode an ideological position that allows Edward to deny responsibility for the hunger and dissatisfaction that result from the unfulfilled desire of body and mind.

The scene in which Sara Pargiter reads *Antigone* pictures the no less problematic response of the common reader. Left at home and lying in bed, she divides her attention between the party that is going on under her windows and Edward's verse translation. She reads at random a line here and a line there. Choosing a line from Creon's speech in which Polyneices is to be punished for leading a rebellion by being left unburied, "a corpse for birds and dogs to eat",[70] she supplements the text by creating her own image of vultures tearing the flesh of the unburied Polyneices. "At first she read a line or two at random; then, from the litter of broken words, scenes rose, quickly, inaccurately, as she skipped. The unburied body of a murdered man lay like a fallen tree-trunk, like a statue, with one foot stark in the air. Vultures gathered. Down they flopped on the silver sand. With a lurch, with a reel, the top-heavy birds came waddling . . ." (*Y* 117). Like others of Woolf's characters she focuses attention on the phrases that allow her to create an image of the death scene. When Antigone is apprehended Sara imagines her taken "to the estimable court of the respected ruler." Reading to the end she discovers that Antigone is in fact buried "in a brick tomb . . . And that's the end, she yawned, shutting the book" (*Y* 118).[71]

Antigone is the text that reveals the ancient lineage of gender distinction as simultaneously inspiring and frustrating desire. From "the litter of broken words" Sara visualizes a play whose ending she imitates by shutting the book and laying out her body in the bed. She positions herself like Antigone in the tomb, in a gesture of imitation as unconscious as Edward's. In complementary responses he reads male sexual desire into the text, she the buried life of a Victorian female. In his reading Antigone is desirable; in hers she is entombed.[72]

The reading of the play also suggests that university education discriminates against men as well as women. Sara lacks the education that might enlarge or diversify a reading in which the play primarily mirrors her personal concerns. North, just back from his farm in Africa, with a yearning to study Greek, is no better off intellectually than the daughter of an educated man. And the translator both discourages the common reader and at the same time sentimentalizes *Antigone*. Its reception reveals the power of the Greek text in the hands of a don to maintain the boundaries of both gender and class on the borders of empire.

The two scenes suggest Woolf's rather unforgiving backward glance at the barriers she had surmounted. She recreates the roles of translator and common reader as though in one sense the struggle that had engaged her for some thirty years had become history. If we take Reuben Brower's suggestion, that a translation is assimilated to contemporary notions of poetic style, Augustan, Victorian, or Modernist, then we may also see the dilemma of reading *Antigone* as Woolf's commentary on the Modernist text. The common reader, estranged from the Greeks by a gendered educational system, puts the play to novel use. Edward's translation frees Sara to invent her own play, in a move that suggests Woolf's license to develop a style that inflects for gender the ancient contest over female authority.

George Steiner's study of *Antigone* frames Edward's and Sara's reading in the context of nineteenth-century European culture. Steiner writes of the play, "It is not obvious that there is another work of literature which has elicited the strengths of philosophic and poetic interest focused on Sophocles' *Antigone* during the late eighteenth and the nineteenth centuries."[73] He attributes the creative response to the play by Hegel, Goethe, Kierkegaard, Hölderlin, and numerous others, in part to "the economy of myth in western thought," and, more to our purpose, to a shift in the emphases of kinship. The play is compelling, he argues, because it emphasizes the love of man and woman as the love of brother and sister. "Between the 1790s and the start of the twentieth century, the radical lines of kinship run horizontally, as between brothers and sisters. In the Freudian construct they run vertically, as between children and parents . . . The shift is momentous; with it Oedipus replaces Antigone."[74]

Although Woolf focuses on British society, her emphases are much the same. *The Years* is a novel which records the decline of family life and the formation of new patterns of kinship. Martin observes of family life that it is built on lies (*Y* 194–5). Delia exclaims " 'It was hell' " (*Y* 365). Eleanor, who recognizes that "this love-making differs from the old" (*Y* 323), would like to have married a man who is twenty years younger and in fact married to her cousin Maggie. Sara responds to Martin's questioning his father's love of her mother with the query, "Are we brother and sister?" (*Y* 216). The narrator takes the long view: "That turn was over – the old-brother-and-sister turn" (*Y* 314), which suggests that the play among siblings has become reduced to theater. It seems appropriate that at the end of the novel the Pargiter brothers and sisters are framed in the window like statues.

Edward holds the key, since he translates the text with the power to reveal the nineteenth-century family to itself. Sara is the most gifted reader, not only during the scene from her girlhood but later in the novel. As North waits for Sara to dress, she pretends to read: " 'He's killed the king,' she said, 'So what'll he do next?' " (*Y* 302). Is that ambiguous allusion sufficient to suggest that the spectacle of the love of brothers and sisters has been replaced, as Steiner suggests, by the Oedipal drama of patricide? And how is the reader to understand the peculiarly helpless position of the translator? Not only is Edward unable to respond either to his siblings or his cousin, but he fares less well in Woolf's hands than does the common reader.

CHAPTER 4

Solar light and darkness: "The Waves"

The perspective against wh. one sees life – is it the stars, or the woods of Elvedon or the British Empire?

(Hol *W* 765)

In *The Waves* (1931) Woolf shows how the subject arose on the ruins of an identity forged by the Imperialist ideology that is apparent in the metaphysics of light and darkness.[1] She invokes two works, Conrad's "Heart of Darkness" (1899) and William Holman Hunt's painting, *The Light of the World* (1853), which figure the process of colonization that precipitates the subject. A larger framework is provided by Martin Heidegger's "The Age of the World Picture," a lecture given in Germany in 1938.[2] His essay suggests the historical context of the emergence of the subject in the novel, and in turn the novel questions the limits of the essay.

Heidegger places anthropology, and by implication Imperialism, in the context of a metaphysics of seeing and being that derives from modern physics: "The fundamental event of the modern age is the conquest of the world as picture."[3] "Research," which Heidegger emphasizes as the defining characteristic of the modern world, gives priority to the importance of representing the world. The world as picture may be confirmed or denied by scientific experimentation, but the priority of mathematical representation is never in question. As a result man as subject comes into existence:

The interweaving of these two events, which for the modern age is decisive – that the world is transformed into picture and man into *subiectum* – throws light at the same time on the grounding event of modern history, an event that at first glance seems almost absurd. Namely, the more extensively and the more effectually the world stands at man's disposal as conquered, and the more objectively the object appears, all the more subjectively, i.e., the more importunately, does the *subiectum* rise up, and all the more impetuously, too, do observation of and teaching about the world change into a doctrine of man, into anthropology. It is no wonder that humanism first arises where the world becomes picture.[4]

In order to trace "the metaphysical ground of research" that determines the modern age, Heidegger goes back to the Greeks. In a series of appendixes to the essay he attempts by means of his reading of Greek philosophy to step outside the paradigms of humanism, as Woolf also attempts to do in *The Waves*. Greek thought in his account is based on a pair of concepts found in Sophism, which in effect prevent subjectivism: "Being is presencing and truth is unconcealment."[5] A horizon exists that may for the moment reveal the "unconcealed" to a particular man. Heidegger argues that for Protagoras man sees in accord with a "horizon of unconcealment" which is accompanied by awareness that the "I" is a restricted position, so that as a result the sophist "acknowledges the insusceptibility to decision of the visible aspect of that which endures as present."[6] Plato and Aristotle introduce a major change. "Precisely as a struggle against sophism and therefore in dependency upon it, this changed interpretation is so decisive that it proves to be the end of Greek thought, an end that at the same time indirectly prepares the possibility of the modern age."[7]

The history of Greek philosophy so formulated permits Heidegger to assert that the experience of the visible in the modern age has undergone fundamental change. Man becomes a subject at the historical moment "in which he frees himself from obligation to Christian revelational truth and Church doctrine."[8] So Neville and Bernard in *The Waves* represent to themselves religious paintings in a way that contrasts their subjectivity. Heidegger epitomizes the experience of freedom in the phrase, "We get the picture," which suggests a system that is normative and binding, and includes the viewer.

Woolf's great achievement in *The Waves* was to discover that the model of the gaze in which the viewer can be both subject and object was the creature of Imperialist notions of race and gender, and that at a different historical moment it might well be remodeled. She represents the reproduction of the gaze primarily in the paired characterizations of Neville and Bernard. Neville experiences the historical moment of Imperialism as a citizen-subject, and consequently does not move beyond the conventions of national and Christian identity which his position in the university effectively reinforces. From a position outside the university Bernard responds to Imperialism in the language of "Heart of Darkness," and experiences its contradictions with less ambiguity than do Marlow or Kurtz. Although at first Bernard is submissive to the discourse of Imperialism, he comes to experience a "division" which destroys the cognitive structure based on an image of the gaze that illumines the dark corners of the world. The solar eclipse which Woolf witnessed while drafting the novel furnished a new model of the gaze in which light comes and goes and the subject witnesses without being seen.

Gillian Beer argues that "for Woolf in the 1930s the language and ideas of the new physics helped to provide pathways out of the impasse of realist fiction."[9] In the language of her novel, astronomy in particular precipitates a new subject position. In June of 1927 Woolf traveled with Leonard and the Nicolsons by train to Yorkshire to witness along with thousands of other amateur observers a solar eclipse. When she wrote up her experience a few days later in her diary, she did not of course describe it from the perspective of an astronomer. Although she and Leonard purchased a telescope in 1930, the year that Pluto was discovered, when an exhibition of astronomical photographs was mounted the same year at the Royal Photographic Society at 35 Russell Square, her diary and letters are mute. Rather she represented the eclipse as a phenomenon whose significance is primarily visual. And so it appears to Bernard in the final section of *The Waves*. Although the moment was transient, it served as an important catalyst in her representation of the visible and the invisible as light and darkness. In *The Waves* she represents Bernard turning from a subject position that is derived from the metaphysics of darkness expressed in the language of "Heart of Darkness" to one dependent on an image of the visual field as constructed by light and imaged by the solar eclipse.

Much of what Woolf understood of the new physics may be inferred from her representation of photography. During the nineteenth century it transformed astronomy. "Photography alone has enabled astronomy to overcome the major obstacles to its progress: the sheer number of the stars, and the faintness of the light we receive from them. The fact that all our ideas on the nature and destiny of the stars have been radically altered . . . is unquestionably due to the use of the photographic plate, in astronomy above all, as the scientist's 'retina.'"[10] By the decade of the 1880s the astronomical community had accepted that the camera might replace the human eye as a recorder of celestial movements. Bernard's figuring his position in terms of a solar eclipse is situated within the cultural moment when it was first understood that film might be more sensitive to light than the retina.

The acceptance of the camera as a tool for recording astronomical events and for research into the position and distance of the stars came after several decades when professional astronomers were reluctant to grant that photographs made largely by amateurs might prove more accurate than visual data. The literature on the subject is not extensive, and here I summarize John Lankford's essay, "The Impact of Photography on Astronomy." From the earliest days of photography the heavens had been an object: a daguerrotype of the moon was obtained in 1840. During the following decade a British amateur, De la Rue, who was an experimentalist as well as a photographer, was able to demonstrate during the total solar eclipse of 1860 that he viewed in Spain, that photographic measurements of the corona were more accurate than visual. But when British photographs of the transit of Venus in 1874 turned out to show distortions, photography was rejected by the international community of astronomers. The decade of the 1880s and the advent of the "new astronomy" is seen as a "watershed," in part because younger astronomers who were trained in physics saw that photography not only recorded celestial events but might serve to make discoveries. By the end of the century, long hours at the telescope had produced "inconclusive results and discordant data," and photographic astronomy remained in the hands of amateurs. Not until photographs recorded the location of the faintest most distant stars with greater precision than statistical measurement was photography accepted by the astronomical profession. Lankford concludes, "By 1920 photography had become a major research tool in most areas of astronomical investigation."[11] And indeed in 1919 *The Times* reported that photographs of the solar eclipse were expected to confirm Einstein's Theory of Relativity.[12]

Alfred North Whitehead in *Science and the Modern World* (1925) argued for the larger significance of scientific developments that had produced a "new mentality" and "altered the metaphysical presuppositions and the imaginative contents of our minds."[13] An indication of this historic change is that the Astronomer Royal was able to verify Einstein's theory of the refraction of light rays in the vicinity of the sun by displaying photographic plates of an eclipse.[14] Arthur

Stanley Eddington in *Stars and Atoms* (1927) refers often to photographic evidence, for instance to demonstrate the behavior of fast-moving atoms and electrons: "I have already shown you photographs of a star, so I ought to show you photographs of an atom. Nowadays that is quite easy." He goes on to describe how the camera tracks fast-moving atoms "which flash by like meteors."[15] It is as though Woolf were present not merely at an eclipse but at the introduction of a new sense of the visible and a new discursive formation. Our task is to discover her response in fiction.

Images of solar light appear throughout Woolf's work, in phrases like "the language of the stars" from "The Mark on the Wall" but without suggesting subjectivity. Susan Dick observes of the beams of the lighthouse that figure in the characterization and structure of *To the Lighthouse*, that "while references to light are frequent in the first draft, Virginia Woolf saw many more opportunities to introduce or further exploit this resonant image as she revised the novel."[16] Yet the possibility that light as well as space determines the visual field, although it is hinted in "Time Passes," undergoes a significant shift of emphasis in *The Waves*. Although Bernard at first apprehends himself as both subject and object of the gaze, when he figures his personal loss in the language of the solar eclipse, suggesting that the visual field is defined by light, he precipitates a new subjectivity. Bernard abandons for the moment a position in which he is interpellated as a storyteller and assumes the position of a witness who sees without being seen.

THE WORLD PICTURE

Criticism of *The Waves* entered a new phase when Jane Marcus first focused attention on Woolf's satire of British colonialism: "Its parody and irony mock the complicity of the hero and the poet in the creation of a collective national subject through an elegy for imperialism . . . *The Waves* undermines humanistic faith in the individual coherent subject while exposing the role writing plays in shoring up *national* subjectivity; it challenges the idea of the artist's integrity."[17] But a study of British Imperialism that takes no account of the way that representation reveals ideology occludes the production of the subject. While Marcus sees Woolf's forebears as the shapers of "British ideology," she does not explain how that ideology was produced, nor does she examine the central significance of

Percival's death, after which Bernard's position splits off from that of the Imperial citizen-subject.

Each of the characters in *The Waves* is characterized by and to some extent imprisoned in a particular mode of vision, but more complex ways of seeing are attributed to the three male characters. In fact their gender seems determined less by physical orientation than by the care which Woolf lavishes on the details of their cooptation by the commercial, religious, and academic institutions in which they spend their lives.

Susan, who glimpses Jinny kissing Louis and Ernest embracing Florrie, creates for herself the solitary position of the child who witnesses the primal scene. It suggests not so much a phase of her childhood as a mode of denying herself subjectivity. In this model someone else articulates on her behalf the meaning of an image which she herself does not translate into words. Although Susan raises children, the male who figures in her discourse is not her husband but her father, as though by continuing to move in his orbit she has denied herself entry into social discourse.[18]

Jinny is restricted to the visible world by her focus on the body: "I pass them, exposed to their gaze, as they are to mine" (*W* 65). The visual image of the body marks her horizon: "I can imagine nothing beyond the circle cast by my body. My body goes before me, like a lantern down a dark lane, bringing one thing after another out of darkness into a ring of light" (*W* 84). She images her body as an instrument of Imperial exploitation. Bernard says of her "she saw nothing that was not there. It was a tree; there was a river" (*W* 169). The visible world that she creates is named but otherwise unrepresented. Fully identified with her image in the looking-glass, her visual impressions restrict her to the Lacanian Imaginary. It has been observed that Jinny and Susan together "represent the two poles of the patriarchal woman as a social construction."[19]

By rejecting the conventions of referentiality and sequestering herself in the codes of the visible world Rhoda creates the isolation which is the condition of her madness. The other students as members of a mathematical community read the numerical figures on the blackboard as the elements of a problem they are asked to solve. Rhoda answers the problem by drawing a figure that represents her position: "the world is looped in it, and I myself am outside the loop" (*W* 11). In Draft 11 of the manuscript the figure six represents her relation to the world: "I am barred out. I cannot do anything . . . Now if I draw the figure six on the page it will enclose the entire world" (Hol *W* 419). Nevertheless she differs from Susan and Jinny in that she is able to represent her subjectivity. The diagram draws her subject position in the code of the visible, suggesting that she herself inscribes the loop that isolates her from the world.[20]

The death of Percival inspires Rhoda to create a geometric image of referentiality, "the thing that lies beneath the semblance of the thing" (*W* 107). What she sees is an oblong laid upon a square, or the reverse, which "liberates understanding" (*W* 107), but again the image that is confined within the visible resists translation into narrative. The figure that she creates represents a kind of geometric sign, its two parts equivalent rather than equal, and neither dominant. The seeing subject notes the square set upon the oblong, the oblong upon the square. Either way, the geometric shapes suggest a new economy of the Imaginary, in which agency may be manifested as an invitation to read difference.

Jane Goldman interprets Rhoda's character as illustrative of "the contradictory position of women in opposition to, yet struggling for better representation within, Empire." Referring to a passage in which Rhoda imagines herself as a Russian ruler ("The diamonds of the Imperial crown blaze on my forehead. I hear the roar of the hostile mob as I step out on to the balcony . . . I am your Empress, people" (*W* 35), she remarks that as Rhoda "imagines becoming the ultimate female imperial subject [she becomes] a counterpart to Percival."[21] Yet the passage in question ends with Rhoda reflecting that "It is not solid; it gives me no satisfaction – this Empress dream. It leaves me, now that it has fallen, here in the passage rather shivering" (*W* 35).

But whereas Goldman resorts to myth to compare Rhoda to Acteon and Orpheus, I prefer to read her female jeopardy in the equally dangerous and more immediate dreams of power bred by Imperialism. In their aftermath Rhoda at first feels deprived, and then in the same paragraph experiences orgasm expressed in the image of her body as a "fertilising" stream (*W* 35). Like Susan's and Jinny's, her sexuality is determined by Imperialist ideology, but the process destroys her mind and life. It prompts her first to a fantasy of authority that mirrors the male and is maintained in the face of hostility, which leads to sexual ecstasy, and in a later passage to a sensual attraction to violence that culminates in her death.

It is primarily in the male characters that we see the coming into existence of the subject on the ruins of an identity that was constructed by the discourses of Imperialist culture. Louis, as an Australian with a keen sense of his alienation from inherited tradition, willfully identifies himself with his function as citizen-subject. His character is clearest in the "Life" chapter, which opens: "'I have signed my name,' said Louis, 'already twenty times. I, and again I, and again I. Clear, firm, unequivocal, there it stands, my name" (*W* 109). The character who identifies so easily and completely with the first person (which Woolf questions in several works) expresses the Imperialist metaphysic of light in commercial terms: "I roll the dark before me, spreading commerce where there was chaos in the far parts of the world" (*W* 110).

Heidegger's view of the increasing irrelevance of the university in an age that is dominated by scientific research puts the characterization of Neville in historical perspective. Heidegger writes of the "humanistic sciences . . . mired in mere erudition," and "the increasingly thin and empty Romanticism of scholarship and the university [that] will still be able to persist for some time."[22] But although he might suggest that Neville's career in classical scholarship safely insulates him, in fact it is the site of major cultural contradictions. Unlike Louis, the most gifted student, who identifies himself with Plato and Socrates, Neville is reluctant to make the easy identification between Greek civilization and his own which as we have seen was so striking a feature of Victorian and Edwardian debates about the uses of classical learning. On the one hand he refuses to "impersonate Catullus, whom I adore" (*W* 56). But when he sees Percival as an emblem of "pagan indifference . . . remote from us all in a pagan universe" (*W* 21) he creates an archaic figure, without impact on contemporary discourse. This image of Percival is a culturally constructed disguise of homosexual desire which elsewhere in the novel Neville expresses more freely.

The conflicted nature of Neville's homosocial Hellenism is suggested when he identifies Percival both with Alcibiades, a man renowned for his beauty, and with two military heroes, Ajax and Hector. He reads all three as versions of Percival: "They loved riding, they risked their lives wantonly, and they were not great readers either" (*W* 119). Ajax and Hector as obstinately brave warriors recall the German scholarship that demonstrated "that paiderastia was martial in origin, closely related to . . . [the]

inspiring warrior ideal." To include in the same list the name of Alcibiades, the wealthy and handsome young man whose relationship with Socrates supported the charge that the latter had corrupted young men, hints at the larger contradiction in Victorian homosocial thought, the "willful denial of the paiderastia so crucial to the Greek culture it otherwise held up to emulation and praise."[23] Neville's list combines warriors and a pederast, the unacknowledged contradictions of whose social functions are masked by the academic nature of his discourse.[24]

Woolf pairs what might be called a mutation of subjectivity in Bernard with a demonstration of the historical moment of the self in Neville. During the reunion dinner at Hampton Court the two characters reflect in the context of a sixteenth-century structure on their place in British history. Bernard's perspective derives from astronomy: "I reflect now that the earth is only a pebble flicked off accidentally from the face of the sun and that there is no life anywhere in the abysses of space" (*W* 150). In that context kings and palaces become like "Our English past – one inch of light" (*W* 151). Neville has a particular sense of himself as the subject of history: "I am beginning to be convinced, as we walk, that the fate of Europe is of immense importance, and, ridiculous as it still seems, that all depends upon the battle of Blenheim. Yes; I declare, as we pass through this gateway, it is the present moment; I am become a subject of King George" (*W* 152). Woolf's note that "without Marlborough we should have been . . . vassals of the French King"[25] makes clear that Neville's conviction of his identity is bound up with that of the nation that won at Blenheim. His understanding of the subject is limited by the relatively brief span of British history, and by his idealized view of the citizen-subject.[26] Woolf's strategy is to profile the historical moment of the nation against the calendar of astronomical time.

Bernard in contrast has carried on his life work outside the university, a position that Woolf had already marked as privileged, and perhaps for that reason he more freely displays the contradictions inherent in Imperialist ideology. Conflict and division in his sense of "identity" are particularly apparent in "The Farewell Dinner" chapter. Bernard, recently engaged to marry, imagines his identity as a train journey toward a specific destination: "We have attained our desire. We have drawn up at the platform" (*W* 72). Although it would seem that marriage confers identity on Bernard as a journey completed, Percival's departure for India precipitates a crisis that complicates Bernard's "identity." His "identity," a term that he uses over a dozen times in the novel, proves powerless against a darkness that he associates with "the sunless territory of non-identity" (*W* 75), and a "solitude that is my undoing" (*W* 144).

The chapters that represent the loss of Percival most vividly, the "Farewell Dinner" chapter, the "Death" chapter, and the "Summing Up" chapter reflect the historical moment of the subject's relationship to the visible that is clarified by comparison with "The Age of the World Picture." Percival is less a character (he does not speak) than the object of desire. He literally vanishes at the convergence of lines of a perspective that focus on him the desire of each of the characters. His image suggests that at some level mathematical perspective governed perception in much the way that Heidegger argues is the primary function of mathematical research, with the difference that what Heidegger presents as prophecy Woolf writes as elegy for the ocular world of perspective.

But whereas Heidegger reads history in a way that occludes the agent of such change, Woolf represents Percival, the Imperial subject, as precipitating Bernard's subjectivity. The male characters of *The Waves* experience Percival in the terms of Lacan's future anterior; what is realized in the history of the subject is "n'est pas le passé defini de ce qui fut puisqu'il n'est plus, ni même le parfait de ce qui a été dans ce que je suis, mais le futur antérieur de ce que j'aurai été pour ce que je suis en train de devenir" [not the past definite of what was, since it is no more, or even the present perfect of what has been in what I am, but the future anterior of what I shall have been for what I am in the process of becoming].[27] The future anterior overrides the segmenting of time, suggesting a sequence of tenses that stresses process. The male characters become subjects to the degree that they see Percival not merely in terms of a shared past, but as in the process of recognizing their separation and loss, they glimpse through him what they might have become. History thus becomes a past that is always yet to come, and closure is indefinitely postponed.[28] One may read the final lines of the novel as Woolf's interpretation of the future anterior in the characterization of Bernard.

As Neville awaits the arrival of Percival at the farewell dinner, his anticipation is figured in a vocabulary of being and order: "Things quiver as if not yet in being . . . The normal is abolished" (*W* 77), and when Percival arrives: "The reign of chaos is over. He has imposed order" (*W* 79). We see that the hunger for order and closure that is frustrated in Bernard's life but achieved in Neville's precludes the future anterior, and hence the kind of subjectivity that Lacan and Heidegger postulate.

In contrast to Neville, Bernard during these three chapters moves towards a clearer sense of the future anterior. Percival's departure becomes at first the occasion of a gaze that imposes order, expressed in the language of seeing from "Heart of Darkness." His "I see India . . . I see the low, long shore; I see the tortuous lanes of stamped mud . . . I see a pair of bullocks" (*W* 88) may be compared with Marlow's "Do you see the story?" (50) or the harlequin's "He made me see things" (91), or Conrad's "Preface" to *The Nigger of the Narcissus:* "My task . . . is to make you *see.*" In Conrad's texts seeing is a project which leads to narrative precisely because it admits of significant difficulties. By contrast Bernard uses the verb "to see" in a manner that stresses its transitive nature, so that seeing becomes the language of execution. He imagines a scene in which Percival, still seated near him, rights a cart in India "by applying the standards of the West, by using the violent language that is natural to him . . . The Oriental problem is solved" (*W* 89). Bernard derives from the Imperial world view an ethic of performative language which he attributes to Percival. Bernard's assertion that Percival is therefore indeed "a God" expresses in simple declarative terms Kurtz's more nuanced assertion that whites may appear to Africans "with the might as of a deity."[29] Unlike Marlow, who never succeeds in integrating the visible with the intelligible, Bernard effortlessly translates sight into language, as though the silent Percival had while still alive already become a signifier.

Keeping in mind Lacan's assertion that the eye is "symbolic of the subject" (*Sem I,* 80), what is the significance of a Bernard who sees more aggressively than either Kurtz or Marlow? As what Bernard terms "the moment of ravenous identity" comes to an end, "Now open in my eyes a thousand eyes of curiosity" (*W* 94). In comparison to Neville's "To read this poem one must have myriad eyes" (*W* 131–2), Bernard's eye colonizes the world. He leaves the restaurant assured that he is not a "slave," but a "creator," and "stride[s] not into chaos, but into a world that our own force can subjugate and make part of the illumined and everlasting road" (*W* 96). The metaphysics of light and darkness have produced in Bernard the voracious Imperial gaze that illumines an otherwise darkened world.

In "the death chapter" Woolf introduces a painting that references the light of the Imperial gaze and suggests the grounds of Neville's inertia. Her notes suggest that she planned to pair Neville and Bernard: "Neville has the actual personal loss . . . Bernard has the speculative . . . " (Hol *W* 755). Each attempts to find consolation for the death of Percival in well-known paintings. Neville's "All is over. The lights of the world have gone out. There stands the tree which I cannot pass" (*W* 98) alludes to Hunt's *The Light of the World*, perhaps the best known nineteenth-century British painting. Conceived during a period of religious fervor in Britain, it is based on a verse from Revelations (3:20, "Behold, I stand at the door and knock; if any one hears my voice and opens the door, I will come in to him and eat with him, and he with me"). In the painting the figure of Christ faces forward holding a lantern in his left hand, while his right knocks at a closed door. The tree in the background and the stigmata on both of his hands prefigure the Crucifixion. The first and larger version hangs in Keble College, Oxford, and the second in the Manchester City Art Gallery.

When Hunt was criticized for representing Christ's spiritual qualities literally as the image of the lantern and halo, he defended his painting, "He who when in body was the LIGHT OF THE WORLD could not be unprovided when in spirit with the means of guiding his followers when it was night."[30] Ruskin, in a lecture about the relationship of science to art, defended the painting as "the most true and useful piece of religious vision which realistic art has yet embodied. But why is the metaphor so necessary, or, rather, how far is it a metaphor at all?"[31] Alluding to the Bible he argues that light has always transcended the distinction on which metaphor is grounded. Lindsay Smith comments on the controversy, that "the central problematic of *The Light of the World* involves a slippage between literal and symbolic – a literalising of the metaphor of light." In his view Hunt, who worked with a fidelity to visual detail that was inspired by photography, subverts the metaphor of light.[32]

Hunt's painting comes to Neville's mind at the moment when he receives word of the death of Percival. Although he registers the death in a way that associates Percival with Christ, the passage represents the authority of a religious ideal that has been replaced by a normative social practice. Neville's "light of the world" is not a title but an echo repeated in the text, part of a vocabulary that speaks Neville. In Heidegger's term Neville "gets the picture" in the sense that the painting represents much more than an image; it represents "a system." He grasps not a picture of the world, but the world as picture, in which the "relationship to oneself . . . [is] the normative realm."[33] Neville's position in an educational institution contributes the paradox of his dominance and inertia.

Woolf records in "22 Hyde Park Gate" (*MB*) that as a young woman she was taken by George Duckworth to Hunt's studio. The copy of *The Light of the World* which she saw on an easel was probably the third version of 1903–4. By this time Hunt was partially blind and the painting that Woolf saw was not entirely his work. The position of Christ's legs as well as the accentuation of light and dark markedly alter the significance of this version.[34] Woolf's description of her visit as the climax of an unsatisfying evening spent with her half-brother George may account for her emphasis on the absurdity of the scene – the famous old painter sipping his cocoa, while his "devout, high-minded" guests tiptoed around the studio (*MB* 176). Her satiric bent would seem to have eclipsed her response to the painting itself.

One of the conditions of the sale of the painting was that it be shown in all the countries of the British Empire; sales of the engraving gave it an even wider circulation. As an icon of Empire *The Light of the World* circulated as we have seen in speech as well. Such was its cultural impact that "there was now a more highly charged connotation to the very word 'light,' with which many a hymn began."[35] And it powerfully reinforced the figure of the Imperialist eye beaming light into the darkness, so that Marlow sees himself as an "emissary of light." We see it as well in Jinny's image of her body: "My body goes before me, like a lantern down a dark lane, bringing one thing after another out of darkness into a ring of light" (*W* 84). Neville's language also reflects its enhanced significance: "The lights of the world have gone out . . . Oh, to crumple this telegram in my fingers – to let the light of the world flood back – to say this has not happened" (*W* 99). This is the same man who "hate[s] ceremonies and lamentations and the sad figure of Christ" (*W* 118), and suggests that "crucifixes are the mark of the devil" (*W*

163), or so I interpret his allusion to Christ's cross as "the tree which I cannot pass" (*W* 98). Perhaps because Neville has assimilated Hunt's painting into his vocabulary, his position as viewer is less active than Bernard's, as though the horizons of his beliefs have been drawn by an ideology of religious and national sentiment which the institution of the university serves to maintain and regulate.

When Bernard receives the news of Percival's death he too seeks spiritual consolation, in a painting hung in the National Gallery, an experience that he recalls in his "summing up." In a passage from Draft 1 Bernard asks himself "those important questions, under the stare of the cold madonnas; To begin with I cease to see him. That obsession . . . of the eye . . . with the fact of death . . . is over. He takes a different form" (Hol *W* 245). The Venetian paintings of the madonna "make no reference whatever . . . Yet Oddly enough, they expand my consciousness of him; they bringing him back in another form. They put our relationship in a better light" (Hol *W* 245–6).[36] Bernard turns to paintings in an attempt to bring to consciousness important questions concerning mimesis and homosocial feeling. The paintings seem to offer him a freedom from the obsessions of the gaze, as well as insight into the manner in which mourning has transformed his viewing. Lacan observes that the painter "gives something for the eye to feed on, but he invites the person to whom this picture is presented to lay down his gaze there as one lays down one's weapons" (*FFC* 101). Bernard discovers that the icon of the madonna assuages his obsession with the injured body of Percival, perhaps by reminding him that the madonna links Jesus' death to his birth, and so allows Bernard to pair the death of his male friend with the birth of his child. But the painting's "perpetual solicitation of the eye" (*W* 103), with its implication of surrender, constrains him.[37]

Like Neville, Bernard performs the funeral rite as a secular experience: "This is my funeral service. We have no ceremonies, only private dirges and no conclusions, only violent sensations, each separate" (*W* 103). The paintings ease the obsession of his mind's eye with Percival's suffering, and serve to remind him of the suffering of others. In the printed version of the passage Woolf added the lines, "Lines and colours almost persuade me that I too can be heroic . . . Now through my own infirmity I recover what he was to me: my opposite" (*W* 102). Without the presence of Percival "my own infirmities oppress me. There is no longer him to oppose them" (*W* 102). The revised museum scene suggests that Bernard responds to Percival as an idealized other, who makes it possible for him to measure his personal "infirmities" against an heroic ideal. In comparison with the moment at the end of the previous chapter when Bernard was prepared to subjugate the world, the experience of the gaze in the museum forces the recognition that the heroism which Bernard has associated with Imperialism is the unattainable object of his desire.

Bernard recalls this moment during his summing up as having produced a short-lived "exaltation . . . But it did not last," and he was once again tormented by "the horrible activity of the mind's eye" (*W* 177). Bernard is a seasoned museum-goer, as familiar with the life and works of Titian as with the experience of viewing. Although religious paintings formerly would "expand my consciousness of him and bring him back to me differently" (*W* 102), the experience now fails. In the interim grief, the sense that "I saw the first morning he would never see" (*W* 176), has transformed his gaze: "To see things without attachment, from the outside . . . pretence and make-believe and unreality are gone, and lightness has come with a kind of transparency, making oneself invisible and things seen through as one walks – how strange" (*W* 176). The passage suggests that the permeation of light everywhere transforms the gaze that had formerly been constructed by viewing paintings. Perhaps it is what Woolf meant by referring to "The Moths" as an "abstract mystical eyeless book" (*D* III:203), or in the language of the drafts as "the perspective of the stars."

The death of Percival prompts in Bernard a meditation on communication with the dead that recalls Septimus Smith's with Evans. "I ask, if I shall never see you again and fix my eyes on that solidity, what form will our communication take? . . . But you exist somewhere. Something of you remains. A judge. That is, if I discover a new vein in myself I shall submit it to you privately. I shall ask, 'What is your verdict?' You shall remain the arbiter" (*W* 101). Bernard's mourning takes the surprising form of submission to the law as the "verdict" of the colonial administrator. But as the decline from "the zenith of an experience" (*W* 101) makes of the colonial moment past history, communication with the dead becomes problematic, and the integrity of Bernard's position comes under increasing pressure. Only later as Bernard sums up does he realize that colonial discourse, for instance in the scene where old men discuss "What is to be done about India, Ireland or Morocco?" (*W* 170), is "a lie" that bifurcates language between that realm and "deep below it . . . a rushing stream of broken dreams, nursery rhymes, street cries, half-finished sentences . . ." (*W* 171).

THE THRESHOLD OF THE VISIBLE . . .

When at the beginning of the "Summing Up" chapter Woolf represents Bernard as someone under the illusion that something "is completed" (*W* 159), a position unavailable to the living self, she prepares the reader for the emergence of the subject and for her version of the future anterior tense. Earlier at the farewell dinner Bernard observes in himself the split in his "identity" that heralds the inauguration of the subject: "I am not part of the street – no, I observe the street. One splits off, therefore" (*W* 74).[38] He figures the position of the participant observer as split between the "I" and the subject as viewer. The position of ethnographer which he assumes remains closely identified with a critical consciousness and with the dominant culture.

In the final chapter, by contrast, the split in Bernard's subjectivity is staged as an address to a figure whose identity is contingent on recognition, whom he does not know but may have met "on board a ship going to Africa" (*W* 158). I argue that the figure of the African traveler is Conrad, and that Woolf represents Bernard's meeting in the manner that Modernist poets have adapted in part from their reading of Dante. Woolf was reading the *Inferno* in Italian from August of 1930, as she was drafting *The Waves*.[39] During a moment of historical crisis, an air raid during World War II, T. S. Eliot also discovered in Dante the image of a silent listener who confirms the subject. In "Little Gidding" (1942) the poet encounters "some dead master" with the eyes of "a familiar compound ghost," who may be identified by the idiom of Yeats and Dante. Although Bernard does not turn to Marlow in the manner of Dante, who seeks guidance from Virgil, he mirrors the authority of the African traveler. We may ask whether Bernard's encounter signifies Woolf's sense of a historical crisis that has so altered the social conditions of speech, that to recognize Conrad as a ghost precipitates the subject.

Once free of his identity Eliot's poet occupies a position in which he may "find words I never thought to speak," and hear what he may neither comprehend nor remember. In a similar fashion Bernard addresses the ghost of Conrad, as he seeks the words with which to assimilate the alien experience of death to the conventions of European discourse. The figure of the African traveler appears again in the final pages of the novel, where Bernard acknowledges what he has achieved "under your gaze," but at the same time gives thanks for his departure: "The face looking at me has gone. The pressure is removed" (*W* 294). The line signifies Bernard's readiness to envision darkness in terms that are independent of Conrad's.

Woolf's admiration of Conrad is well known, especially her praise of the early stories and *Lord Jim*. In her second essay on "Joseph Conrad" (1924), reprinted in *The Common Reader*, she repeated her preference for the earlier work, and she praised "the light of those brilliant eyes." Marlow, a "born observer . . . had a habit of opening his eyes suddenly and looking – at a rubbish heap, at a port, at a shop counter – and then complete in its burning ring of light that thing is flashed bright upon the mysterious background" (*CR* 232). In Conrad we see the power of the visible to motivate narrative.

Shirley Neuman examines the effects of "Heart of Darkness" on Woolf's fiction in *Mrs. Dalloway, The Voyage Out*, and *Between the Acts*: "Remembering *Heart of Darkness* and its ironic reading of the traditional male quest in Marlow's voyage, Woolf further ironizes Conrad's plot to emphasize the colonized over the conquerors." Yet in the area of gender Woolf differs from Conrad in her representation of "authentic spiritual recognition by women."[40] If we move beyond theme and character to include the problem of subjectivity, *The Waves* may be read as a text that is equally deeply engaged with "Heart of Darkness." Percival occupies a position not unlike that of Kurtz, in that his characterization focuses the larger problem of representing the Imperialist subject. Kurtz is represented largely as a "voice"; Percival, who is speechless, largely by his gestures. In both we see that desire for the inscrutable individual serves to organize the passionate attention of the characters, the harlequin and the Intended as well as Marlow, and all of Percival's childhood class-mates. The essentially unknown Imperialist subject dies represented and misrepresented, untruthfulness a part of the truth of what can be known.

At a point in the narrative when Kurtz is still "just a word for me," Marlow asks his listeners, "Do you see him? Do you see the story? Do you see anything? It seems to me that I am trying to tell you a dream" (50). It appears that the problem of communication lies in the area of representation, where the difficulty of representing the seen is conveyed in the image of the dream. Problems of communication simply do not exist for the harlequin, the Intended, and the minor characters. Marlow's preoccupation is heuristic, not only with respect to "Heart of Darkness," but more generally with respect to the Modernist problematic of the sign, as though a rupture in the representation of the visible signified the Imperialist subject which Marlow is here to read.[41]

One may read "Heart of Darkness" as representing Marlow's inability in the context of his African adventure to integrate what he finds intelligible with what he is seeing. As navigator he has been trained to read the surface of the river, but he confesses himself unable to interpret "surface-truth." Part of the difficulty is that he must translate everything he sees into European languages. The helmsman dies "as though he had presently put to us some question in an understandable language." In actuality he would speak if he could in an African language, which Marlow hears as "howls" and "cries." The bifurcation of the intelligible and the visible defines Marlow as Imperial subject, by inhibiting his understanding while simultaneously shielding him from awareness of his position.

His discovery of the seaman's manual, a text with the reader's notes in the margin, figures the semiotic nature of his difficulty. Marlow sees it as filled with "diagrams and repulsive tables of figures." He reads the notes in the margin as cipher until the harlequin identifies them as Russian script. The instructional nature of the manual assumes that the tables and diagrams function as the visible and unproblematic referent of the text, and that the sign is stable. But the wider reading community has generated another, marginal text. The sign has been translated and in the hands of the harlequin, a man without an occupation as seaman or anything else, the significance of the manual is far from evident. Yet Marlow speaks of "these humble pages," as signs of "something unmistakably real." The notes, glosses, and translation in Conrad's text seem to suggest the imagination, not in evidence among his characters, that would be necessary to represent a foreign text or a foreign culture.

Bernard's sense of his marginal position arises as a consequence of recognizing himself as the object of the gaze of the African traveler. "You see me sitting at a table . . . You see me take my napkin . . . You see me pour myself out a glass of wine " (*W* 159). Heretofore

Bernard has been the agent of the gaze, but as object he feels his authority evaporate; his stories, he says, are not true, and his writing but adds "a comment in the margin" of the child's picture book (*W* 159). Rhoda is the character who is capable of imagining the sea and jungle (*W* 135, 137); Bernard will never, he says, see the African jungle or learn Russian (*W* 123). It is sufficient for him as for Marlow that he tell his tale under the gaze of others more familiar with "the dark places of the earth." The Imperialist moment seems to have marginalized the writer by hastening the separation of narrative from experience, and calling in question the power of the text to communicate. The image of marginal notes may stand in Conrad's work and in Woolf's for the limits of empire as an explanatory model, and consequently for their recognition of the writer's obligation to represent a foreign culture from a marginal position.

Bernard's position as citizen-subject is derived from his social and intellectual position as the inheritor of a long tradition that includes Byron, Shelley, Dostoyevsky, and, in draft II, Napoleon (Hol *W* 672), which he has come to see as an "orderly and military progress; a convenience; a lie" (*W* 171). As one of "those who have inherited the spoils of all the ages" (*W* 174), he fantasizes being called on to share in commanding the British Empire. A literary genealogy that Bernard associates with the expropriations of recent history serves to confirm his agency: "called upon to act my part I had no doubt whatever that I could do it" (*W* 175). In the context of Woolf's criticism of British universities, it is not surprising that an education that skimped on the classics contributes to Bernard's sense of authority. He has "nosed around without ever precisely touching the Latin classics" (*W* 163), and of Greek there is no mention.

The death of Percival undermines Bernard's compound social identity, and produces a series of states which figure the destruction of that identity.[42] Instead of an identity shared among his friends he confronts the fission of body and mind into daemon and beast. One self is "that man, the hairy, the ape-like" (*W* 194), the other the resistant self who says "'I will not consent'" (*W* 190). The latter grows silent, withholding phrase and answer: "No echo comes when I speak, no varied words. This is more truly death than the death of friends, than the death of youth. I am the swathed figure in the hairdresser's shop taking up only so much space" (*W* 190). An outline from Woolf's notebook associates this experience with "the loss of identity" (Hol *W* 766). Bernard's self-image echoes Marlow's characterization of the accountant who maintains a European dress code in Africa as "a hairdresser's dummy" (36). As a sign of his dilemma Bernard sees himself as no more than the body he has just glimpsed in the looking-glass of the hairdresser's shop, a functionary of the Imperialist dream.

Leaving the shop Bernard recalls the figure of Rhoda "to serve as opposite to myself" (*W* 188). It is as though the specular identification with the Imperial subject which underlay Bernard's sense of his identity has suddenly been canceled. The loss throws in question his mind/body and male/female identifications, as though without Imperialism gender boundaries might dissolve: "For this is not one life; nor do I always know if I am man or woman " (*W* 188).

WHAT THE EYE CAN DO FOR US

In *The Waves* the solar eclipse becomes the new figure of the visible world. Following the departure of the self with whom Bernard had identified he expresses his loss thus:

The scene beneath me withered. It was like the eclipse when the sun went out and left the earth, flourishing in full summer foliage, withered, brittle, false.

. . .

The woods had vanished; the earth was a waste of shadow. No sound broke the silence of the wintry landscape. No cock crowed; no smoke rose; no train moved. A man without a self, I said. A heavy body leaning on a gate. A dead man . . . How can I proceed now, I said, without a self, weightless and visionless, through a world weightless, without illusion?

. . .

How then does light return to the world after the eclipse of the sun? Miraculously. Fraily. In thin stripes. It hangs like a glass cage. (*W* 191–2)

These passages in which Bernard experiences the death of the self derive from Woolf's account of the total eclipse of the sun which she witnessed on 29 June 1927. Although several solar eclipses had been visible elsewhere during her lifetime, this was "the first visible in England for 200 years."[43]

A few days later she wrote an extended account of her journey by train and car with the Nicolsons and other friends to Yorkshire, where the trajectory was visible: "The 24 seconds were passing. Then one looked back again at the blue: & rapidly, very very quickly, all the colours faded; it became darker & darker as at the beginning of a violent storm; the light sank & sank: we kept saying this is the shadow; & we thought now it is over – this is the shadow when suddenly the light went out. We had fallen. It was extinct. There was no colour. The earth was dead . . . We had seen the world dead. This was within the power of nature" (*D* iii:143–4). As the light was extinguished, the temperature dropped. Afterwards, "what remained was a sense of the comfort which we get used to, of plenty of light & colour" (D iii:144).

It is no surprise that Woolf's approach was quite different from that of professional astronomers. The article, "Eclipse Suggestions," published in the *Journal of the British Astronomical Association* in March 1927 presented some twenty-five pages of advice to viewers, most of it concerning photography, for instance corrections for time when photographing from a mountain top, and advice on types of film, exposure times, and focal length. Color film that required a single exposure was available.[44] The Astronomer Royal reported to the Royal Astronomical Society details of the sequence of twenty-nine colour exposures that he had made of the eclipse. Ironically none were reproduced, since the journal printed its pictures in black and white only.[45]

Woolf's account resembles rather those of the eyewitnesses that were published after the event by the British Astronomical Association. Those observers commented on changes in the color of the oncoming shadow, a deep blue changing to purple and then pink. Others were struck by the sudden return of light: "It was not only very sudden, but the light was extraordinarily warm in colour and reminded me of the effect of switching on the electric light in a cold twilight." One man asserted that the effect of the shadow "rendered the landscape similar to the illustrations of Dante of the Inferno." Another observer who like the Woolfs had traveled to Yorkshire wrote that "Totality came quite suddenly and gave to the heavy clouds the most awe-inspiring effect of falling closer to the Earth by many thousands of feet . . . This strange and indescribable shadow was intensely dark, giving the effect of an appalling purply black. Faces appeared an ashy green; it was like the shadow of death."[46] As biographical subject Woolf shared the consensus among viewers, that however they may have stressed different visual details, the eclipse was made to signify human mortality.

Woolf's account of the eclipse confirms the conditions of the subject that she had derived much earlier from her reading and translation of *Agamemnon*. That is, the transition from one visual circumstance to another creates the split in which the subject briefly emerges. When the eclipse is interpreted as an experience of bereavement, as in her story "Sympathy," its most significant effect is on language. The narrator responds to an obituary in *The Times*: "But how death has changed everything! – as, in an eclipse of the sun, the colours go out, and the trees look thin as paper and livid while the shadow passes . . . Death has done it; death lies behind leaves and houses and the smoke wavering up, composing them into something still in its tranquillity before it has taken on any of the disguises of life" (*CSF* 103–4). Death "had removed the boundaries and fused the separate entities." When the narrator finds herself in error, her friend lives, "the horizon [is] shut in . . . and the coarse strong colours return" (*CSF* 104). The eclipse transforms the understanding of signifier/signified, so that were it to signify death we might welcome the appearance of a horizon capable of widening and contracting, and regret the return to the mundane world now perceived as coarse and shrunken. At the end of *The Waves* Woolf again represents death as an occasion when language can hold closure in abeyance.

"The Sun and the Fish" (1928) is a parable that queries the relationship of the eye/brain to the mind/memory as a phenomenon in the history of the planet.[47] The visual image survives in memory only when linked with another. "So, on this dark winter's morning, when the real world has faded, let us see what the eye can do for us. Show me the eclipse, we say to the eye; let us see that strange spectacle again" (*CDB* 212). But although the dialog is between the "we" and the "eye," the eyes belong to "me." That is, if the editorial "we" is the language of command, the eyes are yet singular. The subject in my argument arises in the conditions of doubleness, when "we" lodge a demand with the "eye/I." The parable asks whether such pairs are biological. That is, memories are paired, as are brain and mind: "the mind's eye is only by courtesy an eye; it is a nerve which hears and smells . . . which is attached to the brain and rouses the mind to discriminate and speculate" (*CDB* 212). The story resembles "The Mark on the Wall," in that it seeks to understand in historical terms the mental process prior to representation. But it widens the scope of history to include the planet.

The command to the eye is followed by a narrative of the eclipse which follows Woolf's account in her diary. If the darkened world be imagined as "dead," those who saw it so were "worshippers at Stonehenge," visitors from the "primeval world" (*CDB* 213–14). In the final paragraph the eye "in pursuit of some logic of its own" represents lizards and fish from the London Zoological Gardens: "In their shape is their reason" (*CDB* 217). It is as though Woolf were rephrasing her questions about the historical conditions of the subject by reorienting them towards the history of the species and the planet.

By far the most detailed interpretation of "The Sun and the Fish" is by Jane Goldman, who argues that Woolf represents the eclipse as "a transitional moment of feminist challenge and change."[48] By noting the differences between the story and Woolf's diary entry, and then identifying the full context in her work of individual words and phrases, Goldman links the story with myth, elegy, Greek tragedy, and the Suffragist movement.

From the perspective of the aquarium, the scene of the eclipse is one of "destruction" and "ruin," but this is revealed as the perspective of the ruling patriarchy, whose "calm . . . steadfastness" and "immortality" have given way to the increasing pressures of the new prismatic feminism . . . But this model must be comprehended by means of her "amusing game" which demonstrates that such a vision is achieved, and survives, only by reference to its contrary.[49]

In Goldman's reading "The Sun and the Fish" tells the story of Woolf's feminism; in mine the story questions the position of the subject in the context not of nations but of the planet. I read the story as a meditation on the relationship of the subject to astronomy and biology. My reading asks whether and under what natural conditions the subject might be said to exist. The gaze cannot be dismissed, since memory appears dependent on the perspective of the gaze, which the subject requires in order to summon scenes to the mind's eye. The lizards and the fish lead the narrator to a meditation on function: "In their shape is their reason. For what other purpose except the sufficient one of perfect existence can they have been thus made?" (*CDB* 217). The eclipse on a larger scale than in "Sympathy" serves to represent the conditions of life, and to suggest that a less than sufficient identification with biological function may be the enabling condition of subjectivity.

When the journal entry of the eclipse was transformed into a simile that figures Bernard's state of mind, the eclipse was made to signify a change in Bernard's subject position. It is revolutionary in the sense that he goes well beyond what he might experience as an individual. The "man without a self" is "a dead man," and to that extent he shares the tendency of his culture to read the eclipse as signifying human mortality (*W* 191). But following the eclipse what Lacan refers to as "the dialectic of the eye and the gaze . . . You never look at me from the place from which I see you" no longer obtains (*FFC* 102f). Once the gaze no longer defines the field of representation, Bernard's world is effectively emptied of echoes, phantoms, and shadows. Light returns but "with this difference; I saw but was not seen . . . Thin as a ghost, leaving no trace where I trod, perceiving merely, I walked alone in a new world, never trodden" (*W* 192).

Without the sense of himself as the subject/object of the gaze an entire cognitive structure collapses. Language is no longer referential. "There are no words. Blue, red – even they distract, even they hide with thickness instead of letting the light through" (*W* 192). His identity is in question: "'Who am I?'" (*W* 193). Since he finds no obstacle beween himself and the dead Percival and Rhoda, he overcomes the notion of "identity."

From this new perspective Bernard once again addresses the figure from Africa in an image of empire, but this time in order to lodge a grievance: "I catch your eye. I, who had been thinking myself so vast, a temple, a church, a whole universe, unconfined and capable of being everywhere on the verge of things and here too, am now nothing but what you see . . . That is the blow you have dealt me" (*W* 196). The departure of the figure with "the power to inflict this insult" (*W* 197) relieves the pressure of the Imperial gaze. The face met "on the gangway of a ship bound for Africa," is figured as "this shadow which has sat by me for an hour or two, this mask from which peep two eyes" (*W* 197). The moment ends in solitude when "the face looking at me has gone. The pressure is removed" (*W* 197). The language of Draft II is more explicit: "Heaven be praised, no one presses upon me, & eyes me; no one looks out of his face into mine; & comes close & peeps in & makes me shiver & makes me laugh & makes me rage" (Hol *W* 738).

As in "Heart of Darkness" the subject comes into existence on "the threshold of the invisible." The helmsman and Kurtz are alike in suggesting at the moment of their death a new meaning for Heidegger's "truth is unconcealment," in the sense that they reveal the limits of the world of work and life. The gaze of the colonized becomes powerful in death; Marlow responds to the death of the helmsman with "an effort to free my eyes from his gaze and attend to the steering" (77–8). Work would appear to be the activity that confines Marlow's attention to the world of the living. After Kurtz has died the horizon once again opens, when Marlow considers his final cry as marking the "moment of time in which we step over the threshold of the invisible" (113–14). Death marks the limits of the gaze that has been established by Imperialist ideology. The narrative suggests that the breaching of its limits is powerful enough to account both for Marlow's astonishing loyalty to Kurtz and his equally astonishing acceptance of the helmsman's gaze as "a claim of distant kinship affirmed in a supreme moment" (85).

In *The Waves* once the gaze of the Conradian figure has been withdrawn, the visual field is seen to be created not by the gaze of the other but by light. Bernard represents the moment in the language of the Watchman in *Agamemnon* adapted to modern astronomy: "I have watched the sky change. I have seen clouds cover the stars, then free the stars, then cover the stars again. Now I look at their changing no more. Now no one sees me and I change no more" (*W* 198). The visual field is no longer defined by the relationship between the colonizer and the colonized, but by a light that comes and goes, independent of human agency.

A STEED THAT KNOWS HIS RIDER

The ending of *The Waves* is problematic. Woolf's diary suggests her doubts and hesitations. The notebook entries suggest some possible lines of inquiry, for instance that she pondered the theme of "identity." She knew that subjectivity is not a train journey, that it is not arrival at the station and cannot be sustained beyond the moment. The notebook shows her working in terms of wave-like repetition: "what can survive?/Then the sense of loneliness again & conflict./Then the complete dying out of identity./Then its return" (Hol *W* 765). When Bernard hears the wave fall on the beach he wonders "Sometimes I think I have escaped identity: that I am free" (Hol *W* 768). But in the printed version he remains imprisoned within its horizons. In the second-to-last paragraph we find him murmuring "I–I–I," and in a significant gesture looking to catch the last train home.

Here again Conrad's darkness serves to position Bernard. In the final interlude darkness falls, and *darkness* is repeated in a context that links "Heart of Darkness" to Romantic metaphor.[50] As Bernard looks up at incipient dawn, "The stars draw back and are extinguished . . . Yes, this is the eternal renewal, the incessant rise and fall and fall and rise again" (*W* 199). He speaks the vocabulary of the interludes that figures the natural world as light and dark and birdsong. The light fades and leaves the world "silent," "empty," and "unseen" (*W* 157–8), but the adjectives, which we recognize as coming from Keats's odes, modify a thrush, a snake skin, and a road. The final paragraph of the interlude represents not the "embalmed darkness" of "Ode to a Nightingale" but darkness as waves that wash and roll over places and persons. Conrad's text has been subsumed into a vocabulary which reassigns Romantic metaphor in order to frame Imperial discourse with an image of the world as planet.

The notebooks imagine a final scene of confrontation: "What this needs is some conflict, so that there can be an end. Death I think must come in as the antagonist: must be an argument between them" (Hol *W* 761). In Draft I Bernard addresses death in the street (Hol *W* 374), and in Draft II addresses death as "my final opponent" (Hol *W* 743). The final lines of the novel in which Bernard experiences "a new desire" and in imitation of Percival rides against death provide conflict, but with a certain satiric note reminiscent of the figure of Mr. Ramsay. His pose is also a comment on Romantic self-dramatization. Since Woolf noted in 1930, when she read Byron's *Childe Harold*, "the inevitable half assumed half genuine tragic note, which comes as a refrain, about death & the loss of friends" (*D* III:288), it is not surprising to catch a hint of the language of Canto III.[51]

Perhaps the clearest example of Woolf's reservations about the discourse of Imperialism in Conrad and Keats occurs earlier, in the "Farewell Dinner" chapter. While Percival is still alive and among them, Louis and Rhoda together figure a scene of savage sacrifice, he in the imagery of "Heart of Darkness," she in the language of Keats's odes. Louis imagines a dance of painted savages. "The flames leap over their painted faces, over the leopard skins and the bleeding limbs which they have torn from the living body" (*W* 92). Rhoda replies with the image of a "festival": "They throw violets. They deck the beloved with garlands and with laurel leaves." We, she says, "are conspirators, withdrawn together to lean over some cold urn" (*W* 141). Louis responds: "'Death is woven in with the violets,' said Louis. 'Death and again death'" (*W* 92). The passage suggests what Laura Doyle argues is Woolf's engagement with the Romantic sublime as "the British subject's sublimation of barbarity – a barbarity at once their own and projected on to those whom they conquer."[52] Louis seizes on the dance as ritual mutilation in a savage culture alien to Europeans; Rhoda uses Romantic metaphor, specifically the funeral urn, to rationalize and poeticize sacrifice. As "conspirators" they appear to be motivated by the departure of Percival to create in companion discourses an acceptable image of the death of others.

In this connection Lacan's assertion that the subject is "a true survival that is abolished by knowledge of itself, and by a discourse in which it is death that sustains existence" would appear not only as an ontological but more significantly as an historically specific formulation (*E* 300). We may see it working as well in *Mrs. Dalloway* in the configuration of the characterizations of Clarissa and Septimus. Her gaze through the window materializes the old woman at the points most necessary to Clarissa, and Septimus although he does not explicitly enact her death wish, plunges to his death along the trajectory of her gaze. In both novels the gaze appears to figure the Imperial will, not merely to subjugate but to murder, under the auspices of a ritual designed to sustain the existence of the speaker.

Woolf's career as self-styled outsider gave her a keen sense of the position of the aspiring artist. We have seen that Bernard's image of splitting echoes the position of the ethnographer as participant observer. And in Draft 1 at the end of the scene at the hairdresser's Bernard wonders "Have I any of the certainty that a mathematician has when his sum ~~call~~ calculation works out, or the planet appears, timed/right to the fraction of a second?" (Hol *W* 363). What Heidegger names as social and professional identities Bernard exhibits as positions in language that he might occupy. Since he distances himself both from the university and from the characteristics of scientific thinking, there may be no social place for Bernard.

Throughout the final chapter Bernard like Marlow has been preoccupied with the question of representing to himself the moment of stepping over "the threshold of the invisible." Bernard asks, "By what name are we to call death? I do not know" (*W* 295). And "Should this be the end of the story? a kind of sigh? a last ripple of the wave?" (*W* 178). Death may be considered as a kind of closure, "the knowledge of limitations" (*W* 180). Or as Bernard ponders his lost identity he asks, "'Was this then, this streaming away mixed with Susan, Jinny, Neville, Rhoda, Louis, a sort of death?'" (*W* 187). In his notebook under "D" he seeks "ways of naming death" (*W* 195). At a moment of such uncertainty it is significant that he clings to the desire to make his language performative: "Death is the enemy. It is death against whom I ride with my spear couched and my hair flying back like a young man's, like Percival's, when he galloped in India. I strike spurs into my horse. Against you I will fling myself, unvanquished and unyielding, O Death!" (*W* 199).

The final passage of Bernard's "summing up" tests the possibility of closure in the language of death and desire. It is initiated by the contradictory nature of his desire, figured as "something rising beneath me like the proud horse whose rider first spurs and then pulls him back." The homoerotic language echoes Plato's *Phaedrus*, and the contrast between the good horse who is noble and ruled by shame, and "the lover's undisciplined horse," who must be reined in by the soul. Seeing the face of the beloved boy, the charioteer remembers that beauty is allied to self-control, "and at the same time has to pull the reins back so fiercely that both horses are set on their haunches." Bernard is the subject divided by desire, both reining in and spurring on his horse, drawn by desire towards death.

The final lines of the novel image his relationship to Percival in the language of the future anterior, the grammar that represents the historical dimension of the subject: "what I shall have been for what I am in the process of becoming." Bernard figuring himself in the position of Percival stages the future as a past yet to come. The image defers closure in the name of the death that is future and fictive. It represents the performative bent of Imperialism at the limits of the imaginary. The faintly ridiculous tone of the line, with its echoes of Mr. Ramsay's romantic posturing, suggests to me that Bernard, like Marlow, has reverted to a position which the novel has worked hard to reveal as riven by serious ethical contradiction. What might have been tragic in an Imperialist narrative the subject as witness rewrites as farce.

CHAPTER 5

The person to whom things happened: "A Sketch of the Past"[1]

The mirror scene in "A Sketch of the Past" offers a remarkable account of the female subject's position in the imaginary, and her coming to subjectivity in a patriarchal culture. I know of nothing comparable in English literature. Coming as Woolf did from a family that included visual artists, it is hardly surprising that she writes "as if I were a painter," and represents her childhood as the visualization of certain spaces, especially the mirror. Seeking relief from the task of writing the life of Roger Fry while withholding her intimate knowledge of him, and from the anxiety of the early days of World War II, she saw autobiography as a kind of retreat, a place to consider "the person to whom things happened," that is often omitted from conventional biography. The mirror puts her family in perspective, while she occupies the position of viewer, and in an extraordinary passage represents her encounter with the Victorian male as the transformation of woman as object into the writing subject. In the field of vision subjectivity arises from its opposite.

In Woolf's fiction the mirror experience is usually feminine. Mrs. Ramsay "avoids her face" in the glass; Mrs. Manresa rouges her lips; Orlando recognizes himself as female in the looking-glass. Moments before he confesses that he may be man or woman Bernard views himself in the hairdresser's glass. In some instances the experience suggests the limitations of the self in the realm of the visible. Jinny, who has an uncomplex notion of the visible, is not disquieted by her reflected image even as she ages.

In "The Mark on the Wall" the looking-glass perpetuates the image of the "romantic figure," and when it breaks reveals "only that shell of a person which is seen by other people . . . A world not to be lived in" (*CSF* 79). It leads into a discussion of the shifting sense of the "real" and the "phantom" that since the war has discredited the romantic self-image. "The Lady in the Looking-glass" (1929) extends the criticism of the romantic self. In it the "stillness and immortality" of the glass are contrasted with the changing light of the surrounding scene. When Isabella Tyson, a rich and cultivated spinster, approaches, the mirror "began to pour over her a light" that revealed not only her aged face, but the "truth" that Isabella "was perfectly empty" (*CSF* 219). The story suggests anxiety that the visible signifies a world restricted to plants and objects, that only the self-scrutiny of the subject assures the significance of the invisible.

Reflection serves a feminist purpose in *A Room of One's Own*, where its implications are figured at the intersection of gender and national history. "Women have served all these centuries as looking-glasses possessing the magic and delicious power of reflecting the figure of man at twice its natural size" (*RO* 35). Reflection is associated with violence: "mirrors are essential to all violent and heroic action. That is why Napoleon and Mussolini both insist so emphatically upon the inferiority of women" (*RO* 36). But although Woolf criticized the violence of patriarchy in European history, she did not until she wrote her autobiography make explicit the connection with the circumstances of her early life. The split consciousness which she notes elsewhere in the essay – "if one is a woman one is often surprised by a splitting off of consciousness" (*RO* 101) is similarly a phenomenon of European history, transformed in "A Sketch" into the painful condition of female subjectivity. In many ways the earlier image of the mirror as reflecting size and scale seems to have been adapted from Lewis Carroll, whose *Collected Works* Woolf was reviewing while writing "A Sketch": "One must get the feeling of everything approaching and then disappearing, getting large, getting small, passing at different rates of speed past the little creature" (*MB* 79). It is significant that "A Sketch" took shape at a moment of crisis among nations, when the scale and speed of what was approaching and disappearing took on a more urgent historical meaning.

The mirror experience in "A Sketch" begins with the circumstances of personal history, memory, and forgetting. In the first sentence Woolf tells an amusing anecdote about Vanessa's reminding her that if she waits until she is eighty-five to write her memoirs, she may, like Lady Strachey, have forgotten more than she remembers. In Lacanian terms the forgotten is the lack of a signifier. "A Sketch" was written under the threat of forgetting, of the erasure of signifiers. Like the trace made by Friday's foot, the signifier is erased but becomes significant not because it was erased, but because the subject marks the place where it was erased. The signifier arises and the subject emerges in the act of marking that place.[2]

"The Mark on the Wall" gives us Woolf's early interpretation of marks and erasure. The story concludes with naming but without the emergence of the subject, perhaps because of an interruption by the other, who brings the narrative to closure by unproblematically naming the mark as a snail. In Lacan's terms "the signifier comes from the Other and returns to the Other."[3] "A Sketch" proposes that autobiography be written so as to change the addressee and so retrieve from the other the act of signifying. It may be read as the problem of assigning the signifier when the signified is fading and the other undergoing redefinition. As we saw in the image of Menelaos and Helen in Chapter 2, these are the conditions that precipitate the subject.

RAIDS ACROSS THE BOUNDARIES

"A Sketch" was written in the intervals of writing the biography of Roger Fry, during the early days of the war. The events of 1939–40 seem to have created the preconditions under which according to George Gusdorf autobiography comes into existence, so that the individual witnesses his entry into history and responds by constructing his story as "the unity of a life across time."[4] Woolf was completing her biography of Roger Fry and uncertain about representing the balance between his public and private life, reading Freud and finding him "upsetting" (*D* v: 250), and anxiously living through the events of 1939. The memoir was begun three days after she wrote in her diary of her "extreme depression," which came, she thought, from illness (influenza), from the "drudgery of writing the biography of Roger Fry," and from her sense that war made life "meaningless" (*D* v: 215). Her diary is punctuated with war news, an air raid in September, and on the 23d the remark that "Poland has been gobbled up." In addition during the period April to November, when the first section of "A Sketch" was written, she and Leonard moved house, and his mother died. By 1940, she wrote, "the French have stopped fighting" (*MB* 107), and the Germans were regularly bombing London. In what seems to me an amazing feat of creative energy she chose a moment of historical turbulence to reflect on the constitution of her subjectivity.

Woolf came to autobiography by way of biography. In "Reminiscences," written when she was twenty-five and ostensibly addressed to the son of Vanessa, she discovered the material of her later autobiographical "Sketch." The emphasis on the life of a sibling, the importance of seeing ("She might not see all, but she did not see what was not there," *MB* 30), and the excitement of looking into the glass are all there in the earlier work, but the narrative is written in the convention of the family history rather than as an exploration of the double nature of the mirror experience. Perhaps the disruptive events of wartime brought her to consider in "A Sketch" a strategy whereby the present provided a "platform" and a perspective from which to write of her past life. (*MB* 75).

The problem of what to conceal from the general public that arose in her writing the biography of Roger Fry seems also to have aided the discovery of her subject position.[5] She complains of the drudgery, presumably an allusion to the burden of reading a lifetime of his correspondence and papers, and to the discomfort as well of writing for a mass readership a life whose intimate details she knew well but could not reveal. Woolf told a half-truth about Vanessa, whom she represents not as Fry's former lover but as a lifelong friend. But Woolf also found Fry fundamentally inscrutable: "Only one subject seemed to escape his insatiable curiosity; and that was himself. Analysis seemed to stop short there" (*RF* 289). So I read her complaint in "A Sketch" of the difficulty of giving "any account of the person to whom things happen" (*MB* 69) as her awareness that the subject is never fully apparent to the self.[6]

The problem of the concealed biographical subject is directly related to the difficulty of representing the autobiographical subject. Woolf's biography of Fry is filled with amusing anecdotes, many of them derived from his correspondence with friends. Although the common reader might gain a good sense of his intellectual gifts and his energy, Woolf conveys less forcefully his professional authority.[7] For instance she uses the titles of two of his books, *Vision and Design* and *Transformations*, as the titles of chapters in which she quotes from his letters rather than from these works. She was pleased by the reviewer who said in effect "that Roger Fry was there and not V. W., which was what I wanted" (*L* VI:479). In an odd collusion with the hidden subject Woolf invented for herself the position of witness, the transparent observer who sees without being seen.

But Woolf gained more than the novelty of the subject position as invisible. In "An Essay on Aesthetics" (1909) Fry drew a significant comparison between the mirror and the cinematograph. The enables the viewer to become the spectator of events in which he might have participated. He drew an analogy between the events that one views in the street and the reflections seen in a mirror:

in the mirror, it is easier to abstract ourselves completely, and look upon the changing scene as a whole. It then, at once, takes on the visionary quality, and we become true spectators, not selecting what we will see, but seeing everything equally . . . The frame of the mirror, then, does to some extent turn the reflected scene from one that belongs to our actual life into one that belongs rather to the imaginative life. The frame of the mirror makes its surface into a very rudimentary work of art, since it helps us to attain to the artistic vision.[8]

Fry uses the frame to offer a material view of the mirror. The adult viewer sees his culture and personal history transformed by the framed reflection into a work of the imagination. The experience of the cinema offers a model of seeing that is analogous to that of the mirror in that it represents the contingency of the imagination on the spectator's awareness that he has access to more than one visual code. The autobiographical aspect of Woolf's biography of Fry is apparent in the way that she represented him as inhabiting her favorite position, that is on the boundary between Imaginary and Symbolic, on the one hand a painter and visionary, and on the other a translator of Mallarmé, and "always making raids across the boundaries" (*RF* 239–40).

As Woolf was reading autobiographies, she came to the realization expressed in "The Leaning Tower" (1940), that they flourished at a certain moment in the history of readership. In the essay she associated the extraordinary production of autobiographies in the decade 1930–40 with a cultural moment when the generation of Dickens and Thackeray was succeeded by the generation of Mac-Neice and Auden, that "leaned" to the left. "By analyzing themselves honestly, with help from Dr. Freud, these writers have done a great deal to free us from nineteenth-century suppressions. The writers of the next generation may inherit from them a whole state of mind, a mind no longer crippled, evasive, divided" (*M* 149). In the diary entry of 11 February she noted, "they have demolished the romance of 'genius' of the great man." As a result she witnessed "the supersession of aristocratic culture by common readers." In a rather cryptic passage of the diary she theorizes the reader's position: "I think there's something in the psychoanaly[s]is idea: that the L.

Tower writer couldn't describe society; had therefore to describe himself, as the product, or victim: a necessary step towards freeing the next generation of repressions" (*D* v: 267). The passage suggests that the autobiographer by revealing himself as produced by social circumstance motivates the reader's potential resistance. In a way that becomes important for reading the character of Gerald in "A Sketch" the passage frames the question of the writer as victim in cultural rather than personal terms.

Shari Benstock reads Woolf's autobiography both against the premises of autobiography, and as part of the project mentioned in the diaries to write her memoirs. Both of our discussions focus on the problematic treatment of the split subject, "who both 'is' and 'is not' the reflected image."[9] But when Benstock writes that the "difficult theoretical questions" posed by Woolf's practice mean that she "finds it impossible to place herself in the position [of subject]," or that the mirror "conceals – and tries to seal itself against – the gap . . . of the unconscious," her definition of the subject suggests the intentions and preoccupations of the self.[10] Lacan's value to my argument is in part his insistence that the subject is located in language, at the moment of contradiction between conscious and unconscious inflections. I share Benstock's sense that the mirror scene is a moment outside memory, "a moment that hangs in a space that is neither dream nor fact, but both."[11] It is central to my interpretation because it genders a perspective on the visible world expressed in the figure of the imaginary.

"A Sketch" lies on the border between public and private writing, neither a draft of a work intended for publication, nor a diary. Woolf herself referred to the work as a "memoir" (*MB* 64, 98), and as "notes" (*MB* 75, 95, 100, 117). John Mepham discusses the status of "A Sketch" at length, observing that it is both memoir and diary, "and gives the lifewriting activity itself a context." He compares it with Woolf's writing the life of Roger Fry, from which she had decided to omit private matters having to do with his sex life. ("Can I mention erection? I asked . . . No you cant" (*D* v: 256). As autobiographer she was free to create a self that did not exclude the female body. Perhaps because Mepham views identity as composite, he treats the mirror passage as no more than one of the "unanalysable experiences" that go to make up human identity: "In this 'sketch,' the writing is not so much designed to record or recall an already established history, as to attempt to create a coherent identity, by holding together in a pattern the various parts of herself, or different identities, that she feels are all authentically part of who she is."[12] In my reading the mirror passage offers not a glimpse at Woolf's "identity," but rather a rare glance at the constitution of the female subject.[13]

"A Sketch" is divided into ten sections corresponding to two periods of composition in 1939 and 1940. The first two, dated two days after 16 April 1939, and 2 May, contain the mirror passage and its context, and the 15 May and 28 May sections concentrate on the face of the mother both living and dead. I am less concerned with the 20 June and 19 July passages on Stella. In June 1940 Woolf rediscovered her manuscript, at a time when German planes were flying over England every night and the Woolfs were contemplating suicide. She completed the memoir in five long passages (dated 19 June, 18 August, 22 September, 11 October and 15 November), while reading the proofs of the Fry biography. Anticipating German victory and the suicide planned with Leonard, she observed in her diary that "the writing 'I' has vanished. No audience. No echo. That's part of one's death" (*D* v: 293). Perhaps for that reason in the 1940 section she is less concerned with herself and returns instead to the position of social historian.

THE GAZE OF THE CHILD

The patriarchal world in which Woolf lived and wrote so idealized the face and gaze of the mother that she had only to avert that gaze to create a sense of loss. "A Sketch" emphasizes significant moments when the child's gaze was not met. Woolf's "first memory" is of sitting on her mother's lap, enroute by train to or from St. Ives. As a child looking at eye-level Woolf seems to have been most aware of the flowers on her mother's breast. But a later scene at St. Ives suggests that not meeting the child's gaze was motivated, and that as Madeline Moore observes, Woolf's relationship to her mother "was like that of an unrequited lover."[14] A later section of "A Sketch" links Woolf's idealization of her mother's "astonishing beauty" with the child's longing. She describes meeting her mother on a path: "I stopped, about to speak to her. But she half turned from us, and lowered her eyes. From that indescribably sad gesture I knew that Philips, the man who had been crushed on the line and whom she had been visiting, was dead . . . I felt that her gesture as a whole was lovely" (*MB* 82). Julia Stephen's turning aside from her daughter in order to mourn forestalls the possibility of an appeal. The child Virginia was momentarily sequestered in a world gone mute, and in later life she recalled that her mother's grief and beauty positioned the child as viewer.

Yet once dead the mother becomes one of the "invisible presences" which locate the subject in time: "if we cannot analyze these invisible presences, we know very little of the subject of the memoir" (*MB* 80). The power of the dead figure becomes clear in the 15 May passage, which ends with the well-known description of Leslie Stephen in the moment immediately after his wife's death. "My father staggered from the bedroom as we came. I stretched out my arms to stop him, but he brushed past me, crying out something I could not catch; distraught" (*MB* 91). Her father repeats the aversion from her glance that earlier in the narrative Woolf had experienced from her mother. When on 28 May Woolf resumed work, she juxtaposed to the deathbed scene an image of her mother's face that was continuous with her experience of parental faces: "Her face looked immeasurably distant, hollow and stern. When I kissed her, it was like kissing cold iron" (*MB* 92). In death Julia's face was both fully exposed to view and her glance finally averted. In the context of Woolf's failure to be seen, I read a quality of her loss that she associates with her mother as both subject and object. Seeking acknowledgment in the gaze of the mother as subject, she encounters a figure whom death has made into an object.[15]

Growing up in a family of visual artists, Woolf learned to look from looking at pictures. The photographic portraits made by her great aunt Julia Margaret Cameron between 1864 and her death in 1879 contributed to Woolf's understanding that the female gaze is historically constructed. In an era when portrait painting was in decline, Cameron like other early photographers revealed a taste for the iconography of painting. Woolf contributed a lively appreciation of Cameron's personality to *Victorian Photographs of Famous Men & Fair Women*, a collection of her work which the Hogarth Press published in 1926. In a companion piece Roger Fry praises the perception of character in Cameron's portraits of such eminent Victorians as Browning, Darwin, and Tennyson. Although occasionally Cameron subtitled male portraits, "A Rembrandt," for instance, or "King Arthur," the tendency to allegorical composition in the manner of George Frederick Watts is more evident in her portraits of women.[16]

Most appear with literary subtitles, for instance "Sappho," "Ophelia," or "Echo." The iconography of "Madonna with Child" or "Madonna with Children" characterizes her female group portraits as well. In "Rosebud Garden of Girls" for instance the gaze of the five women is mysteriously deflected, suggesting the isolation of the women from each other. No two look toward each other and none looks outward toward the viewer. The line of the gaze serves to carve up the photograph into a series of individual studies. The exception is "Death of Elaine," in which the sight lines of three of the five figures converge on the dead face.

Among the many amateur photos of family and friends collected by Vanessa Bell and by Violet Dickinson, a few portraits of the Stephen women made after Cameron's death fit her iconography of the isolated and theatrical female pose. A photograph of Vanessa, Stella, and Virginia (*c*. 1896) from Vanessa's photograph album is a study of three heads.[17] Although the overlapping shoulders suggest a group, each glance is focused on a different horizon. Another photograph shows Mrs. Stephen in profile and Stella facing her but turned slightly towards the viewer.[18] The situation of the heads and Stella's lowered eyelid suggest that although as in "An Unwritten Novel" (see Chapter 1) each woman is positioned in the visual field of the other, something operates to inhibit their exchange of glances.

These portraits show a patriarchal world divided into famous men and sorrowing madonnas. The madonna, writes Julia Kristeva, figures the maternal order within the jurisdiction of the father. In "Stabat Mater" she observes, "motherhood is the *fantasy* that is nurtured by the adult, man or woman, of a lost territory" and an idealized relationship. It intensifies the sense of childhood as lost, and leaves no room for "the war between mother and daughter" which in the photographs is merely hinted by the averted gaze.[19]

THE SIGNIFICANCE OF GERALD

Woolf's mirror frames the moment of entry of the female child into the patriarchal world that the photographic portraits had idealized. It focuses attention on the position of the subject who, when "the writing 'I' has vanished," represents herself before the mirror in an uncertain position. The passage from "A Sketch" includes the same family that appeared in "Reminiscences" (*MB*) and in the photographs, but this time framed by the mirror. Grandfather, mother and father, Stella, Vanessa, Thoby, and Adrian form the gestalt that defines by exclusion. The mirror sets the family in perspective and allows the subject to occupy the position of a viewer who stands outside the frame.

Thomas Brockelman argues that because the imaginary excludes "the place from which representation occurs," it draws responses of both joy and hatred to the mirror experience, which he explains in terms of Lacan's "captation" and "aggressivity."[20] "Captation" is the response to the exclusiveness of the gestalt as an obsessive paralysis. Gestalt in the mirror experience means that the symmetry, size, and exteriority of the image contrast strongly with the uncontrolled movements of the infant (*E* 2). Brockelman interprets Gestalt as "a unity . . . whose form only arises in contrast to an excluded 'ground' against which it appears."[21] In Woolf's representation beauty produced the sense of her captation. The beauty of her mother was "the natural quality that a mother . . . had by virtue of being our mother" (*MB* 82). Stella is largely "unconscious of that [her] beauty" (*MB* 86). Woolf responds to the beauty of her mother and Stella that is assumed as "natural," first by positioning herself as the child viewer, too young herself to have become the beautiful object, and then with reference to her father's "spartan, ascetic" taste, so that "my natural love for beauty was checked by some ancestral dread." In the position of the viewer who uses beauty to mark her separation from the gestalt, she seeks release from captation by claiming a genealogy of those whom she resembles not in face but in mind.

"Aggressivity" is a destructiveness towards the self. Lacan associates it with "images of castration, mutilation, dismemberment, dislocation, evisceration, devouring, bursting open of the body, in short, the *imagos* that I have grouped together under the apparently structural term of *imagos of the fragmented body*" (*E* 11). It is "aimed at destroying the unity of the image so that those chaotic energies suppressed by it can have free rein." In such a move either the mother or a sibling "becomes the victim of a kind of unlimited rage."[22] The object of Woolf's rage is undoubtedly Gerald, the half-brother who molested her.

Louise DeSalvo argues that in "A Sketch" Woolf explored the "possibility that her life might have been otherwise, that the bouts of depression and despair, the suicide attempts, were not an inevitable part of her makeup, but that they were, instead, caused by her reaction to what she had lived through." Under the pressure of the extraordinary circumstances during which Woolf wrote "A Sketch," she recovered the memory of Gerald which until then she had apparently repressed. In the context of research into the behavior patterns of abused children, DeSalvo makes the claim "that sexual abuse was probably the central and most formative feature of her [Woolf's] early life."[23] In letters to her friends as well as in her autobiography she was able to analyze the causes of her lifelong depressions and suicidal feelings, thereby "anticipating, by thirty years or so, inquiry into the relationship between childhood abuse and the formation of personality, between family structure and childhood abuse."[24] DeSalvo makes an unproblematic use of the scene to argue that Woolf's adult self was constituted by the experience with Gerald.

But aside from the question of Gerald's harm to his half-sister, how might his representation figure as part of Woolf's mirror experience? If we accept the statement in her memoir of Julian Bell (1937), that "I am so composed that nothing is real unless I write it," we must preserve the distinction between biography and auto-biography.[25] And it follows that Woolf's representation of the episode has a performative power, in the sense that it contributes to the imaging of her subjectivity.

Richard Gregory observes of the mirror experience, that the child learns that "none of the important properties of things is in the images made by eyes, for these images are but patterns of light. What objects are, for use or to avoid, must be learnt from dangerous experiments."[26] Woolf's autobiographical subject learns the proper-ties of image and object in the particular and painful sense that from a position outside the mirror she discovers from her interaction with Gerald what it means to be object rather than subject.

Gerald is not grouped with the family, but is positioned outside the mirror, at an angle that as I see it blocks the subject's self-reflection. He splits the position of the subject between the victim who does not see and cannot say, and the witness who later represents the action. His presence dramatizes how Woolf's "two people, I now, I then, come out in contrast" (*MB* 75). He initiates a more complex image of the divided subject than we saw in *A Room of One's Own*, and a shift from the emphasis on national history to the history of gender relations.

The representation of Gerald serves a function like that of beauty, to alienate the subject from reflection. He is the focus of a rage expressed in the image of female ancestors: in her distress Virginia Stephen "had from the very first to encounter instincts already acquired by thousands of ancestresses in the past" (*MB* 69).The shame that Woolf felt on looking at her face in the glass and the shame to which Gerald subjected her both prevent identification with the mirror image, what Brockelman calls "the collapse of the subject into the other." Whatever may have been the historical circumstances in Woolf's childhood, in the autobiography Gerald represents a position that is necessary to figure the passage of the female subject out of the imaginary.

Shame plays a significant part in constituting the subject. Lacan refers the reader to Sartre's *Being and Nothingness* (1953), in which shame and the experience of being the object of the gaze are part of his argument that the model of man's being is incomplete without consideration of the existence and role of the Other. Shame illustrates a way of understanding how one may become an object to oneself as subject. Since the face seen by the Other is unknown to the self, the glance becomes the occasion to recognize a self that includes and is larger than the known, and to ask the question, "What sort of relations can I enter into with this being which I am and which shame reveals to me?"[27]

"Shame is not a feeling of being this or that guilty object but in general of being an object; that is, of *recognizing myself* in this degraded, fixed, and dependent being which I am for the Other."[28] Shame, together with the related feelings of fear and pride "are only various ways by which I recognize the Other as a subject beyond reach, and that include within them a comprehension of my selfness which can and must serve as my motivation for constituting the Other as an object."[29] Yet shame in Sartre's argument is a fundamental aspect of identity. Fear, shame, and pride are "nothing more than our way of affectively experiencing our being-for-others."[30]

The genealogical image of ancestresses figures both in the language of captation and aggressivity, obsession and rage, and in the impulse to yield to beauty or to chaos. It complicates the reading of the phrase, that "a woman writing thinks back through her mothers," from *A Room of One's Own*, which conflates the genealogy of the family and of other "ancestresses." It suggests that Woolf's lifelong attention to the aesthetic problems posed by beauty, in *To the*

Lighthouse especially, arose from its power to sequester her within the imaginary. My problem is to ask how the language of "ancestresses" frees the female subject from captation and aggressivity, so as to open a passage into the symbolic.

If as Lacan observes, everything depends on the angle at which one stands before the mirror, would it be sufficient merely to shift the angle? DeSalvo assumes that what took place with Gerald was visible in the mirror: "I strongly suspect that what intensified the horror of the experience was the fact that Virginia was able to see herself in the mirror: she was watching herself being assaulted."[31] But in a passage otherwise devoted to reflection, Woolf presented this experience as a tactile image. Perhaps she was denied a visual perspective. Seated on the slab she faced a larger person, so that if the mirror were opposite she saw the reflection of Gerald's back, or if it were the shelf over which she peered into the mirror, she had her own back to the reflection. Although abused children may be able to allude only indirectly to their abuse, as an adult Woolf could be forthright, as when in "Hyde Park Gate," another memoir, she described her other half-brother, George, entering her bed.

The characterization of Mrs. McNab represents in fiction what is involved in shifting the angle of viewing. In "Time Passes" she is the figure who repairs the destructions of time and war with a mop and a bucket. In the holograph version of the novel she was the focus of Woolf's anti-war and anti-male sentiment. There she is "nothing but a mat for kings & kaisers to tread on." Her role is to "deprecat[e] . . . the scorn or anger which might be of the world," and to preach the "forgiveness of the understanding mind." These qualities were somewhat muted in the typescript, and all but disappeared in the printed version, where the war has become parenthetical and there is no reference to kings, kaisers, or forgiveness. James Haule reasons that in making these revisions Woolf's "desire to explain gives way to a more powerful urge to demonstrate, to represent the darkness and the power of human understanding."[32]

Mrs. McNab is a troubling example of female resistance, marked by references to the Kaiser, and by Woolf's ambivalent attitude towards female domestic servants. She stands at an angle to the mirror: "Rubbing the glass of the long looking-glass and leering sideways at her swinging figure a sound issued from her lips . . . robbed of meaning . . . like the voice of witlessness" (*TL* 142). Lacan comments on the mirror experience that "everything depends on the angle of incidence at the mirror. It's only from within the cone that one can have a clear image. So whether you see the image more or less clearly depends on the inclination of the mirror" (*Sem I,* 140). Curiously although Lacan emphasizes the inclination of the mirror, he does not consider how the subject might be relocated. Mrs. McNab, "the voice of witlessness," has been located at an angle that guarantees her exclusion from the symbolic. The problem, Lacan continues, does not occur during the mirror experience, "but subsequently through our overall relation with others," a problem which he characterizes with such phrases as "the symbolic connection between human beings," and finding "a guide beyond the imaginary" (*Sem I* 140–1). From the point of view of gender the logic seems circular, as though entry into the symbolic depends on acquiring the language of the symbolic. As subject to the "symbolic connection" devised by the male other, Mrs. McNab fails to become a subject, and in the language of the text is imaged as an animal. She "turned aside even from her own face," until "she looked like a tropical fish oaring its way through sun-lanced waters" (*TL* 145). The passage suggests that against a background of the violence of war the working-class female is barred from the symbolic by the way in which her image has been reflected, with the result that her subject position has been assigned by others.

In "A Sketch" Woolf inscribes herself in both positions, that of the woman who writes, and that of the working-class woman whose resistance takes the form of reparation. She combines the role of artist with that of the resister when she defends writing as "far more necessary" than "learning to do something that will be useful if war comes" (*MB* 73). If as George Gusdorf argues, autobiography reveals "the effort of a creator to give the meaning of his own mythic tale," Woolf's tale is the myth of the female coming to subjectivity under patriarchy, where in time of war writing becomes an act of resistance.[33]

THE NAKED CRY

Woolf's study of *Agamemnon* suggests one context in which to consider the genealogy of her ancestresses. At the age of twenty-one Woolf, as discussed in Chapter 2, had seen in her Greek studies "how our minds are all threaded together – how any live mind today is of the very same stuff as Plato's and Euripides'" (*AP* 178). Working at translation every morning in her bedroom isolated her within the domain of the family, and created the position from which she imagined a genealogy of mind. From a position outside the university she situated herself in a line of descent that offered an alternative to her family lineage.

An alternative to patriarchal genealogy appears as well in the characterization of Mrs. Swithin in *Between the Acts*. She stands before the portrait of a male ancestor, "a talk producer," and the picture of an unknown lady, bought by Oliver (*BA* 22). In Elizabeth Abel's reading of the two paintings they frame the patriarchal family, the ancestor's dog replacing the wife who is absent from representation, and "the portrait of the lady [that] makes space sing about prehistory, the canonical locus for the absent mother." Although it is true that the association of the female image with emptiness and silence suggests "a new inability to think or write the mother,"[34] the two portraits also suggest that genealogy can be created outside kinship structures. The purchased portrait suggests that the market offers a freedom unknown in the family to imagine alternatives to patriarchal genealogy. The male is an ancestor; the female is an image which prompts Lucy to recall "the poets from whom we descend by way of the mind" (*BA* 42).[35]

Christine Froula suggests the motivation to seek alternative genealogy in her study of the patriarchal silencing of women. She traces the relationship between the abuse and silencing of women from Woolf's essay, "Professions for Women" to the work of Homer. The scene of Helen and Priam in Book III of the *Iliad* "reveals not Helen's silence but her silencing. Priam in alluding to his battle against the Amazons recalls the daughters who have refused wife and motherhood. "The *Iliad* suggests that women's silence in culture is neither a natural nor an accidental phenomenon but a cultural achievement, indeed, a constitutive accomplishment of male culture."[36]

Froula's argument might be widened to include the sacrificial slayings in *Agamemnon*. The king's sacrifice of his daughter Iphigenia, that is in Froma I. Zeitlin's reading of sacrifice "unlawful . . . the primary cause of woe," becomes the symbol against which we may measure the six other sacrifices represented by clusters of imagery as well as characterization.[37] Cassandra's speech about her father's sacrificial slaughter of sheep before the walls of Troy, which, in the Verrall/Woolf translation, "served not at all/to save the town from such fate as now/it hath" (lines 1169–71) raises a disturbing question.

Is Aeschylus saying that nothing less than the sacrifice of a daughter would satisfy the gods and assure victory? Although Cassandra was safe in her father's hands, she calls in vain on Apollo, paradoxically the god of healing, to spare her the fate she foresees. But her death as a sacrifice is no more efficacious than that before the walls of Troy to alter the curse on the House of Atreus.

"On Not Knowing Greek" discusses *Agamemnon* and other Greek texts in the context of World War I. Writing of the difficulty of expressing the emotion stirred by the war, Woolf asks whether we are "reading into Greek poetry not what they have but what we lack?" (*CR* 36). Cassandra's scene serves to characterize the dramatic immediacy of the play, in which neither "images or allusions of the subtlest or most decorative had got between us and the naked cry" (*CR* 32–3). The phrase refers to Cassandra's first appearance, when she utters the rhythmic speech of the possessed, translated as "Ah! O God! Apollo," a signal to the audience that she is in the realm of the divine. Her speech suggests that personal circumstances apart, the culture offers no escape from the idea of the Father that manifests itself in every utterance of the female. That is the substance of her "naked cry."

Cassandra's violation by Apollo led not to pregnancy as the Chorus suggests that it might have, but to prophecy. The line that Verrall/Woolf translate "Nay it is not as a Saviour that he [Apollo] directs this sentence"[38] suggests that this time a woman's confrontation with the violence of the god will not be averted by her metamorphosis into an animal. In this connection Cassandra expresses nostalgia for the fate of Philomela, who was changed into a nightingale. Verrall/Woolf translate her speech: "Ah, the fate of the musical nightingale/ For her the gods did clothe in a/winged form/ . . . while I must be parted by the/steel's sharp edge" (Berg reel 13, lines 1169–71). As a prophet who is not believed Cassandra would seem in the position of the female speaker who is denied the rhetorical conventions of the public language. Prophecy complicates her understanding of the power of speech, in comparison with Clytemnestra's easy reply to the Chorus's charge that she is arrogant. Verrall/Woolf translate the lines: "Ye challenge me, supposed an unthinking/woman. But I speak with unshaken courage/to those who know, indifferent whether thou/choosest to praise or to blame. This is/Agamemnon, my husband, wrought to/death by the just handicraft of this my hand./So stands the case" (lines 1401–7).

Cassandra's speech has been delivered to a chorus which in large measure fails to understand. Its uneasy command of language prevents its recognition that her prophetic power has revealed a future none can escape. The problem frames a question about Woolf's addressee. Whereas "Reminiscences" had been nominally addressed to Julian Bell, "A Sketch" addressed itself at first to an audience of family and friends, and since its publication to a mass audience. Simon Goldhill, exploring the lack of understanding between Cassandra and the Chorus, writes "The ineffectuality of the Chorus is the logical outcome of their lack of narrative control, their fear that stems from their inability to predict, from their lack of control of the risks of language. Their inability . . . is in ironic tension with Cassandra's predictive vision of the inevitability of things."[39] Cassandra reveals the ineluctable power of the Father, not only when she cries to Apollo, but when she recognizes that the institution of the Father may be occupied by a female, Clytemnestra. It is significant that when she fails to reply to the queen's command to enter the palace, the Chorus sees her not as a prophet, but as an animal sacrifice; in the Verrall/Woolf translation, "She hath the air of a beast new-taken" (line 1063).

The subject seen as animal figures in the incident, possibly a dream, that follows Woolf's molestation by Gerald. "Let me add a dream; for it may refer to the incident of the looking-glass. I dreamt that I was looking in a glass when a horrible face – the face of an animal – suddenly showed over my shoulder" (*MB* 69). One might agree with Thomas Caramagno's identification of "the horrible face" as that of Gerald "acting beastly," if the mirror functioned as it had in *A Room of One's Own* to reflect patriarchal social relations.[40] But if we attempt to read its significance as part of the mirror experience it may be seen to double Woolf's face, so that in effect it juxtaposes the face that is recognized to the face that may be seen. It is the hidden face of her mother: "behind the active [lies] the sad, the silent" (*MB* 83). It is anterior and present, the author *in* and the author *of* the autobiography. It is the face of Julia Stephen behind the photographic image of the madonna, Philomela standing in view of Cassandra, the fish-like Mrs. McNab. Before the looking-glass the female subject appears to herself split between the sacrificed animal and the speaking woman.

Perhaps the most significant of the autobiographical "moments of being" is Woolf's experience of the female confronted not with the behavior of her lineal father but with the institutions of male authority which create the woman as captive animal subject to his desire. That painful genealogy makes it possible to give an "account of the person to whom things happen" (*MB* 69), by precipitating the subject whose voice is heard only by the Chorus. But if we think of the Chorus as the Other to whom the signifier returns, it is important to remember that its position in the play is distinctly non-performative. That is, in contrast with the Messenger and especially with Clytemnestra it hesitates to read the sky as sign. The Chorus as Other suggests the particular suitability of the imaginary to the unpublished autobiographical work.

TO PUT THE SEVERED PARTS TOGETHER

It has been argued that the subject removes the obstacle in "the age-old alternative between being and non-being."[41] Woolf approaches the question of being by narrating moments of childhood experience that revealed to her her capacity to create the sign. Her definition is well known. "Non-being" is the part of the day not lived "consciously"; it included eating, bookbinding, and cooking; it was intensified by illness and fever. The novelists who can convey both being and non-being are the exemplars of realistic fiction: Austen, Thackeray, Dickens, and Tolstoy. Woolf's preoccupation with moments of being, when living is "conscious," underscores the conditions of her alienation from realism.

Three "exceptional moments" of her childhood illustrate the importance of "being." Two concern acts of violence, when non-being is shattered by "a sudden violent shock; something happened so violently that I have remembered it all my life" (*MB* 71). The first is a fight with Thoby which produced what Lacan calls "transitivism": "The child who strikes another says that he has been struck; the child who sees another fall cries" (*E* 19). Transitivisim occurs between pairs of children close in age who in playing exhibit active and passive roles, as master and slave, actor and audience. The ability of an individual to tolerate "an image that alienates him from himself" is tied to the formation of the ego and to the representation of internal conflict. In a discussion of violent shock, Woolf described this phenomenon as it occurred in the fight with Thoby: "We were pommelling each other with our fists. Just as I raised my fist to hit him, I felt: why hurt another person? I dropped my hand instantly, and stood there, and let him beat me. I remember . . . a feeling of hopeless sadness . . . and of my own powerlessness." Unwilling to play either master or slave, stalled between the position of active or passive child, she was unable to create an alternative position. The second moment occurs when she hears that Mr. Valpy has killed himself. That fact alone is sufficient for her to see an apple tree and connect it with suicide. "It seemed to me that the apple tree was connected with the horror of Mr. Valpy's suicide." The third moment is solitary and free of violence: when she looks at a flower, "That is the whole, I said" (*MB* 71).

If one reads the passage for what it says about language, the sign is seen to respond to violence. As a female writer Woolf receives a blow, not as in childhood

simply a blow from an enemy hidden behind the cotton wool of daily life; it is or will become a revelation of some order; it is a token of some real thing behind appearances; and I make it real by putting it into words. It is only by putting it into words that I make it whole; this wholeness means that it has lost its power to hurt me; it gives me, perhaps because by doing so I take away the pain, a great delight to put the severed parts together. Perhaps this is the strongest pleasure known to me. (*MB* 72)

That is, as a writer who is first a seer she restores to signification what has been riven by violent action; the sign is the whole that brings together "the severed parts." Although in an uncontested situation the sign is unproblematic: "That is the whole," the act of writing as putting the severed parts together is more challenging and pleasurable.

Aspects of this process are apparent in Woolf's characterizations. The association of suicide with the apple tree, which suggests Septimus's arbitrary reading of the signs in the sky, seems to me more a signal than a sign, if the sign is understood to have value as communication. In the language of the passage sign-making is carried out as a kind of resistance-as-reparation. The resistance expressed in the character of Mrs. McNab, that seems tinged with absurdity, becomes the condition of the subject that is glimpsed for the moment at the juncture of violent behavior and language. Mrs. McNab, especially in the holograph phrasing, seems the indirect focus of the aggressivity that speaks the woman as animal.

From this experience Woolf arrives at a "philosophy," that the whole world is a work of art, so that "we are the words; we are the music; we are the thing itself. And I see this when I have a shock"

(*MB* 72). The subject become signifier marks its place in representation as a notation of violence. Aggressivity supplies what captation required, an alternative to forgetting and erasure. Captation occurs from looking into the mirror and wishing to resist beauty; aggressivity occurs so as to block the angle of incidence and create the conditions necessary for the formation of the sign. In Lacan's scheme "the sign – with its essential split into two registers – represents the imaginary relationship . . . between ego and image, subject and object."[42]

In "A Sketch" Woolf focuses attention on the imaginary, the site of her struggle to become the subject of representation. Gender is defined by a particular position vis-à-vis the imaginary. It begins with the recognition of the self as object, and at that stage the position may be occupied by a male (Bernard for instance), or by a female. In "A Sketch" the female subject sees the other as beautiful, from a position outside the mirror that is marked as masculine. She experiences aggressivity against the male figure who behaves towards her as though she were simply a member of the family that is reflected in the glass. The experience that genders the female subject precipitates a split between these two positions, female and male, a position within the lineage of the family and outside it as viewer. The female subject manifests itself when it responds to the violence of the opposition by creating the sign.

"A Sketch" reconsiders the question Woolf asked in *A Room of One's Own*, "whether there are two sexes in the mind corresponding to the two sexes in the body," that prefaces her introduction of "the androgynous, of the man-womanly mind" (*RO* 102). The autobiography clearly does not suggest that the subject is a harmonious combination of male and female.[43] But it does suggest a significant modification of the classic account of the move into the symbolic that in Lacan's work marks the successful outcome of the Oedipal struggle. Woolf's female subject seeks not merely to receive but to renegotiate the sign that comes from the other. She does so by redefining the first person which in the essay bored the narrator, "because of the dominance of the letter 'I' and the aridity, which, like the giant beech tree, it casts within its shade. Nothing will grow there" (*RO* 104). When "the writing 'I' has vanished," autobiography enables a retreat to the imaginary. There the mirror splits the "I" so that in memory the symbolic is admitted, but on terms that pair it insistently with the experience of the visible, and distance it from family relations.

CHAPTER 6

"Ruined houses and dead bodies": "Three Guineas" and the Spanish Civil War

> For if people had been aware . . . they would have been able
> with the aid of the photographic camera to *make visible* exist-
> ences which cannot be perceived or taken in by our optical
> instrument, the eye . . .
>
> Laszlo Moholy-Nagy, "Photography"[1]

The Spanish Civil War was the first war to become known to the general public primarily by means of the photographs published in newspapers. In *Three Guineas* Woolf considers the particular significance of the newspaper photograph to women readers. The imagery of the essay suggests that the newspaper enlarged the horizons of the Victorian female by offering her the "unpaid-for culture" that ironically compensated for the "paid-for education" she had been denied at the university (*TG* 214–16). By reading several newspapers she comes to an understanding that "the literature of fact and the literature of opinion, to make a crude distinction, are not pure fact, or pure opinion, but adulterated fact and adulterated opinion" (*TG* 221). Although aware of the attractions of propaganda defined as an unmediated photograph, Woolf rejected this position. Instead in the "Third Guinea" she used photographs to redefine the imaginary as the realm in which women might share with men collective responsibility for evil.

Photographs are central to the argument of *Three Guineas*; in fact Woolf focuses her argument around a question that was suggested by photographs of the war: "What connection is there between the sartorial splendours of the educated man and the photograph of ruined houses and dead bodies?" (*TG* 137–8). The phrase "ruined houses and dead bodies" appears in each of the three "Guineas," and the text mediates two sets of photographs, those of the Spanish Civil War, which she did not publish, and the five photographs of a general, a judge, heralds, professors, and an archbishop, which were printed with the essay. In the "Third Guinea" Woolf's text comes full circle as she weighs the transhistorical qualities of Greek tragedy and the documentary photograph.

The camera reinvented the problematic of the visible in an industrial society. Coming into use around the time of the European revolutions of 1848 it mediated "the shadow of a fading European aristocracy" as it "came to focus the confidence and fears of an ascendent industrial bourgeoisie."[2] Allan Sekula rejects the notion that the photograph is somehow transcultural and transhistorical, arguing instead that it manifests the contradictions between science and aesthetics that are inherent in capitalist culture. Photography attempts to reconcile "human creative energies with a scientifically guided process of mechanization, suggesting that despite the modern industrial division of labor . . . the category of the artist lives on in the exercise of a *purely mental* imaginative command over the camera."[3]

John Tagg demonstrates that the photograph, far from being a record of the seen, derives its meaning from historically specific social practices. In his reading of individual photographs he traces the "world of objects already constructed as a world of uses, values and meanings, though in the perceptual process these may not appear as such but only as qualities discerned in a 'natural' recognition of 'what is there.' "[4] The meaning of the photograph is built up by its interactions with codes of social value. So in the photographs to which Woolf's novels allude, domestic portraits are represented as manifesting certain ideals of family life and a gendered division of labor. The "Third Guinea" is organized by Woolf's critical recognition that even such details as costume in fact manifest the material world that is constructed by ideology.

Jean-Louis Baudry, arguing from a similar perspective, observes that the optical and mechanical nature of the camera seems to grant it the authority and privilege of a scientific instrument, removed from the problems that beset other modes of representation. "Does the technical nature of optical instruments, directly attached to scientific practice, serve to conceal not only their use in ideological products but also the ideological effects which they may themselves provoke."[5] It is the question to which Woolf addressed herself in her essay on the photographs of royalty.

In *Three Guineas* Woolf shows herself well aware of twentieth-century attitudes towards the conditions and uses of photography.

She satirizes the view that the documentary photograph is unmediated. Not only the five photographs which accompanied Woolf's text but her references to war photographs and the development of the narrator as a correspondent reveal her awareness that the photograph has an ideological function. In the "Third Guinea" she refigured the imaginary in order to adapt Greek notions of visibility to the world of photography.

The war in Spain (1936–39) coincided with significant changes in the design of the camera and the social uses of the photograph. In particular the documentary photograph although it might include various uses by the state, had "come to represent the social conscience of liberal sensibility presented in visual imagery."[6] Woolf exploits the popular notion of the documentary photograph, as uncoded when she plays on its capacity to subvert the text it was designed to accompany. The Spanish photographs which play so prominent a part in *Three Guineas* and in my argument are represented rather than reproduced in Woolf's working notes. Their significance seems to me to lie in her recognition that the news photograph has the potential to reveal ideology and consequently to complicate the position of the viewing subject.

The photograph shifted the terms of the conflict between visual codes which in Woolf's earlier work had provided the ground of the subject. It is as though she recognized that the photograph could not be read as either a painting or a dream. It did not so much challenge the territory of the gaze as refigure it, with the effect of relocating the subject in the contradictions between text and photograph. In her novels the domestic photograph represents family members within the familiar visual codes that stress their class and gender. But the photographs of unknown women and children, the casualties of war, posed a new problem for the viewer. It was political and ideological in the sense that it was an appeal to the artist to create propaganda by representing the dead in terms of personal loss. Woolf instead took the opportunity to reopen the question of representation and rethink the difficult but essential negotiation between the visible and the intelligible.[7]

WOOLF AND THE DOMESTIC PHOTOGRAPH

Woolf's novels reflect the changing practice of photography in the nineteenth century, as it gradually supplanted the painted portrait and became widely available to all classes. Photographic portraits of middle-class men and their families represented them within existing cultural conventions of domesticity. Mrs. Chailey, the servant in *The Voyage Out*, decorates her living quarters with "a multitude of tiny photographs, representing downright workmen in their Sunday best, and women holding white babies" (*VO* 26). Clarissa Dalloway's old nurse and Crosby in *The Years* decorate their bedrooms with photographs of their employers' families. In these novels the photograph maintains the institution of the family across class lines.

The photograph reveals as well a special relationship with the dead, often serving, as Christian Metz argues, as a fetish. Not only does the photograph preserve the likeness of the dead person, but the click of the camera shutter abducts the object into another world. "Film gives back to the dead a semblance of life, a fragile semblance but one immediately strengthened by the wishful thinking of the viewer. Photography, on the contrary, by virtue of the objective suggestions of its signifier . . . maintains the memory of the dead *as being dead.*"[8] So above the head of Willoughby Vinrace hangs a photograph of his late wife. Having neglected her in life, Woolf writes, Willoughby now with a gesture in the direction of the photograph abdicates parental responsibility and hands over the education of his daughter, Rachel, to Helen Ambrose. The scene raises the question whether Rachel's death at the end of the novel refigures the fetishized image of the dead mother in the photograph.

Rachel's unwillingness to enter the married state is foreshadowed in a scene in which, while attempting to express to a friend her belief in the material world, she is distracted by two photographs of Evelyn's parents: "Mrs. Murgatroyd looked indeed as if the life had been crushed out of her; she knelt on a chair, gazing piteously from behind the body of a Pomeranian dog which she clasped to her cheek, as if for protection." The companion photograph of the father reveals "a handsome soldier with high regular features and a heavy black moustache; his hand rested on the hilt of his sword" (*VO* 250). These photographs theatrically stage stereotypes of gender. In Woolf's hands they serve to make visible an ideology of gender that links females to animals and males to warfare.

Photographs in *Night and Day* reveal the taste for national monuments. It is no surprise that Mrs. Hilbery, writing a biography of her famous poet father, collects family photographs. In contrast, Ralph Denham's bedroom is decorated with "photographs of bridges and cathedrals" (*ND* 19), and in a later passage with "photographs from the Greek statues" (*ND* 408). In Rodney's room stands "a stack of photographs of statues and pictures" (*ND* 70), and Katharine disguises her uneasiness in his rooms by looking at "a photograph from the Greek" (*ND* 140). Photographs of Greek artifacts appear in *Jacob's Room* as well (*JR* 39). These photographs serve to perpetuate the memory of national monuments and the values of the classical education available to men. The Greek subjects suggest the romantic and antiquarian interests of the 1850s.[9] Not until *The Years* does one of Woolf's novels refer to newspaper photographs (*Y* 330), perhaps because by that time the Spanish Civil War had redirected her interest.

Photography in *Mrs. Dalloway* is an amateur hobby which confers distinctions of class and taste. Lady Bradshaw, whose work "is scarcely to be distinguished from the work of professionals" (*MD* 143), joins the ranks of the amateurs who photograph decaying churches. Her choice of subject reflects the tastes of an earlier generation for images of ruined abbeys and cathedrals in keeping with the guide books and photographs of the 1850s.[10] Until the mid-1850s photography in England was the province of amateurs who often came from influential families with means and education. Their organization as the Photographic Society (1853) and the Antiquarian Photographic Society (1854) helped to preserve an emphasis on picturesque landscape. Their work emerged from a social context in which photography became an art-science.[11] By the end of the decade technical changes led to the lifting of the legal restrictions on commercial photography, and the number of amateurs had also vastly increased.[12] Woolf suggests that Lady Bradshaw aspires to the social distinction of photography as a leisure activity with certain class associations that would make her part of a world where amateurs might become professionals, and science coexisted with art.

Meanwhile Sir William Bradshaw, the son of a tradesman, displays in his consulting room a photograph of Lady Bradshaw "in court dress," an image of a class from which he draws authority while advising Septimus Smith that "Nobody lives for himself alone" (*MD* 85–6). The scene conveys his sentimental reverence for marriage that is severely at odds with the breakdowns to be observed elsewhere in the novel.

The Bradshaws' photographic practice suggests their preoccupation with what John Tagg describes as a cultural production "largely confined to the narrow spaces of the family and commoditised leisure . . . incorporating . . . a familial division of labour, and a stultified repertoire of legitimated subjects and stereotypes."[13] This practice invites some of Woolf's most savage reflections on British culture.

FROM THE BRIDGE TO THE CAMERA

In January of 1931 while in her bath Woolf "conceived an entire new book – a sequel to *A Room of One's Own* – about the sexual life of women: to be called Professions for Women perhaps " (*D* IV:6). On occasion during the next six years she associated "the woman question" with anti-Fascism (*D* IV:273), and Brenda Silver notes that from 1935 on "the desire to write a book on women intersected with another desire – the desire to write an antifascist pamphlet."[14] The Spanish Civil War seems to have been the catalyst that transformed Woolf's essay on women into the anti-war argument of *Three Guineas*.

Three notebooks covering the years 1931–37 contain the reading notes and newspaper clippings on the subjects of male dress and professions for women that Woolf collected over a spectrum of political opinion. They demonstrate the range of her reading. Clippings from *The Times* and *Daily Telegraph* appear with some regularity. These two newspapers were read by the 4.3 percent of families with incomes over five hundred pounds.[15] On occasion she read as well the *Daily Herald*, the newspaper of the Labour movement, 95 percent of whose readership came from the lowest income groups.[16] She clipped articles from the *Evening Standard*, whose editor was a socialist.[17] And she clipped as well on occasion the *New Statesman*, *The Observer*, and *The Listener*. Since the Spanish Civil War was the occasion in Britain for a battle of ideologies, it is important to recognize that Woolf's reading of the news, although largely confined to British newspapers, reveals a mind of broad political range and sympathy at a time when, as we shall see, the reorganization of the newspaper market was narrowing readers' choices.

Although most of the material in the notebooks refers to the position of women, Woolf included several articles about Hitler and the Nazi movement, and one about the bombing of Almeria by German warships on 31 May 1937. One of the most significant documents in the notebooks is *The Martyrdom of Madrid*, a pamphlet translated from the French of Louis Delaprée, the correspondent of *Paris-Soir* whose career was celebrated in *L'Humanité*. It is a series of eyewitness reports of the suffering of noncombatants during the battle of Madrid in November 1936, which suggestively links *Three Guineas* to aspects of European journalism. Woolf's notebooks are silent on the bombing of Guernica on 26 April 1937 and on the death of Julian Bell in Spain on 18 July. They suggest a writer who until 1936 was concerned primarily with local problems of gender and class. The theme of Fascism appeared late in the period of the notebooks, and raises a question about the degree to which her essay integrates the theme of professions for women with wider European political concerns.

The earliest predecessor of *Three Guineas* appears to be a speech that Woolf gave on 21 January 1931 on professions for women, the authoritative text of which, as Jane Marcus points out, is printed in full in *The Pargiters*. "It is about women's violence and its images are angry, military, and murderous . . . positively ferocious."[18] Although the tone of the speech is as angry as that of *Three Guineas*, its horizon is limited to the domestic arrangements of Woolf's class, and by a repeated reference to a woman's experience of her body and her passions. In other words, save for one phrase that connects "the Angel in the House" with "the British Empire, our colonies, Queen Victoria, Lord Tennyson, the growth of the middle class and so on" (*TP* xxx) the terms of the speech are drawn from domestic life. When the Spanish Civil War enlarged the historical horizons of Woolf's argument, she nevertheless maintained in a central position her feminist preoccupation with certain bodies and houses.

Although the holograph and various typescript drafts of the text of *Three Guineas* are so complex that they cannot readily be sorted into an orderly sequence of composition, they suggest that the image of the camera significantly reoriented her essay. Holograph and type-script drafts exist for most of the first and second "Guineas," and there appear to be three manuscript drafts but no typescript of parts of the third. In April 1936 her diary notes that the title was "Two Guineas" (*D* v:22), and in June 1937 she comments several times on the difficulty of "the university chapter," which was "much re-arranged" (*D* v:93). Some passages in the typescript mix text from the first and second "Guineas," and Woolf often began a fresh page by revising several lines of text from the previous. Sentence by sentence the drafts in the Henry W. and Albert A. Berg Collection differ substantially from the printed version and are less well-paced. Overall Woolf expanded the text of each section and shaped the argument both by means of the thematic division into three "Guineas," and a pattern of repeated imagery.

The poetics of composition was also revised. The image of "the bridge which connects the private house with the world of public life," and provides a perspective on patriarchal costume, appears more often in the draft versions. It organized the text around an image of visual perspective as "the educated man's daughter . . . issues from the shadow of the private house, and stands on the bridge which lies between the old world and the new" (*TG* 130–1), and contemplates spending a sixpence. The landscape viewed from a height images the newfound freedom of the daughter, who emerges from the house to find that the horizons of the mind are extended by the range of the gaze as it sweeps backwards and forwards. In the language of "Professions for Women," "she was letting her imagination sweep unchecked round every rock and cranny of the world that lies submerged in our unconscious being" (*TP* xxxviii).

The image of the bridge when it reappears in the "Second Guinea" more specifically refigures the landscape of Wordsworth's "Composed upon Westminster Bridge." Woolf's bridge is "an admirable vantage ground . . . The river flows beneath . . . there on one side are . . . Westminster and the Houses of Parliament. It is a place to stand on by the hour, dreaming. But not now. Now we are pressed for time" (*TG* 183). The passage rewrites "Dull would he be of soul who could pass by/A sight so touching in its majesty" as matter-of-fact prose. It suggests Woolf's impatience with a Romantic ideology of the poet as detached observer, perhaps because the events of 1936–37 had put in question the point of view distant enough to map the world.[19] In the "Third Guinea" Woolf questions the poet's relationship to Dorothy. If in private life brother and sister speak "as if one nightingale called to another . . . Why then . . . should their public relationship, as law and history prove, be so very different?" (*TG* 104–5). The link to Wordsworth's anti-feminist ethics focuses the economic contradictions of the daughter's freedom, and suggests that the Romantic rebellion of the spirit perpetuates a gendered subjectivity.

Although the image of the bridge survives in the printed version of *Three Guineas*, several of its repetitions have been suppressed.[20] To a large extent the image of the photograph takes its place. It shows "your world as it appears to us who see it . . . from the bridge which connects the private house with the world of public life" (*TG* 133). In one sentence Woolf effectively abandons the Romantic image of the mind as the mirror of nature which she had interrogated in "Time Passes," and substitutes an image of the visible world that is produced by the camera. It replaces the mirror image, which suppresses problems of gender and history, with the photograph, which makes visible what the eye cannot see unaided, while effectively concealing the agent.

Three Guineas is also structured by Woolf's representation in her text of photographs of "ruined houses and dead bodies." The image is used in each "Guinea" to question the historical link between patriarchal society and war:

Can we bring out the connection between them [the war photographs] and prostituted culture and intellectual slavery and make it so clear that the one implies the other, that the daughters of educated men will prefer to refuse money and fame, and to be the objects of scorn and ridicule rather than suffer themselves, or allow others to suffer, the penalties there made visible? (*TG* 220)

Whereas Woolf's notebooks document the abuses of British patriarchy, the photographs help to broaden her horizon, so that her question is situated in the larger context of European culture. By so doing she entered the debate which took the Spanish Civil War as the occasion to question the premises of Democracy as well as Fascism.

Pierre Bourdieu observes that dislike of photographs of dead soldiers is part of a working-class aesthetic which is determined by a preference for the agreeable, in fact for "an aesthetic which makes the signifier completely subordinate to the signified."[21] The British press attempted to assimilate its readership to that aesthetic when it spared them the pictures of the Spanish Civil War which were the daily fare of readers of *L'Humanité*. In *Three Guineas* Woolf acknowledges both Spanish censorship and British cultural conventions by not printing the photographs of the dead to which she refers. Rather she plays on the "photograph" as a signifier whose meaning is derived from the relationship both to the photographs which did accompany her text and more generally to the photograph as a sign of what is not there. In effect Woolf seizes on the ideology of the photograph as uncoded to represent it as the visible sign of invisible ideology.

WHEN IN DOUBT LEAVE OUT

Between 1890 and 1920 changes in the ownership and readership of the British press reorganized the industry in ways that greatly affected the management and presentation of foreign news. "Between 1920 and 1939 the combined circulation of the national daily press rose from 5.4 million to 10.6 million." At the same time ownership was concentrated in the hands of a few "press barons," so that by 1937 three men, Lord Rothermere, Lord Beaverbrook, and G. Cadbury controlled half of national daily circulation.[22] The enormous expansion of advertising necessitated an appeal to a less differentiated audience and led to the assumption that British readers did not care to read disturbing news about foreign countries. As a result, according to a survey commissioned by the *News Chronicle* in 1933 "the most-read news in popular daily papers were stories about accidents, crime, divorce, and human interest . . . In contrast most categories of public affairs news had only an average or below-average readership rating . . . Public affairs content was thus, in marketing terms, a commodity with a sectional appeal."[23]

The effect of the reorganization was to increase support among newspapers for conservative values. Papers owned by the press barons "provided cumulative support for conservative values and reinforced opposition, particularly among the middle class, to progressive change."[24] The career of Geoffrey Dawson, who resumed his editorship of *The Times* after the death of Lord North-cliffe in 1922 (1923–41), and worked with little intervention from the new owners, illustrates the point. He has been blamed for supporting a policy of appeasement, which may in fact have resulted in part from his limited knowledge of Europe and his failure to fill the post of Foreign Editor when it fell vacant in 1929.[25] F. R. Gannon writes of *The Times*'s reporting on Germany during the period: "If the duty of a newspaper is to provide its readers with sufficient, relevant, and uncensored information with which to form independent judgements, it cannot be maintained that *The Times* was derelict in this respect."[26] Although it would not be accurate to speak of a policy of British censorship of the news from Spain, Dawson's intellectual limitations may help to account in part for the preoccupation of *The Times* during the Spanish Civil War with British domestic news.

From 1936 to 1939 non-intervention was the key to the British management of the news from Spain. Jill Edwards shows how the British Government favored non-intervention in a conflict that was supported on the Republican side by the French and the USSR and on the Nationalist by the German and Italian dictators. The Non-Intervention Agreement (NIA) offered a way to hedge British support of capitalism and reveals its determination to be on good terms with the victors whether Communist or Fascist. The NIA was never legally binding on its signatories, France, Germany, Italy, the USSR or Britain, and was in any case not funded until early 1937, when it was clearly too late.[27] By July the NIA had in any practical sense ceased to exist.[28] Edwards concludes her study of the British position: "But by turning a blind eye both to the intervention of the dictators and to the need for firm protection of British shipping to Spain the British Government aided Franco as decisively as if it had sent arms to him."[29] Her argument reflects the view of Stephen Spender, Woolf's friend, that the Non-Intervention Committee was "concerned with faking politics in order to cover up a deal."[30]

Leonard Woolf had organized in 1935 "For Intellectual Liberty,"(FIL) a group dedicated "to campaign for 'united action in defence of peace, liberty, and culture," that included Virginia among its five hundred members.[31] But as David Bradshaw has demonstrated, Woolf became increasingly disenchanted with the aims and values of FIL: "Woolf was all too aware that in English society intellectual liberty was a gendered privilege not a cultural touchstone." Accordingly she participated "only when something more concrete than 'moral indignation' was at stake."[32] Leonard, although more actively engaged in the activities of FIL, also expressed skepticism of the government's posture. His analysis of Non-intervention appears in a letter that he wrote in November 1936 to Julian Bell, who was then in China:

Spain was the first test case of the new dispensation of a world without the League. The corollary of isolation was non-intervention; the corollary of alliance was to support the Spanish Government, to get France and the USSR to do the same, and to risk war or trouble with Germany and/or Italy. Our Government was of course in favour of non-intervention, for it is really in its shilly-shallying way isolationist, and in any case is not sufficiently anti-fascist as to be pro-socialist.[33]

In order to control the war news, General Franco imposed censorship on all foreign journalists. Foreign reporters in Nationalist Spain were accredited by Franco's press office, and sent their dispatches either from Government telegraph offices, or, more rarely, by courier across the French border.[34] And since photographs might be used as evidence of bomb attacks, they too were censored. But hundreds of photographs were taken, and although *The Times* and *The Daily Express*, for instance, printed only a few, war photographs appeared regularly in the pages of *L'Humanité* and other French newspapers.

We can form an impression of the way that events of the Civil War were made to signify by comparing *The Times* with *L'Humanité* in the aftermath of two battles which were extensively reported, the Battle of Madrid in November and December 1936, and the destruction of Guernica on 26 April 1937. Throughout the war *The Times* carried daily reports of the fighting, usually illustrated with a map. But foreign news was subordinated to domestic coverage of the Abdication of King Edward VIII on 10 December and, when Guernica was bombed, to the Coronation of King George VI on 11 May. Although *The Times* did not print front-page stories, it included a daily page of several photographs, devoted mainly during this period to the activities of the new king. He was photographed reviewing the boy scouts (26 April), inspecting the Cadets of the Royal Military College (3 May), reviewing overseas troops (15 May), and with the fleet (21 May). He was photographed with the Queen visiting St. Paul's, the Chelsea Flower Show, and the Royal Tournament. By contrast photographs of the bombing of Madrid were few. Photographs appeared in the issues of 9, 10, 18 and 21 November, and 3 December 1936, and one photograph of the bombed Guernica appeared, on 30 April 1937. One editor, H. N. Brailsford of the *Reynolds News*, a veteran journalist and a socialist, complained of the Abdication, "Against the background of this sour comedy, looms up the tragedy of Madrid."[35] Woolf too noted in her *Diary* that the international news was "elbowed out. The marriage stretches from one end of the paper to another" (*D* v:39).

L'Humanité represented the news of the war in picture and print in a different format. News from Spain appeared regularly on the front page, as well as the photographs of dead Spanish children which were ignored by the British press. The newspaper carried as well the stories of the Abdication and Coronation, European and American labor news, and regular reports on the USSR. The representation of the war was clearly partisan, hostile to German and Italian Fascism, and critical of British foreign policy. Republican troops were consistently represented as either victorious or holding their positions. Maps of Spain were rare, but in their place the front page usually carried a photograph that showed refugee women and children as the targets of Fascist attack, bombed buildings, or soldiers on active duty although rarely firing their weapons. The newspaper printed numerous photographs of "dead bodies" with their faces exposed, or crumpled on the ground (see 11, 17 November 1936; 5 March, 2, 6, 28 April, 10 May 1937). Photographs of people who had been wounded or killed in domestic accidents also appeared, as though in response to a different cultural code about the propriety of viewing a corpse.

In fact the French had already demonstrated the ability to translate a corpse into an item of public interest. Vanessa R. Schwartz has described the activities at the Paris morgue, where in the nineteenth century the public came to view (through glass in the rebuilt morgue) various unidentified corpses that had been fished out of the Seine. And in 1877 morgue officials began photographing them, so as to prolong the viewing after decomposition had set in. She prints the photographs of various dead children that appeared in French newspapers of 1886.[36] Clearly then French readers of *L'Humanité* might respond very differently than English ones to the Spanish photographs.

L'Humanité created a reader whose allegiance was not in question, and who saw history as an often mortal struggle. Whereas the maps in *The Times* suggest a Wordsworthian reader educated in detachment who notes movements and identifies locations, the French reader, for whom Spain was geographically more familiar, saw in the daily photographs a world divided between brave soldiers and frightened women and children. It is ironic that the world created by the appeal across language to compassion was so rigidly gendered.

Leonard and Virginia visited France 7–25 May 1937, in order, as Virginia joked with several correspondents, to avoid reading about the Coronation. Apparently they did not visit the Spanish Pavilion of the Paris Exposition where they might have seen Picasso's *Guernica*, which Vanessa had seen in Paris,[37] and where they might also have seen photographs of dead Spanish children. But they moved closer to the Civil War in the sense of moving into a culture where the newspaper photograph suggested an attitude to death as neither distant nor unrepresentable. Woolf sounds very British when two months later she wrote of her nephew Julian's death in Spain, as though he had been merely censored. She could not think of him as dead, "rather as if he were jerked abruptly out of sight without rhyme or reason: so violent & absurd that one cant fit his death into any scheme" (*D* v:122). For Virginia the photographs sent by the Spanish Government represented the Civil War in terms that were not generally available in the British press, and the emphasis on the suffering of women and children must have reinforced her sense of gender as structuring as well as structured by a society at war.

Woolf included among the newspaper clippings in her notebooks a pamphlet, *The Martyrdom of Madrid*, by Louis Delaprée. According to a *L'Humanité* article written after his death, Delaprée was sent to Spain in mid-November, when the fall of Madrid was anticipated, in order to describe the triumphal entry of General Franco. Although instructed to represent both sides, when it became apparent that the citizens of Madrid were mobilizing, Delaprée bore witness to their resistance. The pamphlet is a series of eyewitness reports of the bravery and suffering of civilians in response to "the methodical massacre of the civil population."[38] Increasingly disillusioned by the failure of his editors to publish his work, he protested the displacement of the war by news of the Abdication: "Le massacre de cent gosses espagnols est moins interessant qu'un soupir de Mrs Simpson, putain royale."[39] On 8 December, in the course of an aerial attack on the plane that was to take him to Toulouse, Delaprée received the injuries of which he died in France three days later.[40]

So Woolf was aware how a journalist on the European left covered the battle of Madrid. And in a sense her phrasing echoes the English translation of Delaprée's "I number the ruins, I count the dead, I weigh the blood spilt. All the images of Madrid suffering martyrdom, which I shall try to put under your eyes – and which most of the time challenge description – I have seen them. I can be believed. I demand to be believed."[41] His language represents the ideology of the unmediated photographic image, his prose the lens that brings before the eyes of the reader the houses and bodies that he has seen. In an atmosphere of accusation and counter-accusation, images that bear witness gain in authority.

But as the controversy in the French press over the murder of

L'Humanité, 11 November 1936, front page. Reprinted with the permission of the editor.

Spanish children reveals, Woolf considered and then rejected the demand to write propaganda. For several days beginning on 11 November *L'Humanité* published on the front page photographs of the faces of children killed by Franco, "Tueur d'enfants."[42] Each was a full face portrait of an individual child identified by a number (see figure). Their faces are bloodied, their clothing disordered, their wounds gaping. The images and the reaction to them suggest how the newspaper photograph, which normally stabilizes ideological conflict, on this occasion transported to a new site the contradictions between public and domestic, male and female, war and peace. Two visual codes are at war: whereas the pictures suggest the aesthetics of the family portrait, not only the frame and the frontal image, but the sense of fetishizing the dead, the number displayed below reveals the objectivity of the body count. The accompanying text makes of the photograph an occasion to accuse "la presse bourgeoise" of using "la politique de non-intervention" to justify the government's failure to take action against a bombardment of the civilian population of Madrid by German and Italian planes. It was a response that Woolf specifically rejected.

According to Caroline Brothers, who studied three thousand British and French photographs of the Spanish Civil War, the French press often represented the fate of children during the war, while British publications scarcely mentioned them.[43] In her survey, which did not include *L'Humanité*, she distinguishes newspapers which supported the Republicans and the Insurgents. Pro-Republican weeklies in France were *Vu* and *Regards*, and in England the Communist *The Daily Worker*, the Labor Party's *Daily Herald*, the Cooperative Movement's *Reynolds News*, and *Picture Post*.[44] Brothers's broad research suggests how swiftly photographs circulated across frontiers of culture and language. She reads the publication of the photographs of the dead children as evidence of the willingness of the press to exploit atrocities. Nine photographs of the children were published in *Regards*; five appeared in *The Daily Worker* of 12 November, with a contrasting picture of an English child at play in her peaceful garden.[45] When Woolf wrote to Julian Bell on 14 November of the "packet of photographs from Spain all of dead children, killed by bombs" (*L* vi: 83), she was alluding to these shocking photographs that were first printed in France, in *L'Humanité* and *Regards*, and a day or two later in England, in *The Daily Worker*.

Apparently these images and their interpretation strengthened her resistance to writing propaganda. Among her notes for *Three Guineas* is this curious, undated meditation: "The horror of war . . . /The Spanish photographs./Maimed, mauled./ Death . . . /Yes. only too easy to be moved./How easy to give way to emotion when/ the story has ben [sic] prepared. [one word illegible]/But you dont want tear . . . You want/a suggestion how to prevent war . . . /The difficulty of making a suggestion." And in the penultimate line she wrote: "The war of 1914."[46] The note gives an intimate glimpse of the mind of the writer struggling with the temptation to write propaganda, to provide emotional relief rather than analysis. As subject she is not free to make her suggestion until she has resisted the demands on her social position. "If we use art to propagate political opinion," she wrote in *Three Guineas*, "we must force the artist to clip and cabin his gift to do us a cheap and passing service."[47]

The passage also suggests the problematic of the documentary photograph, which "carries information about a group of powerless people to another group addressed as socially powerful."[48] In the encounter with images of the victims of war Woolf seeks to resist the conventions of the text that accompanies photographs of the wounded, the suffering, or the dead. Acting for the moment like Lily Briscoe, Woolf rejects the vocabulary of mastery on the grounds that it would disable her as an artist. As a result the Spanish photographs become disturbances in the text rather than unproblematic illustrations of human suffering.

Her essay "Why Art Today Follows Politics," which she published in *The Daily Worker* on 14 December 1936, was apparently under way by 10 November when she noted in her *Diary*, "The Daily Worker article. Madrid not fallen. Chaos. Slaughter" (*D* v: 32).

In the letter to Julian Bell written a few days later she promises to omit the news from Spain in order to give him the latest gossip, but the news was too urgent. She felt compelled not only to mention her article and Leonard's "Intellectual libertarians" but the photographs of dead children as well. The essay figures present events as an intrusion on her customary preoccupations: "The historian today is writing not about Greece and Rome in the past, but about Germany and Spain in the present . . . the poet introduces communism and fascism into his lyrics" (*CE* II, 230). Yet in this climate she was determined to resist the demand to write propaganda, to "Celebrate fascism; celebrate communism. Preach what we bid you preach" (*CE*

II, 232). That Woolf maintained her position in the face of the first documentary photographs of war atrocities (and in the face of Leonard's more active war resistance) may help to account for what Brenda Silver terms "the poetics of anger."[49]

Picasso's attitude to *Guernica* reveals a similarly troubled response to the appeal to create propaganda. Although the mural shares some qualities of the poster and of photography, it is far from making a didactic political statement. In fact the motifs of the bull fight and the weeping woman may be found everywhere in Picasso's earlier work. In Paris *Guernica* was championed by the Surrealists against its Republican critics, who demanded that it be removed and in its place in the Spanish Pavilion a "realistic work in which both dead children and ruins were shown" be substituted.[50] In an interview with Jerome Seckler in 1945 Picasso denied that he was a Surrealist, and addressed the question of propaganda: "My work is not symbolic . . . Only the *Guernica* mural is symbolic. But in the case of the mural, that is allegoric. That's the reason I've used the horse, the bull, and so on. The mural is for the definite expression and solution of a problem and that is why I used symbolism."[51] Yet Picasso strongly resisted the suggestion that the bull represents fascism: "The bull is a bull . . . Darkness and brutality, yes, but not fascism."[52] In my reading Picasso in retrospect separates his intentions in painting *Guernica* from its reception, and by splitting his position as painter–viewer leaves unresolved the degree of the artist's political agency.

Woolf's selection of photographic images to accompany the text of *Three Guineas* raises questions about her awareness of the problems of representation as they related to the policies of her government. Specifically did she recognize the relationship of the documentary photograph to the policy of non-intervention? *L'Humanité* used war photographs to accuse the French and British governments of passivity in the face of Fascism, yet their infrequent appearance in *The Times* eloquently manifests denial of the question. Woolf's attitude seems to me rather occluded. The letter to Julian does not reveal how she responded to the photographs of the dead children which she had seen, and they do not appear among the materials that she preserved in her notebooks. Yet both her brief note and her *Daily Worker* essay reveal their central significance in the development of her subject position in *Three Guineas*.[53]

"THE PRESS PHOTOGRAPH IS A MESSAGE"

Although the camera was invented in 1839, it was not, writes John Berger, "until the 20th century and the period between the two world wars that the photograph became the dominant . . . way of referring to appearances."[54] During the Spanish Civil War changes in the design of the camera enhanced its social function. In the nineteenth and early twentieth centuries cameras were set on tripods and the photographer posed his subject. Photo-reportage began in the mid-twenties with the introduction of "new equipment which made it possible to seize fleeting expressions and movements, and even to take indoor photographs in poor lighting conditions."[55] Successive changes in camera design after this time made possible the use of the photograph to record scenes of actual warfare.

Radical changes occurred in the physical and the cultural nature of photography beginning after World War I and accelerating in the succeeding decades. The development of high-speed shutters and increasingly more sensitive film resulted in an economy and ease of execution that would make obsolete the posed or staged approach to the camera's subject. A gradual and yet dramatic shift occurred from the carefully framed, and often either panoramic or symmetrically composed photographic images, to a kind of image that could be an intimate close-up of a face, or an instantaneous freezing of bodies in violent motion. This profoundly divergent set of new pictorial attitudes inevitably altered our perceptions about what the world was like through the camera lens."[56]

The older style in which the subject is posed facing the camera is apparent in *The Times*'s photographs of the new king, which suggest the ideology of monarchy. Stuart Hall argues that the newspaper reproduces ideology when "it *translates* the legitimations of the social order into faces, expressions, subjects, settings and legends."[57] Pictures of the King commanding the troops and the fleet confirm England's military strength. The King represented in his domestic role helps to suppress the distinction between the private and public spheres. If as Bourdieu argues, "In the language of every aesthetic, frontality means eternity,"[58] then the image of the King posed in the older photographic tradition, full-face and motionless, signifies divine command and the mythical aspects of monarchy. Printing the photographs on a separate page helped to deflect any suggestion that the photograph conveyed a message that might contradict the text it was supposedly designed to illustrate.

Newspaper photographs of dukes and kings, Woolf wrote in her 1939 essay on "Royalty" satisfy our desire: "the picture papers show us what we want to see, and the picture papers are full of Dukes and Kings" (*M* 229). She laments that in the last few years the dukes and kings have let us down by loving a Smith and a Simpson, and suggests that the camera turn its attention instead to science. "The camera has an immense power in its eye, if it would only turn that eye in rather a different direction. It might wean us by degrees from the Princess to the panda, and shunt us past religion to pay homage to Science, as some think a more venerable royal house than the House of Windsor" (*M* 233). Beneath the playful tone, one might read Woolf's essay as evidence of her awareness that photography is caught between the ideological demands of desire and fact.

The older frontal representation of the face and the human figure was in a strange way accommodated by war photography. Bernd Hüppauf writes of war photography that its "moral commitment is linked more often than not to a visual code which clashes with the requirements of visualizing a highly abstract modern reality. Juxtapositions of the human face and images of the destructive technological violence of modern warfare suffer in film and photography from an intrinsic contradiction: they aim to maintain a dichotomy between war and civilization."[59] He recounts the efforts of one World War I photographer to reconcile the scale of modern warfare with the camera's traditional emphasis on the human face and figure by conflating several negatives, as though he were responding to the need to compose a beautiful image. The discrepancy between visual codes was exacerbated by the aerial photograph, which cannot reveal objects below a certain size, and recreates the landscape as vast and abstract. "Aerial photographs are symptoms of and at the same time forces in the process of changing the mode of perception by fusing pure aesthetic effects and highly functional military information. Their space is emptied of experience and moral content."[60]

The Spanish Civil War, Hüppauf argues, was an exceptional example of these disparate effects of photographic representation. On the one hand it was a war of modern technology in which the camera and the aeroplane played a significant role, and on the other the Republican position was represented, as we have seen in *L'Humanité* for instance, as a heroic defense. Although a modern war it is remembered for what he calls its "archaic images" of suffering and endurance. "Among the many wars which were fought in Spain between 1936 and 1939, it is the image of the technological war machine against the human face which shaped public memory and reinforced a visual code for the perception of modern wars."[61] I read the text of *Three Guineas* in the context of the contradictory functions of the documentary photograph of bodies and houses in times of war and peace as testimony of Woolf's growing awareness that photographs of all kinds had permanently transformed the problematic of the visible.

Recognizing the capacity of the photograph to signify independently of the text, European and American governments censored war photography. Photographs that revealed information about troop movements or specific war materiel for instance were taboo. During World War I in the U.S. no photographs of dead soldiers and only those that showed wounded soldiers receiving treatment behind the lines could be printed.[62] In Britain it was forbidden to photograph corpses or scenes of combat.[63] The result was that although the war was pivotal in the development of photojournalism, its representation created a class of civilian spectators who had little understanding until the war ended of the actual experience of soldiering. A line of invisibility separated soldiers from their families and from British society.

Much of the argument about what had happened when Guernica was attacked depended on photographic evidence. The authoritative report on the bombing was filed by George Lowther Steer, who visited the town on the evening of the attack; *The Times* printed his account on 27 April 1937.[64] This article and an interview with Father Alberto de Onaindia that appeared in several British newspapers on 3 May were the basic documents for the view that German pilots of the Condor Legion flying German planes had destroyed the Basques' capital city.[65] In the days following, General Franco, in an attempt to deny that his forces had destroyed the civilian population of an "open town," alleged that Guernica had been torched by retreating Republican troops. Survivors subsequently confirmed the story of successive waves of aerial bombardment that first drove the population into shelters, then machine-gunned people who tried to run away, and finally rained thermite bombs which, burning at 3000 degrees centigrade, consumed bodies and houses alike.[66]

Photographs were central to the disagreement among governments over what had occurred at Guernica. A Nationalist sympathizer obtained photographs made on the day following the raid, when fog would have prohibited planes from flying.[67] Photographs taken by Basques reveal clear differences between the destruction of the town of Durango, which was hit by explosive bombs, and Guernica by incendiary. *The Times* and *L'Humanité* printed photographs of the documents obtained from captured German pilots, but neither printed the aerial photographs in question. Hüppauf's argument about the discrepancy between the visual codes revealed in wartime photographs would appear to be confirmed by the practices of both newspapers, which printed the photograph that invites a personal response, rather than the aerial photographs which demand the ability to read and interpret evidence.

Although *L'Humanité* printed news and a photograph from Spain daily during the war, its violence was not represented by images of men in combat. Soldiers in uniform were depicted in peaceful activities, filing down a country road, standing side by side with captured enemy soldiers, or eating a meal and writing while seated at their posts. A viewer might conclude that whereas Franco and the Insurgent forces produced dead bodies and ruined houses, the Republicans were in fact civilians living and working peacefully in male-only communities. A text that reports on war accompanied by photographs of peaceful men points to a contradiction which in effect displaces the ideology of war onto gender. While the news text reported Republican victories, the photographs suggest that in response to Insurgent attacks Republicans became not violent, but more exclusively male.

The five black-and-white photographs that illustrate *Three Guineas* are archival photographs of a general, four heralds, a university procession, a judge, and an archbishop, printed on separate pages throughout the text. A letter in the Hogarth Press archives identifies the general as Lord Baden-Powell, the judge as Lord Hewart, the archbishop as William Cosmo Gordon Lang, Archbishop of Canterbury, and Earl Baldwin in "A University Procession." Readers of *The Times* would have recognized them as "the reigning 'chiefs' of the patriarchal enterprise spanning Empire, Government, Justice, and Religion."[68]

Each photograph represents the costume of the "educated man in his public capacity," enhanced by wigs, medals, and embroidery. The photographs stress the disjunction between the incumbent and his gorgeous insignia, as though in a phrase from *Orlando*, "Clothes wear us." Helen Wussow, comparing Woolf's use of photographs with Lytton Strachey's in *Eminent Victorians*, comments that both "extend and reverse [Julia Margaret] Cameron's penchant for portraying notable men and women in the clothes of greatness. Their subjects become travesties of power, their photographic images contradictions of significance."[69] To the extent that these photographs call in question the text's "dead bodies and ruined houses" they play on the contradictions that were customary in the layout of the newspaper.

The photographs suggest that the common reader has access to just so much of the life of the great religious, legal, military, and academic institutions as can be made visible. Whereas in *A Room of One's Own* Woolf wrote of the exclusion of women from the university, here exclusion takes on a broader cultural significance. In the sense of showing the scenes that we might have seen for ourselves, the camera represents to a mass audience knowledge outside institutions. It breeches the walls to reveal men in motion in the public space of the city street, where separated from their official functions they and their costumes become more vulnerable to Woolf's satiric gaze. The daughters of educated men, excluded from the university, educate themselves by comparing several newspaper accounts of an event, and by implication by comparing the text with its illustrations.

Stuart Hall observes that the newspaper reproduces "the major ideological themes of society" by means of a "double articulation" of news value and ideological treatment.[70] But whereas news value may be apparent, it is more difficult to understand just what creates the ideological content of the photograph. The invisibility of ideology is a function of its redundancy, the "imaginary distortion" which is our customary way of viewing the world. "The ideological concepts embodied in photos and texts in a newspaper, then, do not produce new knowledge about the world. They produce *recognitions* of the world as we have already learned to appropriate it."[71] Woolf's method was to make ideology visible by creating a new and unfamiliar context for the news photograph. In effect she deconstructs the relationship of image to text when she represents the functions of institutions not as generals, judges, and professors, but as decorations and costumes. The unprinted war photographs in comparison are the photographs of those without institutional clothing, the bodies whose images ideology regularly conceals from sight.

The news value of the Spanish photographs is that they document the killing of civilians. Their ideological value is more difficult to grasp. On the one hand "The most salient, operational 'news value' in the domain of political news is certainly that of *violence*."[72] Yet the photograph of a violent action engages contradictions which, in John Berger's view, effectively block recognition of the historical context. Events from culture are represented as occurring in nature, as though "the moment of agony" transcends national boundaries to signify the human condition.[73] Yet as we have seen, propaganda assumes the transcendence of such moments.

Woolf's suppression of the Spanish war photographs suggests the politics of the invisible body as expendable. It is in this sense that her emphasis in "Professions for Women" on women's bodies seems to inhabit her indignation on behalf of the war dead. The female imagination lives "in a state of fury . . . because the conventions are still very strong. If I were to overcome the conventions [and write about the passions of a woman's body] I should need the courage of a hero, and I am not a hero" (*TP* xxxviii–xxxix). On one level then the phrase "dead bodies and ruined houses" is Woolf's sign for patriarchal ideology. It enforces the invisibility of women's bodies and has created as we see in *To the Lighthouse* a private house that is ripe for ruin. "And" activates as a question the relationship between the nouns and their adjectives: why should bodies be dead or houses ruined? What Woolf gives the reader is not "new knowledge" but a fresh recognition of the violent grammar of the familiar patriarchal world. "The most transient visitor to this planet," she wrote in *A Room of One's Own*, "who picked up this paper could not fail to be aware . . . that England is under the rule of a patriarchy" (*RO* 33).

If Virginia in fact shared the sentiments of Leonard I might argue that the photograph of dead bodies images the illusions of non-intervention, a policy complicit with the murder of civilians which the British emphasis on the sanctity of the institutions of monarchy and marriage worked to conceal. But in fact her attitude especially in her published work was far from straightforward. The images of "the dead bodies and ruined houses" that she saw were problematic, in the sense of forcing thought, which in her work often takes the form of an attempt to see something as yet invisible. For this task she fashioned the narrator as correspondent, and incorporated the materials of her argument – the letter of appeal, memoirs, and newspaper articles and photographs. *Three Guineas* by refusing to transform the material of history into narrative, insists on the questions that arise from reading documents. It is situated closer to Woolf's reading than to her writing, and closer as well to her sympathy for the position of Delaprée and European Communists than to the attitude of civilized detachment which she manifested in other circumstances.

"THREE GUINEAS"

Much of the force of the "Third Guinea" is achieved by Woolf's argument that the dictator is evidence of a patriarchy that has persisted since the time of the Greeks. It is an insight accorded to women, who have been excluded from the university. She expresses over and over her sense of that exclusion in terms of not knowing Greek: "we, who have been shut out from the universities so repeatedly, and are only now admitted so restrictedly; we who have received no paid-for education whatsoever, or so little that we can only read our own tongue and write our own language" (*TG* 212). But as the reader has come to expect, Woolf converts the position of outsider into a rhetorical advantage. She relegates the language of the letter of appeal, "culture," and "intellectual liberty," to the realm of "abstract words," when it is compared with the "facts" reported in the newspaper (*TG* 213). In this construction of the poles of discourse the female finds herself positioned between what she later calls "dead words," that is the public language created by university education, and the newspaper. The female reader who is conditioned by exclusion from the language of educated men turns to the newspapers and educates herself by comparing accounts of the same event. In this context the experience of the female reader suggests that ideology may be located in the contradiction implied in Woolf's ironic disclaimer, "since you assure us that there is a connection between those rather abstract words and these very positive photographs – the photographs of dead bodies and ruined houses" (*TG* 210).

In response to the threat of war, she suggests, the "daughters of educated men" must form a new society, "the Society of Outsiders." The term, which she repeats some twenty times throughout the essay, first appeared in Woolf's comments on her reading of the *Baccae* in Greek. In notes written on the life of Euripides in 1923–24[74] she compares him to Alcibiades and Socrates, and comments that he may have left Athens to live in the Macedonian capital in order to avoid a fate like theirs. "[John Pentland] Mahaffy aptly calls him 'the great outsider.'"[75] Mahaffy in his monograph on Euripides paints a picture of the dramatist as a scholarly recluse, "that sort of broad-minded sympathetic thinker who refuses to adopt the views of any party, but holds sometimes with the one and sometimes with the other. . . So the great outsider would be cheered by opposite sides of the house, but make enemies everywhere."[76] Comparing him with Sophocles, Woolf notes that whereas the latter "deals with action," Euripides is a poet of thought and metaphor: "Euripides had the beginning of the subjective mind in him."[77]

Woolf finds herself in the position of the historian she had described in "The Artist and Politics," who in the light of events in Spain is called on to "change his angle of vision. Either he focuses his sight upon the immediate problem; or he brings his subject matter into relation with the present; or in some cases, so paralysed is he by the agitations of the moment that he remains silent" (*CE* II: 230). In *Three Guineas* Woolf faced those same choices. In October of 1935 she was mistrustful of public rhetoric and yet reluctant to become active. The diary gives one definition of the outsider: "Happily, uneducated & voteless, I am not responsible for the state of society" (*D* IV:346). Yet in this mood she entitled her essay "Next War" (*D* IV:346, 348). Nor was she satisfied to be a member of the group For Intellectual Liberty. David Bradshaw notes that her repeated phrase "culture and intellectual liberty" parodies the language about the "defence of peace, liberty and culture" from the group Resolution and suggests her disillusionment.[78]

In the "Third Guinea" she attempts to translate the "outsider," a term associated with Greek tragedy, a reluctance to take sides in political debate, and her sense of exclusion from the intellectual resistance of her class, into the context of an argument about women's political resistance to the Spanish Civil War. To the extent that she shared Mahaffy's view of Euripides' character her argument is weakened, as though she had reacted to the demand to write propaganda with a retreat into aesthetics. And in fact, to add a performative dimension to the term "outsider" significantly alters its implications. As Brenda Silver and Christine Froula have discovered, working women found the Outsiders' Society "impractible."[79] Woolf found herself lodged in the difficult position of negotiating between propaganda and an aesthetics removed from social action.

In the same "Guinea" Woolf brings Sophocles "into relation with the present." The "Guinea" concludes with a modern political interpretation of Creon, who, she writes, might as well have shut Antigone up in a concentration camp as a tomb.

And Creon we read brought ruin on his house, and scattered the land with the bodies of the dead. It seems, Sir, as we listen to the voices of the past, as if we were looking at the photograph again, at the picture of dead bodies and ruined houses that the Spanish Government sends us almost weekly. Things repeat themselves it seems. (*TG* 269–70)

It is consistent with the feminist impulse observable in Woolf's earliest reading of the Greeks, that she read *Antigone* in the service of a transhistorical feminism. Yet although she read a translation her reading is more ambitious and challenging than that of either Edward or Sara Pargiter. It translates the drama of Antigone from the Victorian household onto the stage of European history. Yet in my view it is a thematic reading that does not have the emotional force of the images that Woolf derived from her translation of *Agamemnon*.

In the face of events in Spain and Europe during the last few years of her life, Woolf used the photograph to image the ideology of gender that she had first recognized in her notes on the Greeks.[80] Readers nowadays may find that the newspaper photograph better represents the transhistorical ideology of gender which in Woolf's view has obtained in Western society since the time of the Greeks. In her essay the photograph has the power to make that visible by representing the invisible world that previously was seen only by the mad and the gods.

In the "First Guinea" Woolf acknowledged the view that the photograph has the potential to bypass ideological differences by an unmediated appeal to the eye, when she suggests that war photographs offer an alternative to biography and history. "These photographs are not an argument; they are simply a crude statement of fact addressed to the eye. But the eye is connected with the brain; the brain with the nervous system" (*TG* 125). This position is consistent with the idea of the "documentary photograph," which when it first came into wide use in the 1920s was believed to offer an alternative discourse. Abigail Solomon-Godeau observes that "the paradox that underlies those documentary practices that have defined themselves as critical of the status quo, or at very least reformist in intention, is that they normally operate within larger systems that function to limit, contain, and ultimately neutralize them."[81] The problem does not concern appropriation so much as the imagined capacity of the photograph to circumvent the ideology within which it is inscribed. Woolf's representation of the photograph as "a crude statement of fact addressed to the eye" refers to what had been hoped of the documentary photograph before it was subjected to criticism by Walter Benjamin.

In "A Short History of Photography" (1931)[82] Benjamin surveyed the history of the camera from the vantage point of Surrealism. Although in his history the photograph always created an image mediated by its social function, Surrealism succeeded in showing the human figure fundamentally alienated from its environment. The visual "authenticity" of the photograph, he writes, cannot be linked to "reportage." "At this point captions must begin to function, captions which understand the photography which turns all the relations of life into literature, and without which all photographic construction must remain bound in coincidences."[83] Once again Benjamin's analysis identifies Woolf's position as viewing subject. But whereas Benjamin writes as a historian, in *Three Guineas* Woolf is a polemicist. What Benjamin represents as a moment in nineteenth-century history Woolf interrogates as the connection between war photographs and a history that goes back to the Greeks.

The "Third Guinea" reorients Woolf's essay. The textual practices that I discussed earlier in the chapter, and in particular the lack of a typescript, lead me to surmise that it had a somewhat different history, and in particular that the "Third Guinea" may have been a later addition to a manuscript that had been planned around two "Guineas." The substantive difference concerns Woolf's creation in language of a "picture" to represent the ideological functions of the photograph. It juxtaposes the photographs which illustrate her text to those that she represents as the signs of war. The "figure of a man," who may represent "Man himself, the quintessence of virility," the "Tyrant or Dictator," equally at home in German, Italian, or British culture, is posed before a scene of "ruined houses and dead bodies – men, women and children . . . It suggests that the public and the private worlds are inseparably connected" (*TG* 270). The "picture" superimposes the man in uniform, who represents the photographs which accompany the text, over the war photographs which Woolf has seen but does not reproduce. Its composition suggests the older style of photography with its focus on the immobile frontal pose, which relegates houses and unidentified bodies to the background. The "picture" is composite, in the sense that it combines the photographic and the textual image, but not in the service of a beautiful composition.

Then with a phrase Woolf articulates a position which dispels the illusion of passivity suggested by the Society of Outsiders and by the mirror experience, and at the same time offers an alternative to the temptation to write propaganda. She makes the remarkable suggestion that the subject may refigure the imaginary in terms of the newspaper photograph. Although we may view it "from different angles," the picture is "the picture of evil" (*TG* 271). Woolf carefully denies its value as propaganda: "we have not laid that picture before you in order to excite once more the sterile emotion of hate" (*TG* 270). Instead she asks that we incorporate it into the world of the imaginary by treating it as an image, albeit alienating, of ourselves: "we cannot dissociate ourselves from that figure but are ourselves that figure. It suggests that we are not passive spectators doomed to unresisting obedience but by our thoughts and actions can ourselves change that figure" (*TG* 271). By inscribing in the imaginary a harsh image of the other as male and evil Woolf creates an ethics of the imaginary which by bringing gender into play not only goes beyond Lacan, but offers an alternative to propaganda.

Until the "Third Guinea" Woolf's position had been complicated and apparently contradictory, as though in the language of *A Room of One's Own* she were concerned only "to do what I can to show you how I arrived at this opinion" (*RO* 4). But if one grants the argument that the photograph reveals the invisible workings of ideology, then the terms of resistance differ from those evoked by propaganda. They involve a recognition of complicity that overrides the gender difference that has obtained since the time of Sophocles. To leave the form "unsigned" suggests her continued distrust of symbolic transactions as though she preferred to function within an imaginary that had been redefined by the photograph. She rejects ventriloquism and asks for a new vocabulary: "we can best help you to prevent war not by repeating your words and following your methods but by finding new words and creating new methods" (*TG* 272). Resistance once again takes the form of seeking a position on the threshold of the symbolic.

War photographs gave a new meaning to the world imaged by the

Greeks. The invisible is no longer the realm reserved in the mundane world for the eyes of the insane, for the camera speaks for those who have become invisible in a new sense. Benjamin suggests that the camera image shows us what the eye does not see, the invisible behind the visible, so that it creates what he calls "the optical unconscious."[84] Sounding like Lacan at this point he sees the camera as a model of the mental function of subjectivity which comes into existence at the point of contradiction between two visual codes. Lacan instances the rainbow, a subjective phenomenon which can nevertheless be photographed, Benjamin the photographic enlargements of pictures of plants that reveal images of architectural forms. Neither sees what Woolf discovered, that the photograph may reveal the invisible workings of ideology. She arrived at this point by refusing a subject position in which the documentary photograph becomes the occasion for propaganda, and by embracing the newspaper's problematic separation of text and photograph. Her subject position is represented as that of the female correspondent who addresses the one presumed to know. In that role she is able to maintain the urgency of the unanswered question while keeping before the reader a set of illustrative photographs and another set of photographs that is more disturbing because it is invisible in the text. Her sense of ideology would appear to be that which disquiets by its very invisibility.

Notes

1 THE HIDING PLACES OF MY POWER: WOOLF'S OPTICS

1 William Wordsworth, *The Prelude*, Book XI, lines 279–80.
2 Martin Jay introduces his analysis of the denigration of the hegemony of vision in twentieth-century French thought with a comprehensive survey of "the cultural variability of ocular experience" from classical Greece to the present, *Downcast Eyes: The Denigration of Vision in Twentieth Century French Thought* (Berkeley and Los Angeles: The University of California Press, 1994), p. 4. Jonathan Crary writes about the "historical construction" of vision before 1850, *Techniques of the Observer: On Vision and Modernity in the Nineteenth Century* (Cambridge, Mass. and London: MIT Press, 1990), and "Modernizing Vision," *Vision and Visuality*, ed. Hal Foster (Seattle: Bay Press, 1988), pp. 29–43. Woolf gives us what Rosalind E. Krauss calls "a bridge moment between a nineteenth century psychophysiological theory of vision and a later, psychoanalytic one," *The Optical Unconscious* (Cambridge, Mass. and London: MIT Press, 1993), p. 135.
3 Insofar as Lacan identifies with Descartes the autonomous subject who derives a sense of identity from his thought and consciousness, "il faut dire qu'elle nous oppose à toute philosophie issue directement du *Cogito*" (*E* 93). It is an experience that leads us to oppose any philosophy directly issuing from the *Cogito* (trans. Alan Sheridan, *E* 1).
4 René Descartes, *Selected Philosophical Writings*, ed. John Cottingham, Robert Stoothoff, Dugald Murdoch, trans., John Cottingham, Robert Stoothoff (Cambridge: Cambridge University Press, 1988), p. 85.
5 David Michael Levin, *The Philosopher's Gaze: Modernity in the Shadows of Enlightenment* (Berkeley, Los Angeles and London: University of California Press, 1999), p. 44, and Part III, section 1 "Descartes's Window."
6 Erwin Panofsky, *Perspective as Symbolic Form*, trans. Christopher S. Wood (New York: Zone Books, 1991), p. 27.
7 Alberti, *De Pictura* (1435), Book I, quoted in Joel Snyder, "Picturing Vision," *Critical Inquiry* 6 (1980), 519.
8 Panofsky, *Perspective as Symbolic Form*, p. 31.

9 Ibid., p. 67. In *Ways of Seeing* John Berger notes that "the convention of perspective, which is unique to European art and which was first established in the early Renaissance, centres everything on the eye of the beholder. It is like a beam from a lighthouse." (London: BBC and Penguin, 1972), p. 16.

10 Hubert Damisch, *The Origin of Perspective*, trans. John Goodman (Cambridge, Mass. and London: MIT Press, 1994). Damisch notes in particular Fritz Novotny's *Cézanne and the End of Scientific Perspective* (n.p., 1936), p. 31n. 11. See also Lawrence Wright's discussion of the use of perspective by the Surrealists, in *Perspective in Perspective* (London, Boston, Melbourne and Henley: Routledge & Kegan Paul, 1983), pp. 307–12.

11 Roger Fry, *Cézanne: A Study of His Development* (New York: The Macmillan Company, 1927), p. x.

12 Roger Fry, "The Art of Florence," *Vision and Design* (London: Chatto & Windus, 1920; Oxford University Press reprint, 1981), p. 127.

13 Fry, *Cézanne*, p. 26.

14 Snyder, "Picturing Vision," 512.

15 "The subject says, and saying, becomes subject and disappears. Before the act, it did not exist, and after the act, it does not exist any longer." Juan-David Nasio, "The Concept of the Subject of the Unconscious," *Disseminating Lacan*, ed. David Pettigrew and François Raffoul (State University of New York Press, 1996), p. 29.

16 For instance in "The Lady in the Looking-Glass: A Reflection": "Here was the woman herself . . . Isabella was perfectly empty," (*CSF* 219).

17 Walter Benjamin, *Selected Writings, Volume 1: 1913–1926*, ed. Marcus Bullock and Michael W. Jennings (Cambridge, Mass.: Harvard University Press, 1996), p. 85.

18 Hermione Lee, *Virginia Woolf* (London: Chatto & Windus, 1996), p. 375.

19 Lacan writes of *Repräsentanz*, distinguishing "for example, the representative of France," from *Vorstellung*, "in which is situated the subjectivity on which the theory of knowledge is suspended" (*FFC* 221).

20 Harvena Richter writes that it is the "emphasis on the subject's experience of the object which separates Virginia Woolf most clearly from her contemporaries." *Virginia Woolf: The Inward Voyage* (Princeton: Princeton University Press, 1970), p. viii.

21 Jacques Lacan, "Position of the Unconscious," in French edition of *Ecrits* (Paris: Editions de Seuil, 1966), pp. 829–50.

22 Douglas Mao focuses his study of "the problem of production under modernity" in Woolf's work on "Solid Objects." He traces the themes of consumption, domination, and leisure class guilt in the story and in her major novels, *Solid Objects: Modernism and the Test of Production* (Princeton: Princeton University Press, 1998), ch. 1, pp. 26–89.

23 Toril Moi, *Sexual/Textual Politics: Feminist Literary Theory* (London and New York: Routledge, 1985), pp. 1–8.

24 It is the assumption of many of Woolf's critics, expressed by Alex Zwerdling in *Virginia Woolf and the Real World* (Berkeley, Los Angeles, London: University of California Press, 1986), pp. 24, 31.

25 Woolf spent her life among visual artists and their work. One of her earliest critics, Winifred Holtby, noted that "She is at home in the painter's world of form and colour. Her own imagination seems to be visual rather than aural," *Virginia Woolf* (London: Wishart, 1932), p. 16. Diane F. Gillespie writes that Woolf's awareness of the schools of Victorian and modern painting emerged from her knowledge of Vanessa's professional activity. She includes several of Woolf's own copies and sketches in *The Sisters' Arts: The Writing and Painting of Virginia Woolf and Vanessa Bell* (Syracuse: Syracuse University Press, 1988), p. 307.

26 Jean-Paul Sartre's study of the gaze predates Lacan's, and the gaze is a central focus of the work of Michel Foucault. But Lacan's formulation of the subject at the intersection of the visible and the intelligible lies closer to Woolf's ideas.

27 Richter, *Virginia Woolf*, p. 75.

28 Makiko Minow-Pinkney, *Virginia Woolf and the Problem of the Subject* (New Brunswick: Rutgers University Press, 1987), p. 15.

29 For instance the first sentence of "Hours in a Library" (1916): "Let us begin by clearing up the old confusion between the man who loves learning and the man who loves reading, and point out that there is no connexion whatever between the two," or the first sentence of "Phases of Fiction" (1929): "The following pages attempt to record the impressions made upon the mind by reading a certain number of novels in succession." *CE* ii: 34, 56.

30 Daniel Ferrer, *Virginia Woolf and the Madness of Language*, trans. Geoffrey Bennington and Rachel Bowlby (London and New York: Routledge, 1990), p. 57.

31 Bruce Fink argues that Lacan's return to Plato was an attempt to avoid the anthropologist's reading of the other merely as a reflection of his own beliefs, a "psychologization" of the subject, *The Lacanian Subject: Between Language and Jouissance* (Princeton: Princeton University Press, 1995), p. 60.

32 Samuel Weber, *Return to Freud: Jacques Lacan's Dislocation of Psychoanalysis*, trans. Michael Levine (Cambridge: Cambridge University Press, 1991), pp. 99–100.

33 Mark Hussey discusses Woolf's representation of identity, self, and soul, as potential and realized, in "Identity and Self," ch. 2 of *The Singing of the Real World: The Philosophy of Virginia Woolf's Fiction* (Columbus: Ohio State University Press, 1986).

34 Given that Nietzsche's work was in several aspects anticipated by the Victorians it may come as no surprise that Woolf's notion of the subject is similar in outline. Perhaps the most telling among several of the

studies and fragments which make up *The Will to Power* is No. 548 (1885–86): "Our bad habit of taking a mnemonic, an abbreviative formula, to be an entity, finally as a cause, e.g., to say of lightning 'it flashes.' Or the little word 'I.' To make a kind of perspective in seeing the cause of seeing: that was what happened in the invention of the 'subject,' the 'I.' " See also Nos. 481 and 549.

35 Weber, *Return to Freud*, p. 55, refers to a passage in *E*, 505.

36 Weber, *Return to Freud*, p. 108.

37 Quoted in Quentin Bell, *Virginia Woolf: A Biography*, vol. II (London: The Hogarth Press, 1972), pp. 128–9.

38 Pamela L. Caughie, *Virginia Woolf and Postmodernism: Literature in Quest and Question of Itself* (Urbana and Chicago: University of Illinois Press, 1991), p. 37.

39 In others of Woolf's novels England or the king is a symbol; mathematicians and philosophers love their symbols.

40 Patrick McGee, *Telling the Other: The Question of Value in Modern and Postcolonial Writing* (Ithaca and London: Cornell University Press, 1992), p. 113.

41 Weber, *Return to Freud*, p. 109.

42 Elizabeth Abel, *Virginia Woolf and the Fictions of Psychoanalysis* (Chicago and London: The University of Chicago Press, 1989), p. 47.

43 Ibid., pp. 66, 77.

44 Ibid., pp. 76, 79.

45 Ibid., p. 79.

46 Ibid., p. 80.

47 Weber, *Return to Freud*, p. 90, translates Lacan: "là où je ne suis pas parce que je ne peux pas m'y situer" [there where I am not because I cannot situate myself there] (*E* 517).

48 Abel, *Virginia Woolf*, p. 69.

49 Weber, *Return to Freud*, p. 90. He translates Lacan's "Je ne suis pas, là où je suis le jouet de ma pensée; je pense à ce que je suis, là où je ne pense pas penser," [I am not, wherever I am the plaything of my thought; I think of what I am, wherever I do not think [that I am] thinking]. (*E* 517–18).

50 Caughie, *Virginia Woolf and Postmodernism*, pp. 28–32.

51 Book XI, lines 279–80.

2 ON THE FAR SIDE OF LANGUAGE: GREEK STUDIES AND "JACOB'S ROOM"

1 Plato, *The Republic*, Book VI, trans. Paul Shorey (Cambridge, Mass.: Harvard University Press, and London: William Heinemann Ltd, 1935), p. 211.

2 Leonard Woolf, *Beginning Again: An Autobiography of the Year 1911 to 1918* (New York: Harcourt, Brace & World, 1963, 1964), p. 164.

3 Quentin Bell, *Virginia Woolf: A Biography*, vol. 1 (London: The Hogarth Press, 1972), pp. 89–90.

4 Roger Poole, *The Unknown Virginia Woolf* (Cambridge: Cambridge University Press, 1978), p. 175.

5 In her notes on line 565 of the *Bacchae* Woolf wrote: "Here are the originals which have been sounding through literature ever since. Orpheus & the nightingale," Berg Reel 13, fol. 29.

6 Birdsong figures as well in the interludes of *The Waves*, and in her notebook entry on the conclusion of the novel Woolf wrote "The tram stopped & the nightingale went on singing," as though to suggest the continuation of the female voice beyond time (Hol *W* 761).

7 Poole notes that Woolf had read T. S. Eliot's *The Waste Land*, which contains a passage about Philomel, and indeed in *The Waves* Jinny says: "Jug, jug, jug, I sing like the nightingale . . ." (*W* 117). In May 1918 Woolf wrote simply about the nightingale: "Last night at Charleston I lay with my window open listening to a nightingale" (*D* 1:151).

8 Since I can find no mention of a date of composition for "Old Bloomsbury" in Woolf's diaries, I rely on Quentin Bell's assertion that it was read to the Memoir Club "in about 1922," *Virginia Woolf*, vol. 1, p. 125n.

9 Kenneth J. Reckford, *Aristophanes' Old-and-New Comedy, Vol. I: Six Essays in Perspective* (Chapel Hill: University of North Carolina Press, 1987), pp. 24, 56.

10 Christine Perkell, "On The Two Voices of The Birds in *Birds*," *Ramus* 22 (1993), 6–7.

11 Ibid., 7.

12 Ibid., 11.

13 F. E. Romer, "Good Intentions and the ὁδὸς ἡ ἐς κόρακας," *The City as Comedy: Society and Representation in Athenian Drama*, ed. Gregory W. Dobrov (Chapel Hill and London: The University of North Carolina Press, 1997), p. 56.

14 Ibid., p. 59.

15 Woolf translation, line 1254. Birds and the nightingale figure as well in *The Waves*, where they suggest a link between individual characterizations and astronomical rhythms.

16 Harvena Richter associates Cassandra with Septimus Smith, in *Virginia Woolf: The Inward Voyage* (Princeton: Princeton University Press, 1970), p. 120.

17 Berg reel 6, vol. 1, fol. 65.

18 Bell, *Virginia Woolf*, vol. 1, p. 90.

19 Walter Benjamin, "The Task of the Translator," *Illuminations*, trans. Harry Zohn (New York: Harcourt, Brace & World, Inc., 1968), pp. 69–82.

20 I am indebted for this reading to Paul deMan's "Conclusions: Walter Benjamin's 'The Task of the Translator,'" *Yale French Studies* 69 (1985), 25–46.

21 Ibid., 81.
22 Christopher Stray, *Classics Transformed: Schools, Universities, and Society in England, 1839–1960* (Oxford: Clarendon Press, 1998), p. 27.
23 Ibid., p. 29.
24 Roy Lowe, "The Expansion of Higher Education in England," *The Transformation of Higher Learning 1860–1930: Expansion, Diversification, Social Opening, and Professionalization in England, Germany, Russia, and the U.S.*, ed. Konrad J. Jarausch (Chicago: University of Chicago Press, 1983), pp. 51–3.
25 For a discussion of Platonic ideals of leadership that survived in twentieth-century British education, see Gary McCulloch, *Philosophers and Kings: Education for Leadership in Modern England* (Cambridge: Cambridge University Press, 1991).
26 Reba N. Soffer writes in her study of Newnham College that Eleanor Sidgwick, the head of "the first women's college to become integrated into a traditional university," and her husband Henry Sidgwick "were prepared to relinquish Greek and Latin not only for women, but also for men, because they believed that more modern languages would serve them all better in the real world. But they were especially willing to delete ancient languages as a requirement for women's matriculation in the university since it served essentially to exclude intelligent girls who had never been to preparatory schools where the ancient languages were taught." "Authority in the University: Balliol, Newnham and the New Mythology," *Myths of the English*, ed. Roy Porter (Cambridge and Cambridge, Mass.: Polity Press, 1992), pp. 194, 202.
27 George Spater and Ian Parsons write that Virginia "except for a few miscellaneous courses which she took at King's College London, did not go out of the house for her education. She was largely self-taught, with some help from her parents, and from tutors who came to Hyde Park Gate. Her exuberant imagination had not been dulled by academic discipline, and her natural sensitivity had not been blunted by association with less sensitive schoolfellows." *A Marriage of True Minds: An Intimate Portrait of Leonard and Virginia Woolf* (New York and London: Harcourt Brace Jovanovich, 1977), p. 25. But in *Three Guineas* Woolf lamented that unpaid for education restricts a woman to "reading and writing our own tongue" (*TG* 214).
28 Garnett McCoy, *Reading Records: A Researcher's Guide to the Archives of American Art* (Washington, D.C.: Smithsonian Institution, 1997), p. 25. The letter was acquired under the mistaken assumption that it had been addressed to the American painter John F. Weir, the head of the school of fine arts at Yale University. I am indebted to Professor Pat Hills of Boston University for the reference.
29 Perry Meisel, *The Absent Father: Virginia Woolf and Walter Pater* (New Haven and London: Yale University Press, 1980), pp. 17–18n. 25.
30 Bell, *Virginia Woolf*, vol. I, p. 68. Christopher Stray has discovered in the

archives of the Cambridge University Library that Case played the role of the goddess Athena in the *Eumenides*, the Cambridge Greek Play for 1885, *Classics Transformed*, pp. 160–1.

31 Brenda Silver, ed., *Virginia Woolf's Reading Notebooks* (Princeton: Princeton University Press, 1983), pp. 124, 133.

32 Alfred Zimmern, *The Greek Commonwealth: Politics & Economics in Fifth-Century Athens* (London: Oxford University Press, 1911), p. 343. Benjamin Jowett, the head of Balliol and also an editor and translator of Plato, wrote of Socrates as an Oxford colleague "walking into the clubs and courts of law, appearing in society, talking with our statesmen, instructing our artists, reasoning with our divines and men of science, ready to argue about all things human and divine with young men everywhere." "The Character of Socrates" in *Essays on Men and Manners* (1895), quoted by Reba N. Soffer, "Authority in the University," p. 199.

33 Zimmern, *The Greek Commonwealth*, p. 336.

34 Ibid., pp. 341–2.

35 Berg reel x, fol. 36.

36 G. R. F. Ferrari, *Listening to the Cicadas: A study of Platos's "Phaedrus"* (Cambridge: Cambridge University Press, 1987), p. 148. But see Martha Nussbaum, "The Window: Knowledge of Other Minds in Virginia Woolf's *To the Lighthouse*," *New Literary History* 26 (1995), 731–53.

37 Meisel, *The Absent Father*, pp. 16–17n. 24.

38 Walter Pater, *Plato and Platonism* (New York and London: Macmillan, 1893), p. 143. Perry Meisel in his study of Woolf pays less attention to this than others of Pater's works.

39 Ibid., p. 141.

40 Meisel, *The Absent Father*, pp. 39–40.

41 Silver, *Reading Notebooks*, p. 125.

42 Walter Headlam, *On Editing Aeschylus: A Criticism* (London: D. Nutt, 1891), p. 4.

43 A. W. Verrall, *"On Editing Aeschylus" A Reply* (London and New York: Macmillan, 1892), pp. 6–7.

44 Bell, *Virginia Woolf*, vol. i, p. 118.

45 In 1920 Woolf wrote that she had put Walter Headlam into *Night and Day*: "If there was a dash of anybody in Rodney [   ], I think it must have been Walter Headlam" (*L* ii:414).

46 Walter Headlam, *"Agamemnon" of Aeschylus with Verse Translation*, Introduction and Notes (Cambridge: Cambridge, University Press, 1910), p. 75.

47 Berg reel 13.

48 Silver, *Reading Notebooks*, pp. 109–10.

49 *Three Guineas*, p. 303n. 40.

50 Berg reel 13, fols. 34, 36.

51 Soffer, "Authority in the University," p. 193.

52 For instance Simon Goldhill sketches the link between ecphrasis and a

"shift in the epistemological status of viewing" in Hellenistic culture, and concludes that "writing about viewing art is to engage in the construction of the viewing subject." "The Naive and Knowing Eye: Ecphrasis and the Culture of Viewing in the Hellenistic World," in *Art and Text in Ancient Greek Culture*, ed. Simon Goldhill (Cambridge: Cambridge University Press, 1994), pp. 209, 216.

53 Jean-Pierre Vernant, *Mortals and Immortals: Collected Essays*, trans. Froma I. Zeitlin (Princeton: Princeton University Press, 1991), p. 164.

54 Ibid., p. 174.

55 Ibid., p. 168.

56 Ibid., p. 168.

57 Vernant, *Mortals and Immortals*, p. 181.

58 Like other women of her generation Woolf used Greek material as "a way of talking about gender and sexuality." Writers like Mary Butts and Mary Renault, choosing to set their historical novels in Greece, "were plunging into contested waters, setting up their own 'Greece' to compete with those constructs that in the past had served, implicitly if not explicitly, to disempower women," Ruth Hoberman, *Gendering Classicism: The Ancient World in Twentieth-Century Women's Historical Fiction* (Albany: State University of New York Press, 1997), p. 23.

59 Woolf, "Virginia Woolf: A Dialogue upon Mount Pentelicus," ed. S. P. Rosenbaum, *Times Literary Supplement* (11–17 Sept. 1987), 979.

60 Patrick McGee, *Telling the Other: The Question of Value in Modern and Postcolonial Writing* (Ithaca and London: Cornell University Press, 1992), p. 101.

61 Ibid., pp. 101–2.

62 Claire Kahane, *Passions of the Voice: Hysteria, Narrative, and the Figure of the Speaking Woman, 1850–1915* (Baltimore and London: The Johns Hopkins University Press, 1995), p. 114.

63 Ibid., p. 118. Elizabeth Heine, ed., *VO*, includes earlier and substantially different drafts of this important passage, pp. 440–2.

64 Rosalind Krauss, *The Optical Unconscious* (Cambridge, Mass.: MIT Press, 1994), p. 114.

65 Ibid., p. 140.

66 Bruce Fink, *The Lacanian Subject: Between Language and Jouissance* (Princeton: Princeton University Press, 1995), p. 77.

67 Silver, *Reading Notebooks*, pp. 166–9.

68 Ibid., pp. 166–9.

69 Clive Bell, writing in 1911–12, defined "significant form," a quality that he saw in Cézanne, in part by distinguishing it from "beauty." He rejected the term because of its popular association with sensuality and desire: "A beautiful picture is a photograph of a pretty girl," *Art* (New York: Capricorn Books, 1958 reprint), p. 21.

70 Berg reel 13, fol. 57.

71 David M. Halperin, "Why is Diotima a Woman? Platonic *Eros* and the

Figuration of Gender," *Before Sexuality: The Construction of Erotic Experience in the Ancient Greek World*, ed. David M. Halperin, John J. Winkler, and Froma I. Zeitlin (Princeton: Princeton University Press, 1990), p. 281.

72 The Cambridge group known as the Apostles referred to themselves as "brothers of Plato," and save for Leonard Woolf the group was composed largely of homosexual men. George Spater and Ian Parsons, *A Marriage of True Minds: An Intimate Portrait of Leonard and Virginia Woolf* (New York and London: Harcourt Brace Jovanovich), p. 29.

73 Halperin, "Why is Diotima a Woman?", p. 289. Adriana Cavarero reaches much the same conclusion in her discussion of Diotima, in *In Spite of Plato: A Feminist Rewriting of Ancient Philosophy*, trans. Serena Anderlini-D'Onofrio and Aine O'Healy (Oxford: Oxford University Press, 1995), p. 94.

74 Berg reel 13, fol. 59.

75 Louis Althusser, "Ideology and Ideological State Apparatuses (Notes towards an Investigation)," *Lenin and Philosophy and Other Essays*, trans. Ben Brewster (New York: Monthly Review Press, 1971).

76 Rachel Bowlby, *Virginia Woolf: Feminist Destinations* (Oxford and New York: Blackwell, 1988), pp. 110–11.

77 Woolf's view of Jacob's "manly beauty" was undoubtedly complicated by her protest over the celebration of Rupert Brooke after his death: "So much has been written of his personal beauty that to state one's own first impression of him in that respect needs some audacity", "Rupert Brooke," (*E* II:279).

78 Ferrari, *Listening to the Cicadas*, p. 154. In "The Intellectual Status of Women," which appeared in the correspondence columns of the *New Statesman*, Woolf chose Sappho to reply to Arnold Bennett's assertion in *Our Women* (1920) that women are the intellectual inferiors of men. See Appendix III of *D* II: 339–42.

79 Ferrari, *Listening to the Cicadas*, p. 163.

80 Makiko Minow-Pinkney reads the song as "the voice of the mother, issuing from 'a mere hole in the earth,'" offering "an alternative, 'feminist' view of evolution to set against the patriarchal social Darwinism of Sir William Bradshaw," *Virginia Woolf and the Problem of the Subject* (New Brunswick: Rutgers University Press, 1987), p. 73.

81 Brenda Lyons, "Virginia Woolf and Plato: The Platonic Background of *Jacob's Room*," *Platonism and the English Imagination*, ed. Anna Baldwin and Sarah Hutton (Cambridge: Cambridge University Press, 1994), 290.

82 Ibid., p. 296.

83 Bell, *Virginia Woolf*, vol. I, pp. 35f.

84 James Kenneth Stephen, *The Living Languages: A Defence of the Compulsory Study of Greek at Cambridge* (Cambridge: Macmillan and Bowes, 1891), p. 47.

85 Ibid., p. 42.

86 Ibid., p. 13.

87 Her essay appears to respond as well to an idea in J. W. Mackail's "Greek and Latin in Human Life": "Rome we know . . . Greece is in contrast something which we are so far from knowing that we hardly have a name for it," *Classical Studies* (London: J. Murray, 1925), p. 7.

88 Frank M. Turner, *The Greek Heritage in Victorian Britain* (New Haven and London: Yale University Press, 1981), p. 381.

89 Ibid., pp. 431–2.

90 Berg reel 13.

91 George Devereux, *Dreams in Greek Tragedy: An Ethno-Psycho-Analytical Study* (Berkeley, University of California Press, 1976), p. 63.

92 Ibid., pp. 62–4.

93 Ibid., p. 97.

94 Ibid., p. 110.

95 Ibid., p. 124.

96 Ibid., pp. 129–30.

97 Mark Spilka reads the scene as the return of Julia's first husband, "The Robber in the Bedroom," in *Virginia Woolf's Quarrel with Grieving* (Lincoln and London: University of Nebraska Press, 1980), ch. 1.

98 Makiko Minow-Pinkney reads the connection between the two novels as the "images of the absent son and the grieving mother," in *Virginia Woolf and the Problem of the Subject*, p. 79.

3 NO GOD OF HEALING IN THIS STORY: "MRS. DALLOWAY" AND "TO THE LIGHTHOUSE"

1 Berg, reel 13. Woolf's translation consists of lines 1–1550.

2 Froma I. Zeitlin, *Playing the Other: Gender and Society in Classical Greek Literature* (Chicago: University of Chicago Press, 1996), p. 90.

3 Ibid., p. 94.

4 Ibid., p. 119.

5 "The war that she [Woolf] wants to claim a cultural and personal stake in is also one that she problematically reproduces as a site from which she is ignorant and excluded, raising, as well as a set of ideological difficulties, a crisis in narrative confidence." Tracy Hargreaves, "The Grotesque and the Great War in *To the Lighthouse*," *Women's Fiction and the Great War*, ed. Suzanne Raitt and Trudi Tate (Oxford: Clarendon Press, 1997), p. 134.

6 Other telling instances may be found in Aeschylus, *The Complete Greek Tragedies*, trans. Richmond Lattimore (Chicago: University of Chicago Press, 1953), at lines 480, 684, 1080, and 1215.

7 Simon Goldhill, *Language, Sexuality, Narrative: The Oresteia* (Cambridge: Cambridge University Press, 1984), p. 48.

8 Alex Zwerdling writes of *Mrs. Dalloway*: "Though they have never exchanged a word, on the deepest level Septimus and Clarissa are kin." "*Mrs. Dalloway* and the Social System," *PMLA* 92 (1977), 81.

9 They are included in the Berg Collection on microfilm reel 6 (M 18).
10 Verso fol. 131.
11 Verso fol. 133.
12 The notebook is in the Berg Collection.
13 Mark Hussey, *The Singing of the Real World: The Philosophy of Virginia Woolf's Fiction* (Columbus: Ohio State University Press, 1986), ch. 2.
14 Ruth Padel, *Whom Gods Destroy: Elements of Greek and Tragic Madness* (Princeton: Princeton University Press, 1995), p. 74.
15 As for instance in *A Midsummer Night's Dream*, V:1.
16 Monks House papers, University of Sussex, 6 reels of microfilm; reel 6, vol. 1, fols. 64–6.
17 In this connection it is of interest that in the manuscript Septimus appears twice as "Bernard."
18 Gillian Beer, "The Island and the Aeroplane: The Case of Virginia Woolf," *Nation and Narration*, ed. Homi K. Bhabha (London: Routledge, 1990), pp. 265–90.
19 Jennifer Wicke, in an argument about the contribution of Bloomsbury to a change in market consciousness, reads the aeroplane as "a portentous reminder of the pan-European nature of the First World War and the importance of airplane technology to its devastation." The skywriting is "an ineluctable feature of modernity capable of hiero-glyphic play, of hierophantic writing." "*Mrs. Dalloway* Goes to Market: Woolf, Keynes, and Modern Markets," *Novel* 28 (1994), 15.
20 Goldhill, *Language, Sexuality, Narrative*, p. 19.
21 Suzette A. Henke writes of the ritual sacrifice in the novel: "Septimus dies that Clarissa may live," "*Mrs. Dalloway*: The Communion of Saints," *New Feminist Essays on Virginia Woolf*, ed. Jane Marcus (Lincoln: University of Nebraska Press, 1981), pp. 125–47.
22 Pierre Vidal-Naquet, "Chasse et sacrifice dans l'*Orestie* d'Eschyle," *Mythe et tragédie en Grèce ancienne*, ed. J. P. Vernant and P. Vidal-Naquet (Paris, Editions Maspero, 1981), pp. 135–6.
23 Ibid., p. 138.
24 Ibid., p. 146.
25 Charles Segal, *Interpreting Greek Tragedy: Myth, Poetry, Text* (Ithaca: Cornell University Press, 1986), p. 40.
26 J. Hillis Miller's sense of the chthonic powers in the novel, for instance that the characters "rise from the dead to come to Clarissa's party," is focused on the song "Allseseelen," by Richard Strauss. *Fiction and Repetition: Seven English Novels* (Cambridge, Mass.: Harvard University Press, 1982), p. 190.
27 Jean-Pierre Vernant, *Tragedy and Myth in Ancient Greece*, trans. Janet Lloyd (Brighton, Sussex: Harvester Press, 1981) p. 56.
28 In this behavior she suggests the troubled sense of "kinship" that Marlow feels towards the dead helmsman in Conrad, "Heart of Darkness."

29 Miller, *Fiction and Repetition*, p. 196.
30 Froma I. Zeitlin in a discussion of identity in *Ion* points out that "likemindedness . . . between apparent strangers seems to be a prerequisite to formal recognition . . . Affinity and affiliation go together." *Playing the Other*, p. 293.
31 Bennett Simon, *Tragic Drama and the Family: Psychoanalytic Studies from Aeschylus to Beckett* (New Haven and London: Yale University Press, 1988), p. 55.
32 Ibid., p. 49.
33 Jay Winter derives from anthropology a distinction between blood kinship and "fictive kinship," in order to describe the response of communities in mourning to returning soldiers, and the families of the wounded and slain, after World War I. *Sites of Memory, Sites of Mourning: The Great War in European Cultural History* (Cambridge: Cambridge University Press, 1995), ch. 2.
34 Goldhill, *Language, Sexuality, Narrative*, p. 129.
35 Ibid., p. 131. In a discussion of *Ion* Nicole Loraux writes that Ion recognizes his mother Kreousa only after an extensive deciphering of visual signs that include his infant clothes, a basket, golden snakes, and a crown made from the olive tree. "Kreousa the Autochthon: A Study of Euripides' *Ion*," *Nothing to Do with Dionysos? Athenian Drama in Its Social Context*, ed. John J. Winkler and Froma I. Zeitlin (Princeton: Princeton University Press, 1990), p. 171.
36 Zeitlin, *Playing the Other*, p. 353.
37 Ibid., p. 362.
38 Vernant, *Tragedy and Myth*, p. 18.
39 Makiko Minow-Pinkney, *Virginia Woolf and the Problem of the Subject* (New Brunswick: Rutgers University Press, 1987), p. 78.
40 Harvena Richter writes that "Septimus Smith can be seen as Clarissa's double on two counts. He is the irrational, uncontrolled unconscious as opposed to her controlled rational conscious . . . In another sense, Septimus is the prophet, possessed of a divine madness as he raves against a wicked generation and foresees a future world in which there is 'universal love' and 'no crime.'" *Virginia Woolf: The Inward Voyage* (Princeton: Princeton University Press, 1970), p. 120.
41 The phrase "Communication is health; communication is truth; communication is happiness" is translated by Woolf from Montaigne, in the context of his "attempt to communicate a soul." "Montaigne," *CR* 66.
42 Were it not for the somber tone of *Mrs. Dalloway* it would be tempting to read Clarissa's visual encounter with the old woman in the terms of Maurice Merleau-Ponty's "reversibility," the sense that the gaze is meaningful because "it is not *I* who sees, not *he* who sees, because an anonymous visibility inhabits both of us." In the work of Merleau-Ponty the encounter with the gaze is the occasion of a utopian vision of kinship: "the seer and the visible reciprocate one another and we no

longer know which sees and which is seen." *The Visible and the Invisible* (1948), trans. Alfonso Lingis (Evanston: Northwestern University Press, 1973, 1997), pp. 142 and 139. It is a dimension of Merleau-Ponty's work that Lacan does not acknowledge.

43 Samuel Weber translates Lacan's passage in *Return to Freud: Jacques Lacan's Dislocation of Psychoanalyses*, trans. Michael Levine (Cambridge: Cambridge University Press, 1991), and discusses the future anterior, pp. 7–11.

44 Merleau-Ponty, *The Visible and the Invisible*, p. 27.

45 John Maynard Keynes, "My Early Beliefs," *The Bloomsbury Group: A Collection of Memoirs, Commentary and Criticism*, ed. S. P. Rosenbaum (Buffalo: University of Toronto Press, 1975), 59–63.

46 Seth Benardete, *The Being of the Beautiful: Plato's Theaetetus, Sophist, and Statesman*, transl. with Commentary by Seth Benardete (Chicago and London: University of Chicago Press, 1984), p. xxxiv.

47 Johann Winckelmann, *Reflections on the Imitation of Greek Works in Painting and Sculpture: Complete German Text, with a New English Translation by Elfriede Heyer and Roger C. Norton* (La Salle, Illinois: Open Court, 1987), p. 21.

48 Eugene W. Holland in his study of Baudelaire's "La Beauté" and other poems of the cycle of beauty poems argues that the poet's decoding of Romantic metaphor situates the revised poems "between metaphor and metonymy, between a romanticism being abandoned and a modernism still in the making." *Baudelaire and Schizoanalysis: The Sociopoetics of Modernism* (Cambridge: Cambridge University Press, 1993), p. 76.

49 Charles Baudelaire, "Le Peintre de la vie moderne," *Curiosités esthétiques: L'Art romantique et autres oeuvres critiques*, ed. Henri Lemaitre (Paris: Éditions Garnier Frères, 1962), pp. 455–6.

50 Ibid., p. 467.

51 The line appears in the American editions only.

52 Jürgen Habermas, *The Philosophical Discourse of Modernity*, trans. Frederick Lawrence (Cambridge, Mass.: MIT Press, 1987), pp. 8–9.

53 Ibid., p. 9.

54 Kathy Alexis Psomiades, "Beauty's Body: Gender Ideology and British Aestheticism," *Victorian Studies*, 35 (1992), 32.

55 Ibid., p. 33.

56 Bruce Fink, *The Lacanian Subject: Between Language and Jouissance* (Princeton: Princeton University Press, 1995), p. 77.

57 Hans-Georg Gadamer, "The Relevance of the Beautiful," in *The Relevance of the Beautiful and Other Essays*, trans. Nicholas Walker, ed. Robert Bernasconi (Cambridge: Cambridge University Press, 1986), pp. 26–7.

58 William Wordsworth, "Preface to *Lyrical Ballads* (1802)," in *William Wordsworth*, ed. Stephen Gill (Oxford, New York: Oxford University Press, 1984), p. 606.

59 Duncan Wu in *Wordsworth's Reading 1770–1799* (Cambridge: Cambridge

University Press, 1993) discusses Wordsworth's classical education. He includes Plato's *Apology* in "a speculative list of authors that an able pupil at a good Grammar School like Hawkshead can be expected to have read, on the basis of what is known of the syllabus at other schools," pp. 165–6. See also *Wordsworth's Reading 1800–1815* (Cambridge: Cambridge University Press, 1995), pp. 167–8. A complex argument, beyond the scope of my discussion, is Theresa M. Kelley's, *Wordsworth's Revisionary Aesthetics* (Cambridge: Cambridge University Press, 1988): "This longing for the beautiful as a refuge from the sublime structures Wordsworth's most sustained representations of this aesthetic conflict, beginning in the 1790s . . ." p. 61. See also the wording of the "Prospectus" to *The Recluse*, "Beauty, whose living home is the green earth,/Surpassing the most fair ideal Forms . . ." quoted in Kelly, p. 44.

60 Ellen Tremper, *"Who Lived at Alfoxton?": Virginia Woolf and English Romanticism* (Lewisburg: Bucknell University Press, 1998), pp. 35–7.

61 Quoted in Stephen Gill, *Wordsworth and the Victorians* (Oxford: Clarendon Press, 1998), p. 215.

62 Ibid., pp. 235–6.

63 Ellen Tremper traces echoes of Wordsworth's poetry in the characterizations of Cam and Lily, and of "Time Passes" she writes: "This section of poetic prose is . . . a critique of the Wordsworthian apprehension of the natural world." "In Her Father's House: *To the Lighthouse* as a Record of Virginia Woolf's Literary Patrimony," *Texas Studies in Literature and Language* 34 (1992), 13. See also Tremper, *"Who Lived at Alfoxton?",* ch. 5.

64 Woolf wrote of the mourning for her mother, that "it made her unreal," "A Sketch of the Past" (*MB* 95).

65 Habermas, *The Philosophical Discourse of Modernity*, p. 9.

66 Gilbert D. Chaitin, *Rhetoric and Culture in Lacan* (Cambridge: Cambridge University Press, 1996), pp. 5 and 46.

67 Sybil Oldfield prints and discusses Woolf's notes on *Antigone*, in the University of Sussex Library, in "Virginia Woolf and Antigone – Thinking Against the Current," *The South Carolina Review* 29 (1996), 45–57.

68 R. C. Jebb, ed. and trans., *Sophocles: The Plays and Fragments, part III: The Antigone* (Cambridge: Cambridge University Press, 1891), line 524.

69 Jane Marcus, *Virginia Woolf and the Languages of Patriarchy* (Bloomington: Indiana University Press, 1987), p. 44.

70 Jebb, ed., *The Antigone*, line 205.

71 Diana L. Swanson writes that "in the thirties Woolf was revising the Western tradition to develop a vision of a new world of altered relations between the sexes and a new language for communicating about it," and of the scene of Sara's reading, that it indicates "that the daughter is in effect buried alive in the patriarchal home." "An Antigone Complex?

The Political Psychology of *The Years* and *Three Guineas*," *Woolf Studies Annual* 3 (1997), 31, 34.

72 R. P. Winnington-Ingram interprets the role of Eros in *Antigone* in *Sophocles: An Interpretation* (Cambridge: Cambridge University Press, 1980), especially ch. 5, "Sophocles and the Irrational: Three Odes in *Antigone.*"

73 George Steiner, *Antigones* (New York and Oxford: Oxford University Press, 1984), p. 103.

74 Ibid., p. 18.

4 SOLAR LIGHT AND DARKNESS: "THE WAVES"

1 I share Makiko Minow-Pinkney's reading of *The Waves* as inscribing "the emergence of subjectivity and the process of its consolidation." But Woolf's keen sense of historical/ideological context exceeds the psychoanalytic paradigm. *Virginia Woolf and the Problem of the Subject* (New Brunswick: Rutgers University Press, 1987), p. 156.

2 Mark Hussey draws attention to "the remarkable similarities in the contours of Woolf's and Heidegger's thinking about being," especially in her concern with "the nature of the self" and a "point of departure [that] is always a simple, but radical wonder in the face of being at all." *The Singing of the Real World: The Philosophy of Virginia Woolf's Fiction* (Columbus: Ohio State University Press, 1986), pp. xiv–xv, p. 159. See also Holly Henry, "Nebulous Networks: Woolf's Rethinking of Jeans's Analogy of the Scientist as Artist," *Virginia Woolf and the Arts: Selected Papers from the Sixth Annual Conference on Virginia Woolf*, ed. Diane F. Gillespie and Leslie K. Hankins (New York: Pace University Press, 1997), pp. 268–76.

3 Martin Heidegger, "The Age of the World Picture," *The Question Concerning Technology and other Essays*, trans. William Lovitt (New York and London: Garland Publishing, 1977), p. 134.

4 Ibid., p. 133. Heidegger like Lacan distinguishes the subject from the self and the "I," translating the Greek *hypokeimenon* as the naming of "that-which-lies-before, which, as ground, gathers everything onto itself," p. 128. Lacan translated Heidegger's "Logos" in the first issue of *Psychanalyse* (1956).

5 Heidegger, "The Age of the World Picture," p. 147.

6 Ibid., p. 146.

7 Ibid., p. 143.

8 Ibid., p. 148.

9 Gillian Beer, "Physics, Sound, and Substance: Later Woolf," *Open Fields: Science in Cultural Encounter* (Oxford: Clarendon Press, 1996), p. 113.

10 Gérard deVaucouleurs, *Astronomical Photography: From the Daguerrotype to the Electron Camera* (London and New York: Macmillan, 1961), pp. 11–12.

11 John Lankford, "The Impact of Photography on Astronomy," _The General History of Astronomy_, ed. Owen Gingerich (Cambridge: Cambridge University Press, 1984), vol. IV, 16–39.

12 Recorded by Jane Goldman in _The Feminist Aesthetics of Virginia Woolf: Modernism, Post-Impressionism and the Politics of the Visual_ (Cambridge: Cambridge University Press, 1998), p. 27.

13 Alfred North Whitehead, _Science and the Modern World: Lowell Lectures, 1925._ (New York: The Macmillan Company, 1925), p. 3.

14 Ibid., p. 15.

15 Arthur Stanley Eddington, _Stars and Atoms_ (New Haven: Yale University Press, 1927), p. 17. Sir James Jeans, who argues that the universe "looks more like a great thought than like a great machine," illustrates his chapter "Modern Physics" with three photographs in _The Mysterious Universe_ (New York: The Macmillan Company, 1930), p. 186 and photographs facing p. 50.

16 Susan Dick, ed., _Virginia Woolf / To the Lighthouse / The Original Holograph Draft_ (Toronto and Buffalo: University of Toronto Press, 1982), p. 18.

17 Jane Marcus, "Britannia Rules _The Waves_," in _Decolonizing Tradition: New Views of Twentieth-Century 'British' Literary Canons_, ed. Karen Lawrence (Urbana and Chicago: University of Illinois Press, 1992), p. 145.

18 Their intimacy is made more explicit in Draft 1 of the novel, where becoming the daughter involves a mind that "would begin to bow itself like a flame before his ~~need~~ tiredness, or sadness" (Hol _W_, 190).

19 Patrick McGee, "The Politics of Modernist Form: or, Who Rules _The Waves?_," _Modern Fiction Studies_ 38 (1992), 637.

20 Lacan characterizes the preformation of the subject as "the level at which there is counting, things are counted, and in this counting he who counts is already included. It is only later that the subject has to recognize himself as such, recognize himself as he who counts" (_FFC_ 20).

21 Goldman, _The Feminist Aesthetics of Virginia Woolf_, p. 195.

22 Heidegger, "The Age of the World Picture," p. 125.

23 Linda Dowling, _Hellenism and Homosexuality in Victorian Oxford_ (Ithaca and London: Cornell University Press, 1994), pp. 79, 88, and _passim_.

24 Ruth Vanita notes that Neville and Bernard also respond in different ways to Shakespeare's sonnets, in "Gender Crossings: _The Waves_," _Re: Reading, Re: Writing, Re: Teaching Virginia Woolf: Selected Papers from the Fourth Annual Conference on Virginia Woolf_ (New York: Pace University Press, 1995), p. 301.

25 Kate Flint, ed., _The Waves_ (London: Penguin, 1992) p. 237n. 61.

26 Étienne Balibar traces the concept of the subject in the work of Marx and Spinoza, and offers the phrase "becoming-subject of the citizen" to describe a subject that is "not an ontological figure . . . but a legal, political, theological, and moral figure . . . a dependent, believing, and obedient individual," in other words a citizen. "The puzzling nature of

what is called 'modernity' is that the individual can be a citizen effectively only if he or she *becomes a subject again*." "The Infinite Contradiction," *Yale French Studies* 88 (1995), 149–53.

27 Translated by Alan Sheridan (*E* 300).

28 See Samuel Weber, ch. 2, "Mistaken Identity: Lacan's Theory of the 'mirror stage,'" *Return to Freud: Jacques Lacan's Dislocation of Physchoanalysis*, trans. Michael Levine (Cambridge: Cambridge University Press, 1991).

29 Flint, ed., *The Waves*, p. 83. Subsequent references appear in the text.

30 Quoted in Lindsay Smith, *Victorian Photography, Painting and Poetry: The Enigma of Visibility in Ruskin, Morris and the Pre-Raphaelites* (Cambridge: Cambridge University Press, 1995), p. 111.

31 John Ruskin, "The Relation to Art of the Science of Light," *The Works of John Ruskin*, ed. E. T. Cook and Alexander Wedderburn eds., vol. XXII (London: George Allen, 1906), pp. 203–4.

32 Smith, *Victorian Photography*, p. 111.

33 Heidegger, "The Age of the World Picture," pp. 129, 131.

34 Jeremy Maas, *Holman Hunt and the Light of the World* (London and Berkeley, Scolar Press, 1984), p. 106 and *passim*.

35 Ibid., p. 78.

36 The printed version is less explicit: "Let them lay to rest the incessant activity of the mind's eye, the bandaged head, the men with ropes, so that I may find something unvisual beneath. Here are gardens; and Venus among her flowers; here are saints and blue madonnas. Mercifully these pictures make no reference; they do not nudge; they do not point. Thus they expand my consciousness of him and bring him back to me differently" (*W* 102).

37 In a second working of the passage in Draft II Woolf identifies the painter as "of the school of Titian," and the paintings those "in the Italian room at the National Gallery" (Hol *W* 570). The details in the text, "ruffled fur against the olive green lining, or the morning intensity of the sky against the aqueduct/arches; or the yellow light behind the pricked ears of the olive trees" (Hol W 571) more clearly suggest Giorgione's *Adoration of the Kings*, which hangs in the same room.

38 The companion passage from *A Room of One's Own* reads: "Again if one is a woman one is often surprised by a sudden splitting off of consciousness, say in walking down Whitehall, when from being the natural inheritor of that civilisation, she becomes, on the contrary, outside of it, alien and critical." Michelle Barrett (ed.), *"A Room of One's Own" and "Three Guineas"* (London: Penguin, 1993) p. 88.

39 Brenda Silver, *Virginia Woolf's Reading Notebooks* (Princeton: Princeton University Press, 1983), p. 79. See also *D* III:313, 320, 326, 339n; and *D* IV:5, 264, 274, 275.

40 Shirley Neuman, "'Heart of Darkness,' Virginia Woolf and the Spectre

of Domination," *Virginia Woolf: New Critical Essays*, ed. Patricia Clements and Isobel Grundy (Totowa, New Jersey: Barnes & Noble Books, 1983), pp. 57–76. Marianne DeKoven discusses *The Voyage Out* in *Rich and Strange: Gender, History, Modernism* (Princeton: Princeton University Press, 1991), ch. 4. Allen McLaurin notes the connection between *Victory* and *Night and Day*, in *Virginia Woolf: The Echoes Enslaved* (Cambridge: Cambridge University Press, 1973), pp. 34–7.

41 The well-known passage from "Modern Fiction" (1919) in which Woolf defends her preference for "life," as opposed to the realism of Arnold Bennett, "Life is not a series of gig lamps symmetrically arranged; but a luminous halo, a semi-transparent envelope surrounding us from the beginning of consciousness to the end" (*CR* 154), seems to me to owe something to the characterization of Marlow's narrative in which "the meaning of an episode was not inside like a kernel but outside, enveloping the tale which brought it out only as a glow brings out a haze, in the likeness of one of those misty halos that sometimes are made visible by the spectral illumination of moonshine" ("Heart of Darkness," p. 18).

42 Minow-Pinkney observes that "Continual alternation between an integrated assertion of identity and its dissolution makes Bernard a would-be novelist," *Virginia Woolf and the Problem of the Subject*, p. 158. That alternation is substantially modified by the departure of the Conrad figure.

43 "Report of the Annual General Meeting on October 26, 1927," *Journal of the British Astronomical Association*, vol. 38 (Oct 1927–Sept 1928), 204.

44 Ibid., 37, 194–219.

45 *Monthly Notices of the Royal Astronomical Association*, 88 (1928), 142–4.

46 *Journal of the British Astronomical Association*, 38, 19.

47 Mark Hussey notes that "'the world seen without a self' almost certainly derives from Woolf's experience of a solar eclipse in 1927 . . . 'The Sun and the Fish' demonstrates the enormous scope the eclipse had in Woolf's imagination as she appropriates Christian terminology for cosmic significance." *The Singing of the Real World*, p. 166 n. 9.

48 *The Feminist Aesthetics of Virginia Woolf*, p. 10.

49 Ibid., p. 106.

50 In Draft ii Woolf notes "the spectral landscape wh. becomes visible in the last ch" (Hol *W* 758).

51 Marcus notes that "*The Waves* is the swan song of the white Western male author with his Romantic notions of individual genius, and his Cartesian confidence in the unitary self. Byronic man, the Romantic artist-hero, sings his last aria against death," "Britannia Rules *The Waves*," p. 145.

52 Laura Doyle, "Sublime Barbarians in the Narrative of Empire; Or, Longinus at Sea in *The Waves*," *Modern Fiction Studies* 42 (1996), 340.

5 THE PERSON TO WHOM THINGS HAPPENED: "A SKETCH OF
THE PAST"

1 A somewhat different version of this chapter appeared as "Ideology
into Fiction: Virginia Woolf's 'A Sketch of the Past,'" *Novel: A Forum on
Fiction* 27 (Winter 1994), 174–95.
2 Juan-David Nasio, "The Concept of the Subject of the Unconscious,"
Disseminating Lacan, ed. David Pettigrew and François Raffoul (Albany:
State University of New York Press, 1996), p. 39.
3 Ibid., p. 29.
4 George Gusdorf, "Conditions and Limits of Autobiography," *Autobiography: Essays Theoretical and Critical*, ed. James Olney (Princeton:
Princeton University Press, 1980), pp. 30–7.
5 Allen McLaurin devotes Part One of *Virginia Woolf: The Echoes Enslaved*
(Cambridge: Cambridge University Press, 1973) to a study of the
"common *problems*" faced by Fry and Woolf in representation,
pp. 17–94.
6 Some years earlier, in October 1934, Woolf noted in her diary, "Yeats
said that in writing his memoirs he had to leave out himself, because no
man could tell the truth about the women in his life" (*D* IV: 257).
7 Lorraine Janzen Kooistra reads Woolf's biography of Fry as a eulogy of
Bloomsbury: "her interest is not so much in Fry's achievements as in
their origins and effects." "Virginia Woolf's *Roger Fry*: A Bloomsbury
Memorial," *Woolf Studies Annual* 2 (1996), 30.
8 Roger Fry, "An Essay on Aesthetics," in *Vision and Design* (London:
Chatto & Windus, 1920), reprint Oxford University Press, 1981,
pp. 14–15.
9 Shari Benstock, ed., "Authorizing the Autobiographical," *The Private
Self: Theory and Practice of Women's Autobiographical Writings* (Chapel Hill
and London: University of North Carolina Press, 1988), p. 15.
10 Ibid., 25–9.
11 Ibid., 14.
12 John Mepham, *Virginia Woolf: A Literary Life* (New York: St. Martin's
Press, 1991), pp. 181–3.
13 Françoise Defromont writes of the mirror that it "is not only a theme,
it is the sore point, where all the unconscious currents which run
through the text meet up." "Mirrors and Fragments," in *Virginia
Woolf*, ed. Rachel Bowlby (New York: Longman Publishing, 1992),
p. 62.
14 Madeline Moore, *The Short Season Between Two Silences* (Boston: George
Allen & Unwin, 1984), p. 12.
15 Defromont writes of the mirror, that "because of the absence of the
maternal figure, the ego does not succeed in organising itself into a
coherent whole, or in constituting for itself a satisfactory narcissistic
image. This ultimately provokes an uncertainty as to sexual identity . . .

as though her [the mother's] absence had deprived the writer of a female figure to identify with." "Mirrors and Fragments," p. 66.

16 *Victorian Photographs of Famous Men & Fair Women by Julia Margaret Cameron*, Introduction by Virginia Woolf and Roger Fry (London: Hogarth Press, 1926), pp. 9–15.

17 Quentin Bell, *Virginia Woolf: A Biography*, vol. 1 (London: The Hogarth Press, 1972) facing p. 44.

18 The photograph is reproduced in Louise DeSalvo, *Virginia Woolf: The Impact of Childhood Sexual Abuse on Her Life and Work* (New York: Ballantine Books, 1989), p. 232.

19 Julia Kristeva, *Histoire d'amour* (Paris: Denoel, 1983), trans. Arthur Goldhammer, reprinted in *The Kristeva Reader*, ed. Toril Moi (New York: Columbia University Press, 1986), pp. 161, 183–5.

20 Thomas Brockelman, "Lacan and Modernism: Representation and its Vicissitudes," *Disseminating Lacan*, ed. David Pettigrew and François Raffoul (Albany: State University of New York, 1996), pp. 207–37. Jacqueline Rose addresses the question of identity formation as incorporating resistance, so that the female is neither wholly the victim nor the agent of ideology. In her reading of "Le Stade du Miroir" she stresses "the paradox that the subject finds or recognises itself through an image which simultaneously alienates it, and hence, potentially, *confronts* it." *Sexuality in the Field of Vision* (London: Verso, 1986), p. 174.

21 Brockleman, "Lacan and Modernism," p. 15.

22 Ibid., p. 216.

23 Louise DeSalvo, *Virginia Woolf: The Impact of Childhood Sexual Abuse on her Life and Work* (New York: Ballantine Books, 1989), pp. 100–1.

24 Ibid., p. 124.

25 Quoted in Bell, *Virginia Woolf*, vol. 11, p. 255.

26 Richard Gregory, *Mirrors in Mind* (Oxford, New York, Heidelberg: W. H. Freeman/Spektrum, 1997), p. x.

27 Jean-Paul Sartre, *Being and Nothingness: An Essay on Phenomenological Ontology*, trans. Hazel E. Barnes (New York: Philosophical Library, n.d.), p. 261.

28 Ibid., p. 288.

29 Ibid., p. 291.

30 Ibid., p. 288.

31 DeSalvo, *Virginia Woolf: The Impact of Childhood Sexual Abuse*, p. 105.

32 James Haule, "*To the Lighthouse* and the Great War: The Evidence of Virginia Woolf's Revision of 'Time Passes,'" *Virginia Woolf and War: Fiction, Reality, and Myth*, ed. Mark Hussey (Syracuse: Syracuse University Press, 1991), pp. 166–70, 178.

33 Gusdorf, "Conditions and Limits of Autobiography," p. 48.

34 Elizabeth Abel, *Virginia Woolf and the Fictions of Psychoanalysis*, pp. 116–18.

35 McLaurin associates genealogy with Woolf's difficulty in writing

biography, and notes in her *Flush* "a mock genealogy of the dog," *Virginia Woolf*, pp. 65–6.

36 Christine Froula, "The Daughter's Seduction: Sexual Violence and Literary History," *Signs* 11 (1986), 621–44.

37 Froma I. Zeitlin, "The Motif of the Corrupted Sacrifice in Aeschylus' *Oresteia*," *Proceedings of the American Philological Association* 96 (1965), 489.

38 Richmond Lattimore translates it: "there is no god of healing in this story" in (Aeschylus), *The Complete Greek Tragedies* (Chicago: University of Chicago Press, 1953), *Agamemnon*, line 1248.

39 Simon Goldhill, *Language, Sexuality, Narrative: The "Oresteia"* (Cambridge: Cambridge University Press, 1984), p. 88.

40 Thomas C. Caramagno, *The Flight of the Mind: Virginia Woolf's Art and Manic-Depressive Illness* (Berkeley, University of California Press, 1992), p. 200.

41 Nasio, "The Concept of the Subject of the Unconscious," p. 33.

42 Brockelman, "Lacan and Modernism," p. 218.

43 Woolf seems to me close to the formulation of Jacqueline Rose, who writes in *Sexuality in the Field of Vision*, of a woman's search for "a language which allows us to recognise our part in intolerable structures – but in a way which renders us neither the pure victims nor the sole agents of our distress," p. 14.

6 "RUINED HOUSES AND DEAD BODIES": "THREE GUINEAS" AND THE SPANISH CIVIL WAR

1 Laszlo Moholy-Nagy, *"Photography," Painting, Photography, Film*, trans. Janet Seligman (London: Lund Humphries Publications, 1969), repr. in *Classic Essays on Photography*, ed. Alan Trachtenberg (New Haven: Leete's Island Buola, 1980), p. 166.

2 Allan Sekula, "Traffic in Photographs," *Photography Against the Grain: Essays and Photo Works 1973–1983* (Halifax: The Press of the Nova Scotia College of Art and Design, 1984), p. 96.

3 Ibid., pp. 78–9.

4 John Tagg, *The Burden of Representation: Essays on Photographies and Histories* (Amherst: The University of Massachusetts Press, 1988), p. 187.

5 Jean-Louis Baudry, "Ideological Effects of the Basic Cinematographic Apparatus," *Narrative, Apparatus, Ideology: A Film Theory Reader*, ed. Philip Rosen (New York: Columbia University Press, 1986), pp. 286–7.

6 Martha Rosler, "in, around, and afterthoughts (on documentary photography)," *3 works* (Halifax, Canada: The Press of NSCAD, 1981), p. 71.

7 Jane Marcus discusses Woolf's use of the Spanish photographs: "What is the connection she was trying to make? . . . We are meant to put the patriarchal horse before the Fascist cart. It is a very clever device." "'No more horses': Virginia Woolf on Art and Propaganda," *Women's Studies* 4 (1977), 275.

8 Christian Metz, "Photography and Fetish," *October* 34 (1985), 84.

9 Grace Seiberling with Carolyn Bloore, *Amateurs, Photography, and the Mid-Victorian Imagination* (Chicago and London: University of Chicago Press, 1986), ch. 3.

10 David Harris, "Photography and Topography: Tintern Abbey," in *British Photography in the Nineteenth Century: The Fine Art Tradition*, ed. Mike Weaver (Cambridge: Cambridge University Press, 1989), pp. 95–101.

11 Seiberling, *Amateurs*, p. 18.

12 Ibid., pp. 1–13.

13 John Tagg, *The Burden of Representation*, p. 18.

14 Brenda Silver, "'Three Guineas' Before and After," *Virginia Woolf: A Feminist Slant*, ed. Jane Marcus (Lincoln and London: University of Nebraska Press, 1983), p. 257.

15 *Report on the British Press* (London: Political and Economic Planning, 1938), p. 141.

16 Franklin Reid Gannon, *The British Press and Germany 1935–1939* (Oxford: Clarendon Press, 1971), p. 42.

17 James Curran and Jean Seaton, *Power Without Responsibility: The Press and Broadcasting in Britain*, Third edition (London: Routledge, 1988), p. 52.

18 Jane Marcus, *Art and Anger: Reading Like a Woman* (Columbus: Ohio State University Press, 1988), p. 137.

19 The image of the bridge appears elsewhere in Wordsworth's poems, in "The Evening Walk," "The Excursion," and more ominously in "Lucy Gray."

20 For instance in the typescript of the "Second Guinea," on fols. 101, 107, 119.

21 Pierre Bourdieu, "The Social Definition of Photography," trans. Shaun Whiteside, *Photography: A Middle-brow Art* (Stanford: Stanford University Press, 1990), p. 86.

22 Curran and Seaton, *Power Without Responsibility*, pp. 50–2.

23 Ibid., p. 57.

24 Ibid., p. 61.

25 Gannon, *The British Press*, pp. 58, 61.

26 Ibid., p. 68.

27 Jill Edwards, *The British Government and the Spanish Civil War, 1936–1939* (London: Macmillan Press, 1979), pp. 41, 56.

28 Ibid., p. 63.

29 Ibid. p. 215.

30 Valentine Cunningham, *Spanish Front: Writers on the Civil War* (Oxford: Oxford University Press, 1986), p. 80.

31 Tom Buchanan, *Britain and the Spanish Civil War* (Cambridge: Cambridge University Press, 1997), pp. 149–50.

32 David Bradshaw, "British Writers and Anti-Fascism in the 1930s, Part II: Under the Hawk's Wings," *Woolf Studies Annual* 4 (1998), 41. See also his "British Writers and Anti-Fascism in the 1930s, Part I: The

Bray and Drone of Tortured Voices," *Woolf Studies Annual* 3 (1997), 3–27.

33 Leonard Woolf, *Letters of Leonard Woolf*, ed. Frederic Spotts (New York: Harcourt Brace Jovanovich, 1989), p. 409.

34 Herbert Rutledge Southworth, *Guernica! Guernica!: A Study of Journalism, Diplomacy, Propaganda, and History* (Berkeley: University of California Press, 1977), p. 45.

35 Stephen Koss, *The Rise and Fall of the Political Press in Britain*, vol. II, *The Twentieth Century* (London: Hamish Hamilton, 1984), p. 567.

36 Vanessa R. Schwartz, *Spectacular Realities: Early Mass Culture in Fin-de-Siècle Paris* (Berkeley, Los Angeles, London: University of California Press, 1998), pp. 58, 76, and ch. 2 *passim*.

37 "Earlier Duncan Grant with Vanessa and Quentin Bell visited Picasso at his studio in Paris where they saw, but were not especially impressed by, the unfinished *Guernica*." The finished painting was exhibited in London, Leeds, and Oxford in 1938, in order to raise money "to pay for a food ship for Spain." Woolf was one of the patrons. John Mepham, *Virginia Woolf: A Literary Life* (New York: St. Martin's Press, 1991), pp. 166–8.

38 Delaprée, *The Martyrdom of Madrid*, p. 21.

39 Quoted in *L'Humanité*, 31 December 1936.

40 *L'Humanité*, 12 December 1936.

41 Delaprée, *The Martyrdom of Madrid*, p. 21. Patricia Laurence has analyzed Woolf's notes for the essay, and writes that her "preoccupation with two of Delaprée's tropes of war – the murder of innocent women and children and ruined houses – is evident in that these images will reoccur throughout *Three Guineas*." "The Facts and Fugue of War From *Three Guineas* to *Between the Acts*," *Virginia Woolf and War: Fiction, Reality, and Myth*, ed. Mark Hussey (Syracuse: Syracuse University Press, 1991), 236.

42 In the issues of 11, 17, 18 November 1936.

43 Caroline Brothers, *War and Photography: A Cultural History* (London and New York: Routledge, 1997), p. 124.

44 Ibid., p. 4.

45 Ibid., pp. 175–8.

46 Monks House MS B 16a, undated. Patricia Laurence prints a facsimile in "The Facts and Fugues of War From *Three Guineas* to *Between the Acts*." Some of the wording crept into the phrases of the "Second Guinea," p. 199, which suggests an approximate date of composition.

47 Jane Marcus takes this sentence as the text of her argument that Woolf wrote propaganda in the tradition of Milton and Swift. "'No more horses': Virginia Woolf on Art and Propaganda," *Women's Studies* 4 (1977), 265–90.

48 Rosler, *3 works*, p. 73.

49 Brenda Silver, "The Authority of Anger: *Three Guineas* as Case Study," *Signs* 16 (1991), 368.

50 Catherine Blanto Freedberg, *The Spanish Pavilion at the Paris World's Fair* (New York and London: Garland Publishing, 1986), vol. 1, p. 633.

51 Excerpted from an interview with Jerome Seckler, "Picasso Explains," *New Masses* (13 March 1945), reprinted in *Theories of Modern Art: A Source Book by Artists and Critics*, ed. Herschel B. Chipp (Berkeley and Los Angeles: University of California Press, 1968), p. 487.

52 Ibid., p. 489.

53 Diane Gillespie writes "Instead of showing us the pictures designed to win sympathy for even the more appealing side in a complex and violent power struggle, Woolf imprints upon our minds visual images of the overriding source of the problem, the patriarchy on parade. In this way the five photographs are central to the argument of the book." "'Her Kodak Pointed at His Head': Virginia Woolf and Photography," *The Multiple Muses of Virginia Woolf*, Diane F. Gillespie, ed. (Columbia and London: University of Missouri Press, 1993), p. 138.

54 John Berger, *About Looking* (New York: Pantheon Books, 1980), p. 48.

55 Helmut Gernsheim in collaboration with Alison Gernsheim, *A Concise History of Photography* (New York: Grosset & Dunlap, 1965), p. 245.

56 Jane Livingston, "Thoughts on War Photography," *The Indelible Image: Photographs of War–1846 to the Present* (New York: Harry N. Abrams, 1985), p. 13.

57 Stuart Hall, "The Determinations of News Photographs," in *The Manufacture of News*, Revised edition, ed. Stanley Cohen and Jock Young (London: Constable, 1981), p. 234.

58 Bourdieu, "The Social Definition of Photography," p. 76.

59 Bernd Hüppauf, "Experiences of Modern Warfare and the Crisis of Representation," *New German Critique* 59 (1993), 46.

60 Ibid., 59. Gillian Beer writes of the aeroplane that its advent "reordered the axes of experience" in Woolf's work. She comments on the appearance of planes near the end of *Between the Acts*: "The sombre untranslatability of the planes here is part of the new meaning of the aeroplanes after the Spanish Civil War." "The Island and the Aeroplane: The Case of Virginia Woolf," *Nation and Narration*, ed. Homi K. Bhabha (London: Routledge, 1990), pp. 265–90.

61 Hüppauf, "Experiences of Modern Warfare," p. 69.

62 Susan D. Moeller, *Shooting War: Photography and the American Experience of Combat* (New York: Basic Books, 1989), p. 136.

63 Samuel Hynes, *A War Imagined: The First World War and English Culture* (New York: Collier-Macmillan, 1992), p. 80.

64 It is reprinted in Southworth, *Guernica! Guernica!*, pp. 14–16.

65 Ibid., pp. 137–41 and 451.

66 Ibid., p. 367.

67 Ibid., p. 103.

68 Alice Stavely identifies the figures and argues that in printing them

"Woolf here flirts with sedition," "Name That Face," *Virginia Woolf Miscellany*, No. 51 (Spring 1998), 4–5.

69 Helen Wussow, "Travesties of Excellence: Julia Margaret Cameron, Lytton Strachey, Virginia Woolf, and the Photographic Image," *Virginia Woolf and the Arts: Selected Papers from the Sixth Annual Conference on Virginia Woolf*, ed. Diane F. Gillespie and Leslie K. Hankins (New York: Pace University Press, 1997), p. 51.

70 Hall, "The determinations of news photographs," p. 234.

71 Ibid., p. 239.

72 Ibid., p. 237.

73 Berger, *About Looking*, p. 40.

74 Silver, *Reading Notebooks*, p. 99.

75 Berg reel 13, fol. 26.

76 J[ohn] P[entland] Mahaffy, *Euripedes* (New York: D. Appleton, 1879), pp. 37f.

77 Bradshaw, "British Writers and Anti-Fascism in the 1930s: Part II," 48.

78 " 'Three Guineas' Before and After," *Virginia Woolf: A Feminist Slant* (Lincoln and London: University of Nebraska Press, 1983). pp. 263–4; and Christine Froula, "St. Virginia's Epistle to an English Gentleman; or, Sex, Violence, and the Public Sphere in Woolf's *Three Guineas*," *Tulsa Studies in Women's Literature* 3 (1994), 41. See also Mary M. Childers, who opposes feminist readings of *Three Guineas* by noting the limitations of class in Woolf's essay, and her preference for aesthetic categories rather than political argument. "Virginia Woolf on the Outside Looking Down: Reflections on the Class of Women," *Modern Fiction Studies* 38 (1992), 61–79.

79 See my discussion of Woolf's notes on Zimmern's *The Greek Commonwealth*, in ch. 2.

80 Abigail Solomon-Godeau, *Photography at the Dock: Essays on Photographic History, Institutions, and Practices* (Minneapolis: University of Minnesota Press, 1991), p. 171.

81 Ibid., pp. 169, 176.

82 The essay, which first appeared in *Literarische Welt*, has been translated in *Classic Essays on Photography*, ed. Alan Trachtenberg (New Haven: Leete's Island Books, 1980), p. 215.

83 Ibid., p. 203.

Bibliography

Abel, Elizabeth. *Virginia Woolf and the Fictions of Psychoanalysis.* Chicago and London: University of Chicago Press, 1989.

Aeschylus. *The Complete Greek Tragedies.* Trans. Richmond Lattimore. Chicago: University of Chicago Press, 1953.

Althusser, Louis. *For Marx.* Trans. Ben Brewster. London: New Left Books, 1977.

"Ideology and Ideological State Apparatuses (Notes towards an Investigation)." *Lenin and Philosophy and Other Essays.* Trans. Ben Brewster. New York and London: Monthly Review Press, 1971, pp. 127–86.

Aristophanes's Plays. Ed. B. B. Rogers. London: William Heinemann, 1924.

Balibar, Etienne. "The Infinite Contradiction." *Yale French Studies* 88 (1995), 142–64.

Baudelaire, Charles. *Curiosités esthétiques: L'art romantique et autres oeuvres critiques.* Paris: Éditions Garnier Frères, 1962.

Baudry, Jean-Louis. "Ideological Effects of the Basic Cinematographic Apparatus." *Narrative, Apparatus, Ideology: A Film Theory Reader.* Ed. Philip Rosen. New York: Columbia University Press, 1986, pp. 286–98.

Beer, Gillian. "The Island and the Aeroplane: The Case of Virginia Woolf." *Nation and Narration.* Ed. Homi K. Bhabha. London: Routledge, 1990, pp. 265–90.

"Physics, Sound, and Substance: Later Woolf." *Open Fields: Science in Cultural Encounter.* Oxford: Clarendon Press, 1996, pp. 115–45.

Bell, Clive. *Art.* New York: Capricorn Books, 1958 reprint.

Bell, Quentin. *Virginia Woolf: A Biography.* 2 vols. London: The Hogarth Press, 1972.

Benardete, Seth. *The Being of the Beautiful: Plato's Theaetetus, Sophist, and Statesman.* Trans. with commentary, Seth Benardete. Chicago and London: University of Chicago Press, 1984.

Benjamin, Walter. "A Short History of Photography." *Screen* (1972), reprinted in *Classic Essays on Photography.* Ed. Alan Trachtenberg. New Haven: Leete's Island Books, 1980, pp. 199–216.

"The Author as Producer." in *Thinking Photography.* Ed. Victor Burgin. London: The Macmillan Press, 1982, pp. 15–31.

"Printing or Signs and Marks." *Selected Writings, Volume I: 1913–1926*. Ed. Marcus Bullock and Michael W. Jennings. 3 vols. Cambridge, Mass: Harvard University Press, 1996, pp. 83–6.

"The Task of the Translator." *Illuminations*. Trans. Harry Zohn. New York: Harcourt, Brace & World, 1968, pp. 69–82.

Benstock, Shari. "Authorizing the Autobiographical." *The Private Self: Theory and Practice of Women's Autobiographical Writings*. Chapel Hill and London: University of North Carolina Press, 1988, pp. 10–33.

Berger, John. *About Looking*. New York: Pantheon Books, 1980.

Ways of Seeing. London: Penguin, 1972.

Bourdieu, Pierre. "The Social Definition of Photography." Trans. Shaun Whiteside. *Photography: a Middle-brow Art*. Stanford: Stanford University Press, 1990, pp. 73–98.

Bowlby, Rachel. *Virginia Woolf: Feminist Destinations*. Oxford and New York: Blackwell, 1988.

ed. *Virginia Woolf*. New York: Longman Publishing, 1992.

Bradshaw, David. "British Writers and Anti-Fascism in the 1930s, Part I: The Bray and Drone of Tortured Voices." *Woolf Studies Annual 3* (1997), 3–27.

"British Writers and Anti-Fascism in the 1930s, Part II: Under the Hawk's Wings." *Woolf Studies Annual 4* (1998), 41–66.

Brockelman, Thomas. "Lacan and Modernism: Representation and Its Vicissitudes." *Disseminating Lacan*. Ed. David Pettigrew and François Raffoul. Albany: State University of New York Press, 1996, pp. 207–37.

Brothers, Caroline. *War and Photography: A Cultural History*. London and New York: Routledge, 1997.

Brower, Reuben. "Seven *Agamemnons*." *On Translation*. Ed. Reuben Brower. Cambridge, Mass.: Harvard University Press, 1959, pp. 173–95.

Buchanan, Tom. *Britain and the Spanish Civil War*. Cambridge: Cambridge University Press, 1997.

Burgin, Victor, ed. *Thinking Photography*. London: The Macmillan Press, 1982.

Cameron, Julia Margaret. *Victorian Photographs of Famous Men & Fair Women by Julia Margaret Cameron*. Introduction by Virginia Woolf and Roger Fry. London: Hogarth Press, 1926.

Caramagno, Thomas C. *The Flight of the Mind: Virginia Woolf's Art and Manic-Depressive Illness*. Berkeley: University of California Press, 1992.

Caughie, Pamela L. *Virginia Woolf and Postmodernism: Literature in Quest and Question of Itself*. Urbana and Chicago: University of Illinois Press, 1991.

Cavarero, Adriana. *In Spite of Plato: A Feminist Rewriting of Ancient Philosophy*. Trans. Serena Anderlini-D'Onofrio and Aine O'Healy, Oxford: Oxford University Press, 1995.

Chaitin, Gilbert D. *Rhetoric and Culture in Lacan*. Cambridge: Cambridge University Press, 1996.

Childers, Mary M. "Virginia Woolf on the Outside Looking Down: Reflections on the Class of Women." *Modern Fiction Studies* 38 (1992), 61–79.

Chipp, Herschel B. ed. *Theories of Modern Art: A Source Book by Artists and Critics.* Berkeley and Los Angeles: University of California Press, 1968.

Clements, Patricia and Grundy, Isobel, eds. *Virginia Woolf: New Critical Essays.* Totowa, New Jersey: Barnes & Noble Books, 1983.

Conrad, Joseph. *Heart of Darkness.* Ed. Robert Hampson. London: Penguin, 1995.

Crary, Jonathan. *Techniques of the Observer: On Vision and Modernity in the Nineteenth Century.* Cambridge, Massachusetts and London: MIT Press, 1990.

Cunningham, Valentine. *Spanish Front: Writers on the Civil War.* Oxford: Oxford University Press, 1986.

Curran, James and Seaton, Jean. *Power Without Responsibility: The Press and the Broadcasting in Britain.* Third edition. London: Routledge, 1988.

Damisch, Hubert. *The Origin of Perspective.* Trans. John Goodman. Cambridge, Mass. and London: MIT Press, 1994.

Defromont, Françoise. "Mirrors and Fragments." *Virginia Woolf.* Ed. Rachel Bowlby. New York: Longman, 1992, pp. 62–76.

DeKoven, Marianne. *Rich and Strange: Gender, History, Modernism.* Princeton: Princeton University Press, 1991.

Delaprée, Louis. *The Martyrdom of Madrid.* Madrid, 1937.

DeMan, Paul. "Conclusions: Walter Benjamin's 'The Task of the Translator,'" *Yale French Studies* 69 (1985), 25–46.

DeSalvo, Louise. *Virginia Woolf: The Impact of Childhood Sexual Abuse on Her Life and Work.* New York: Ballantine Books, 1989.

Descartes, René. *Selected Philosophical Writings.* Ed. and trans. John Cottingham, Robert Stoothoff, and Dugald Murdoch. Cambridge: Cambridge University Press, 1988.

DeVaucouleurs, Gérard. *Astronomical Photography: From the Daguerrotype to the Electron Camera.* London and New York: Macmillan, 1961.

Devereux, George. *Dreams in Greek Tragedy: An Ethno-Psycho-Analytical Study.* Berkeley: University of California Press, 1976.

Dick Susan, ed. *Collected Shorter Fiction of Virginia Woolf.* San Diego, New York, London: Harcourt Brace Jovanovich, 1985.

Virginia Woolf / To the Lighthouse / The Original Holograph Draft. Toronto and Buffalo: University of Toronto Press, 1982.

Dowling, Linda. *Hellenism and Homosexuality in Victorian Oxford.* Ithaca and London: Cornell University Press, 1994.

Doyle, Laura. "Sublime Barbarians in the Narrative of Empire; Or, Longinus at Sea in *The Waves,*" *Modern Fiction Studies* 42 (1996), 323–47.

Eddington, Arthur Stanley. *Stars and Atoms.* New Haven: Yale University Press, 1927.

Edwards, Jill. *The British Government and the Spanish Civil War, 1936–1939.* London: Macmillan Press, 1979.

Ferrari, G. R. F. *Listening to the Cicadas: A Study of Plato's "Phaedrus"*. Cambridge: Cambridge University Press, 1987.

Ferrer, Daniel. *Virginia Woolf and the Madness of Language*. Trans. Geoffrey Bennington and Rachel Bowlby. London and New York: Routledge, 1990.

Fink, Bruce. *The Lacanian Subject: Between Language and Jouissance*. Princeton: Princeton University Press, 1995.

"Science and Psychoanalysis." *Reading Seminar* xi. Ed. Richard Feldstein, Bruce Fink, Maire Jaanus. Albany: State University of New York Press, 1995, pp. 55–64.

Flint, Kate, ed. *The Waves*. London: Penguin, 1992.

Freedberg, Catherine Blanto. *The Spanish Pavilion at the Paris World's Fair*. 2 vols. New York and London: Garland Publishing, 1986.

Froula, Christine. "The Daughter's Seduction: Sexual Violence and Literary History." *Signs* 11 (1986), 621–44.

"St. Virginia's Epistle to an English Gentleman; or, Sex, Violence, and the Public Sphere in Woolf's *Three Guineas*," Tulsa Studies in *Women's Literature* 13 (1994), 27–56.

Fry, Roger. *Cezanne: A Study of His Development*. New York: The Macmillan Company, 1927.

Vision and Design. London: Chatto & Windus, 1920. Reprinted by Oxford University Press, 1981.

Gadamer, Hans-Georg. "The Relevance of the Beautiful," *The Relevance of the Beautiful and Other Essays*. Trans. Nicholas Walker, ed. Robert Bernasconi. Cambridge: Cambridge University Press, 1986, pp. 3–53.

Gannon, Franklin Reid. *The British Press and Germany 1935–1939*. Oxford: Clarendon Press, 1971.

Gernsheim, Helmut in collaboration with Gernsheim, Alison. *A Concise History of Photography*. New York: Grosset & Dunlap, 1965.

Gill, Stephen. *Wordsworth and the Victorians*. Oxford: Clarendon Press, 1998.

Gillespie, Diane F. "'Her Kodak Pointed at His Head': Virginia Woolf and Photography." *The Multiple Muses of Virginia Woolf*. Ed. Diane F. Gillespie. Columbia and London: University of Missouri Press, 1993, pp. 113–47.

The Sisters' Arts: The Writing and Painting of Virginia Woolf and Vanessa Bell. Syracuse: Syracuse University Press, 1988.

Gingerich, Owen, ed. *The General History of Astronomy*, vol. iv. Cambridge: Cambridge University Press, 1984.

Goldhill, Simon. *Language, Sexuality, Narrative: The "Oresteia."* Cambridge: Cambridge University Press, 1984.

"The Naive and Knowing Eye: Ecphrasis and the Culture of Viewing in the Hellenistic World." *Art and Text in Ancient Greek Culture*. Ed. Simon Goldhill. Cambridge: Cambridge University Press, 1994, pp. 197–223.

Goldman, Jane. *The Feminist Aesthetics of Virginia Woolf: Modernism, Post-Impressionism and the Politics of The Visual.* Cambridge: Cambridge University Press, 1998.

Gregory, Richard. *Mirrors in Mind.* Oxford, New York, Heidelberg: W. H. Freeman/Spektrum, 1997.

Gusdorf, George. "Conditions and Limits of Autobiography." *Autobiography: Essays Theoretical and Critical.* Ed. James Olney. Princeton: Princeton University Press, 1980, pp. 28–48.

Habermas, Jürgen. "Modernity – An Incomplete Project." Trans. Seyla Ben-Habib. *New German Critique* 22 (1981), 3–14. Reprinted in *The Anti-Aesthetic: Essays on Postmodern Culture.* Ed. Hal Foster. Port Townsend, Washington: Bay Press, 1983, pp. 3–16.

The *Philosophical Discourse of Modernity*, Trans. Frederick Lawrence. Cambridge, Mass.: MIT Press, 1987.

Hall, Stuart. "The Determinations of News Photographs." *The Manufacture of News.* Revised edition. Ed. Stanley Cohen and Jock Young, London: Constable 1981, pp. 226–43.

Halperin, David M. "Why is Diotima a Woman? Platonic Eros and the Figuration of Gender." *Before Sexuality: The Construction of Erotic Experience in the Ancient Greek World.* Ed. David M. Halperin, John J. Winkler, and Froma I. Zeitlin. Princeton: Princeton University Press, 1990, pp. 257–308.

Hargreaves, Tracy. "The Grotesque and the Great War in *To the Lighthouse*," *Women's Fiction and the Great War.* Ed. Suzanne Raitt and Trudi Tate . Oxford: Clarendon Press, 1997, pp. 132–50.

Harris, David. "Photography and Topography: Tintern Abbey." *British Photography in the Nineteenth Century: The Fine Art Tradition.* Ed. Mike Weaver. Cambridge: Cambridge University Press, 1989, pp. 95–101.

Haule, James M. "*To the Lighthouse* and the Great War: The Evidence of Virginia Woolf's Revision of 'Time Passes.'" *Virginia Woolf and War: Fiction, Reality, and Myth.* Ed. Mark Hussey. Syracuse: Syracuse University Press, 1991, pp. 164–79.

Headlam, Walter. *"Agamemnon" of Aeschylus with Verse Translation, Introduction and Notes.* Cambridge: Cambridge University Press, 1910.

On Editing Aeschylus: A Criticism. London: D. Nutt, 1890.

Heidegger, Martin. "The Age of the World Picture." *The Question Concerning Technology and Other Essays.* Trans. William Lovitt. New York and London: Garland Publishing, 1977, pp. 115–54.

Henke, A. Suzette. "De/Colonizing the Subject in Virginia Woolf's *The Voyage Out*: Rachel Vinrace as *La Mysterique.*" *Virginia Woolf: Emerging Perspectives: Selected Papers from the Third Annual Conference on Virginia Woolf.* Ed. Mark Hussey. New York: Pace University Press, 1994, pp. 103–08.

"*Mrs. Dalloway*: The Communion of Saints." *New Feminist Essays on Virginia Woolf.* Ed. Jane Marcus. Lincoln: University of Nebraska Press, 1981, pp. 125–47.

Henry, Holly. "Nebulous Networks: Woolf's Rethinking of Jeans's Analogy of the Scientist as Artist." *Virginia Woolf and the Arts: Selected Papers from the Sixth Annual Conference on Virginia Woolf.* Ed. Diane F. Gillespie and Leslie K. Hankins. New York: Pace University Press, 1997, pp. 268–276.

Hoberman, Ruth. *Gendering Classicism: The Ancient World in Twentieth-Century Women's Historical Fiction.* Albany: State University of New York Press, 1997.

Holland, Eugene W. *Baudelaire and Schizoanalysis: The Sociopoetics of Modernism.* Cambridge: Cambridge University Press, 1993.

Holtby, Winifred. *Virginia Woolf.* London: Wishart, 1932.

Hüppauf, Bernd. "The Emergence of Modern War Imagery in Early Photography." *History and Memory* 5 (1993), 130–51.

"Experiences of Modern Warfare and the Crisis of Representation." *New German Critique* 59 (1993), 41–76.

Hussey, Mark. *The Singing of the Real World: The Philosophy of Virginia Woolf's Fiction.* Columbus: Ohio State University Press, 1986.

"*To the Lighthouse* and Physics: The Cosmology of David Bohm and Virginia Woolf." *New Essays on Virginia Woolf.* Ed. Helen Wussow. Dallas: Contemporary Research Press, 1995, pp. 79–98.

Ed. *Virginia Woolf and War: Fiction, Reality, and Myth.* Syracuse: Syracuse University Press, 1991.

Hynes, Samuel. *A War Imagined: The First World War and English Culture.* New York: Collier-Macmillan, 1992.

Jay, Martin. *Downcast Eyes: The Denigration of Vision in Twentieth-Century French Thought.* Berkeley: University of California Press, 1994.

Jeans, Sir James. *The Mysterious Universe.* New York: The Macmillan Company, 1930.

Jebb, R. C., ed. and trans. *Sophocles: The Plays and Fragments, Part III: The Antigone.* Cambridge: Cambridge University Press, 1891.

Journal of the British Astronomical Association 38 (Oct. 1927–Sept 1928).

Jowett, Benjamin, trans. *The Dialogues of Plato.* Vol 1. London and New York: Macmillan, 1892.

Kahane, Claire. *Passions of the Voice: Hysteria, Narrative, and the Figure of the Speaking Woman, 1850–1915.* Baltimore and London: The Johns Hopkins University Press, 1995.

Kelley, Theresa M. *Wordsworth's Revisionary Aesthetics.* Cambridge: Cambridge University Press, 1988.

Keynes, John Maynard. "My Early Beliefs." *The Bloomsbury Group: A Collection of Memoirs, Commentary and Criticism.* Ed. S. P. Rosenbaum. Buffalo: University of Toronto Press, 1975, pp. 48–64.

Kooistra, Lorraine Janzen. "Virginia Woolf's *Roger Fry*: A Bloomsbury Memorial." *Woolf Studies Annual* 2 (1996), 26–38.

Koss, Stephen. *The Rise and Fall of the Political Press in Britain.* vol. II: *The Twentieth Century.* London: Hamish Hamilton, 1984, 2 vols.

Kracauer, Siegfried. "Photography." *Critical Inquiry* 19 (1993), 421–36.
Krauss, Rosalind. *The Optical Unconscious.* Cambridge, Mass.: MIT Press, 1994.
Kristeva, Julia. "Stabat Mater." *Histoire d'amour.* Trans. Arthur Goldhammer, reprinted in *The Kristeva Reader.* Ed. Toril Moi. New York: Columbia University Press, 1986, pp. 160–86.
Lankford, John. "The Impact of Photography on Astronomy." *The General History of Astronomy.* Ed. Owen Gingerich. Cambridge: Cambridge University Press, 1984, pp. 16–39.
Laurence, Patricia. "The facts and Fugue of War From *Three Guineas* to *Between the Acts.*" *Virginia Woolf and War: Fiction, Reality, and Myth.* Ed. Mark Hussey. Syracuse: Syracuse University Press, 1991, pp. 225–45.
Lawrence, Karen, ed. *Decolonizing Tradition: New Views of Twentieth-Century "British" Literary Canons.* Urbana and Chicago: University of Illinois Press, 1992.
Lee, Hermione. *Virginia Woolf.* London: Chatto & Windus, 1996.
Levin, David Michael. *The Philosopher's Gaze: Modernity in the Shadows of Enlightenment.* Berkeley, Los Angeles and London: University of California Press, 1999.
L'Humanité. Paris: 1936, 1937.
Livingston, Jane. "Thoughts on War Photography." *The Indelible Image: Photographs of War – 1846 to the Present.* New York: Harry N. Abrams, 1985, pp. 13–16.
Loraux, Nicole. "Kreousa the Autochthon: A Study of Euripides' Ion." *Nothing to Do with Dionysos? Athenian Drama in Its Social Context.* Ed. John J. Winkler, and Froma I. Zeitlin. Princeton: Princeton University Press, 1990, pp. 168–206.
Lowe, Roy. "The Expansion of Higher Education in England." *The Transformation of Higher Learning 1860–1930: Expansion, Diversification, Social Opening, and Professionalization in England, Germany, Russia, and the U.S.* Ed. Konrad J. Jarausch. Chicago: University of Chicago Press, 1983, pp. 37–57.
Lyons, Brenda. "Virginia Woolf and Plato: The Platonic Background of *Jacob's Room.*" *Platonism and the English Imagination.* Ed. Anna Baldwin and Sarah Hutton. Cambridge: Cambridge University Press, 1994, pp. 290–7.
Maas, Jeremy. *Holman Hunt and the Light of the World.* London and Berkeley: Scolar Press, 1984.
Mackail, J. W. "Greek and Latin in Human Life." *Classical Studies.* London: J. Murray, 1925.
Mahaffy, J[ohn] P[entland]. *Euripedes.* New York: D. Appleton, 1879.
Mao, Douglas. *Solid Objects: Modernism and the Test of Production.* Princeton: Princeton University Press, 1998.
Marcus, Jane. *Art and Anger: Reading Like a Woman.* Columbus: Ohio State University Press, 1988.

Virginia Woolf and the Languages of Patriarchy. Bloomington: Indiana University Press, 1987.

ed. *New Feminist Essays.* Lincoln: University of Nebraska Press, 1981.

"Britannia Rules *The Waves.*" *Decolonizing Tradition: New Views of Twentieth-Century 'British' Literary Canons.* Ed. Karen R. Lawrence. Urbana: University of Illinois Press, 1992, pp. 136–62.

" 'No more horses': Virginia Woolf on Art and Propaganda." *Women's Studies* 4 (1977), 265–90.

McCoy, Garnett. *Reading Records: A Researcher's Guide to the Archives of American Art: Archives of American Art Journal* 35 (1995), 25.

McCulloch, Gary. *Philosophers and Kings: Education for Leadership in Modern England.* Cambridge: Cambridge University Press, 1991.

McGee, Patrick. "The Politics of Modernist Form: or, Who rules *The Waves?*" *Modern Fiction Studies* 38 (1992), 631–50.

Telling the Other: The Question of Value in Modern and Postcolonial Writing. Ithaca and London: Cornell University Press, 1992.

"Woolf's Other: The University in Her Eye." *Novel: A Forum on Fiction* 23 (1990), 229–46.

McLaurin, Allen. *Virginia Woolf: The Echoes Enslaved.* Cambridge: Cambridge University Press, 1973.

Meisel, Perry. *The Absent Father: Virginia Woolf and Walter Pater.* New Haven and London: Yale University Press, 1980.

Mepham, John. *Virginia Woolf: A Literary Life.* New York: St. Martin's Press, 1991.

Merleau-Ponty, Maurice. *The Primacy of Perception/ And Other Essays on Phenomenological Psychology, the Philosophy of Art, History and Politics.* Ed. James M. Edie. n.p. Northwestern University Press, 1964.

The Visible and the Invisible (1948). Trans. Alfonso Lingis. Evanston: Northwestern University Press, 1973, 1997.

Metz, Christian. "Photography and Fetish." *October* 34 (1985), 81–90.

Miller, J. Hillis. *Fiction and Repetition: Seven English Novels.* Cambridge, Mass.: Harvard University Press, 1982.

Minow-Pinkney, Makiko. *Virginia Woolf and the Problem of the Subject.* New Brunswick: Rutgers University Press, 1987.

Moeller, Susan D. *Shooting War: Photography and the American Experience of Combat.* New York: Basic Books, 1989.

Moi, Toril. *Sexual/Textual Politics: Feminist Literary Theory.* London and New York: Routledge, 1985.

Moore, Madeline. *The Short Season Between Two Silences.* Boston: George Allen & Unwin, 1984.

Nasio, Juan-David. "The Concept of the Subject of the Unconscious." *Disseminating Lacan.* Ed. David Pettigrew and François Raffoul. Albany: State University of New York Press, 1996, pp. 23–42.

Neuman, Shirley. " 'Heart of Darkness,' Virginia Woolf and the Spectre of Domination." *Virginia Woolf: New Critical Essays.* Ed. Patricia Clements and Isobel Grundy. Totowa, New Jersey: Barnes & Noble Books, 1983, pp. 57–76.

Nussbaum, Martha. "The Window: Knowledge of Other Minds in Virginia Woolf's *To the Lighthouse*." *New Literary History* 26 (1995), 731–53.

Oldfield, Sybil. "Virginia Woolf and Antigone – Thinking Against the Current." *The South Carolina Review*. 29 (Fall 1996), 45–57.

Olney, James, ed. *Autobiography: Essays Theoretical and Critical*. Princeton: Princeton University Press, 1980.

Padel, Ruth. *Whom Gods Destroy: Elements of Greek and Tragic Madness*. Princeton: Princeton University Press, 1995.

Panofsky, Erwin. *Perspective as Symbolic Form*. Trans. Christopher S. Wood. New York: Zone Books, 1991.

Pater, Walter. *Plato and Platonism*. New York and London: Macmillan, 1893.

Perkell, Christine. "On The Two Voices of The Birds in *Birds*." *Ramus* 22 (1993), 1–18.

Plato. *Phaedrus*. Trans. Alexander Nehamas, and Paul Woodruff. Indianapolis/Cambridge: Hackett Publishing Company, Inc. 1995.

The Republic, Book VI. Trans. Paul Shorey. Cambridge, Mass.: Harvard University Press; London. William Heinemann Ltd., 1935.

Symposium. Trans. Alexander Nehamas and Paul Woodruff. Indianapolis/Cambridge: Hackett Publishing Company, 1989.

Poole, Roger. *The Unknown Virginia Woolf*. Cambridge: Cambridge University Press, 1978.

Psomiades, Kathy Alexis. "Beauty's Body: Gender Ideology and British Aestheticism." *Victorian Studies* 35 (1992), 31–52.

Reckford, Kenneth J. Aristophanes' *Old-and-New Comedy, Vol. 1, Six Essays in Perspective*. Chapel Hill: University of North Carolina Press, 1987.

Report on the British Press. London: Political and Economic Planning, 1938.

Richter, Harvena. *Virginia Woolf: The Inward Voyage*. Princeton: Princeton University Press, 1970.

Romer, F. E. "Good Intentions and the ὁδὸς ἡ ἐς κόρακας *The City as Comedy: Society and Representation in Athenian Drama*. Ed. Gregory W. Dobrov. Chapel Hill and London: University of North Carolina Press, 1997, pp. 51–74.

Rose, Jacqueline. *Sexuality in the Field of Vision*. London: Verso, 1986.

Rosenbaum, S. P. ed. "A Dialogue upon Mount Pentelicus," *Times Literary Supplement* (1987), 979.

Rosler, Martha. "in, around, and afterthoughts (on documentary photography)." *3 works*. Halifax, Canada: The Press of NSCAD, 1981.

Ruotolo, Lucio P. *The Interrupted Moment: A View of Virginia Woolf's Novels*. Stanford: Stanford University Press, 1986.

Sartre, Jean-Paul. *Being and Nothingness: An Essay on Phenomenological Ontology*. Trans. Hazel E. Barnes. New York: Philosophical Library, n.d.

Schwartz, Vanessa R. *Spectacular Realities: Early Mass Culture in Fin-de-Siècle Paris.* Berkeley, Los Angeles, London: University of California Press, 1998.

Segal, Charles. *Interpreting Greek Tragedy: Myth, Poetry, Text.* Ithaca: Cornell University Press, 1986.

Seiberling, Grace, with Bloore, Carolyn. *Amateurs, Photography, and the Mid-Victorian Imagination.* Chicago and London: The University of Chicago Press, 1986.

Sekula, Allan. *Photography Against the Grain: Essays and Photo Works 1973–1983.* Halifax: The Press of the Nova Scotia College of Art, 1984.

Showalter, Elaine. *The Female Malady: Women, Madness, and English Culture, 1830–1980.* New York: Pantheon Books, 1985.

Silver, Brenda. "The Authority of Anger: *Three Guineas* as Case Study," *Signs* 16 (1991), 340–70.

"'Three Guineas' Before and After." *Virginia Woolf: A Feminist Slant.* Ed. Jane Marcus. Lincoln and London: University of Nebraska Press, 1983, pp. 254–76.

ed. *Virginia Woolf's Reading Notebooks.* Princeton: Princeton University Press, 1983.

Simon, Bennett. *Tragic Drama and the Family: Psychoanalytic Studies from Aeschylus to Beckett.* New Haven and London: Yale University Press, 1988.

Smith, Lindsay. *Victorian Photography, Painting and Poetry: The Enigma of Visibility in Ruskin, Morris and the Pre-Raphaelites.* Cambridge: Cambridge University Press, 1995.

Snyder, Joel. "Picturing Vision." *Critical Inquiry* 6 (1980), 499–526.

Soffer, Reba N. "Authority in the University: Balliol, Newnham and the New Mythology." *Myths of the English.* Ed. Roy Porter. Cambridge and Cambridge, Mass.: Polity Press, 1992, pp. 192–215.

Solomon-Godeau, Abigail. *Photography at the Dock: Essays on Photographic History, Institutions, and Practices.* Minneapolis: University of Minnesota Press, 1991.

Southworth, Herbert Rutledge. *Guernica! Guernica!: A Study of Journalism, Diplomacy, Propaganda, and History.* Berkeley: University of California Press, 1977.

Spater, George and Parsons, Ian. *A Marriage of True Minds: An Intimate Portrait of Leonard and Virginia Woolf.* New York and London: Harcourt Brace Jovanovich, 1977.

Spilka, Mark. *Virginia Woolf's Quarrel with Grieving.* Lincoln and London: University of Nebraska Press, 1980.

Stavely, Alice. "Name That Face." *Virginia Woolf Miscellany*, No. 51 (Spring 1998), 4–5.

Steiner, George. *Antigones.* New York and Oxford: Oxford University Press, 1984.

Stephen, James Kenneth. *The Living Languages: A Defence of the Compulsory Study of Greek at Cambridge.* Cambridge: Macmillan and Bowes, 1891.

Stray, Christopher. *Classics Transformed: Schools, Universities, and Society in England, 1830–1960.* Oxford: Clarendon Press, 1998.

Swanson, Diana L. "An Antigone Complex? The Political Psychology of *The Years* and *Three Guineas.*" *Woolf Studies Annual* 3 (1997), 28–44.

Tagg, John. *The Burden of Representation: Essays on Photographies and Histories.* Amherst: The University of Massachusetts Press, 1988.

The Times. London: 1936, 1937.

Trachtenberg, Alan, ed. *Classics Essays on Photography.* New Haven: Leete's Island Books, 1980.

Tremper, Ellen. "In Her Father's House: *To the Lighthouse* as a Record of Virginia Woolf's Literary Patrimony." *Texas Studies in Literature and Language* 34 (1992), 1–40.

"Who Lived at Alfoxton?" Virginia Woolf and English Romanticism. Lewisburg: Bucknell University Press, 1998.

Turner, Frank M. *The Greek Heritage in Victorian Britain.* New Haven: Yale University Press, 1981.

Vanita, Ruth. "Gender Crossings: *The Waves,*" *Re: Reading, Re: Writing, Re: Teaching Virginia Woolf: Selected Papers from the Fourth Annual Conference on Virginia Woolf.* New York: Pace University Press, 1995, pp. 299–304.

Vernant, Jean-Pierre. *Mortals and Immortals: Collected Essays.* Trans. Froma I. Zeitlin. Princeton: Princeton University Press, 1991.

Tragedy and Myth in Ancient Greece. Trans. Janet Lloyd. Brighton, Sussex: Harvester Press, 1981.

Verrall, R. W. *The* Agamemnon *of Aeschylus* with an introduction, commentary and translation. London and New York: Macmillan, 1889.

"On Editing Aeschylus": A Reply. London and New York: Macmillan, 1892.

Vidal-Naquet, Pierre. "Chasse et sacrifice dans l'Orestie d'Eschyle." *Mythe et tragédie en Grèce ancienne.* Ed. J. P. Vernant and P. Vidal-Naquet. Paris: Editions Maspero, 1981, pp. 135–58.

Weber, Samuel. *Return to Freud: Jacques Lacan's Dislocation of Psychoanalysis.* Trans. Michael Levine. Cambridge: Cambridge University Press, 1991.

Whitehead, Alfred North. *Science and the Modern World: Lowell Lectures, 1925.* New York: The Macmillan Company, 1925.

Wicke, Jennifer. "*Mrs. Dalloway* Goes to Market: Woolf, Keynes, and Modern Markets." *Novel: A Forum on Fiction* 28 (1994), 5–23.

Winckelmann, Johann. *Reflections on the Imitation of Greek Works in painting and Sculpture: Complete German Text, with a New English Translation by Elfreide Heyer and Roger C. Norton.* La Salle, Illinois: Open Court, 1987.

Winnington-Ingram, R. P. *Sophocles: An Interpretation.* Cambridge: Cambridge University Press, 1980.

Winter, Jay. *Sites of Memory, Sites of Mourning: The Great War in European Cultural History.* Cambridge: Cambridge University Press, 1995.

Woolf, Leonard. *Beginning Again: An Autobiography of the Years 1911 to 1918.* New York: Harcourt, Brace & World, 1963, 1964.

Letters of Leonard Woolf. Ed. Frederic Spotts. New York: Harcourt Brace Jovanovich, 1989.

William Wordsworth. Ed. Stephen Gill. Oxford and New York: Oxford University Press, 1984.

Wright, Lawrence. *Perspective in Perspective.* London, Boston, Melbourne and Henley: Routledge & Kegan Paul, 1983.

Wu, Duncan. *Wordsworth's Reading 1770–1799.* Cambridge: Cambridge University Press, 1993.

Wordsworth's Reading 1800–1815. Cambridge: Cambridge University Press, 1995.

Wussow, Helen. "Travesties of Excellence: Julia Margaret Cameron, Lytton Strachey, Virginia Woolf, and the Photographic Image." *Virginia Woolf and the Arts: Selected Papers from the Sixth Annual Conference on Virginia Woolf.* Ed. Diane F. Gillespie and Leslie K. Hankins. New York: Pace University Press, 1997. 48–56.

Zeitlin, Froma I. "The Artful Eye: Vision, Ecphrasis and Spectacle in Euripidean Theatre." *Art and Text in Ancient Greek Culture.* Ed. Simon Goldhill and Robin Osborne. Cambridge: Cambridge University Press, 1994, pp. 138–96.

"The Motif of the Corrupted Sacrifice in Aeschylus' *Oresteia,*" *Proceedings of the American Philological Association* 96 (1965), 463–508.

Playing the Other: Gender and Society in Classical Greek Literature. Chicago: University of Chicago Press, 1996.

Zimmern, Alfred. *The Greek Commonwealth: Politics & Economics in Fifth-Century Athens.* London: Oxford University Press, 1911.

Zwerdling, Alex. "*Mrs. Dalloway* and the Social System. *PMLA* 92 (1977), 69–82.

Virginia Woolf and the Real World. Berkeley, Los Angeles: University of California Press, 1986.

Index